T0326256

BUILDING SOMETHING BETTER

NATURE, SOCIETY, AND CULTURE
Scott Frickel, Series Editor

A sophisticated and wide-ranging sociological literature analyzing nature-society-culture interactions has blossomed in recent decades. This book series provides a platform for showcasing the best of that scholarship: carefully crafted empirical studies of socio-environmental change and the effects such change has on ecosystems, social institutions, historical processes, and cultural practices.

The series aims for topical and theoretical breadth. Anchored in sociological analyses of the environment, Nature, Society, and Culture is home to studies employing a range of disciplinary and interdisciplinary perspectives and investigating the pressing socio-environmental questions of our time—from environmental inequality and risk, to the science and politics of climate change and serial disaster, to the environmental causes and consequences of urbanization and war making, and beyond.

BUILDING SOMETHING BETTER

Environmental Crises and the Promise of Community Change

STEPHANIE A. MALIN
MEGHAN ELIZABETH KALLMAN

RUTGERS UNIVERSITY PRESS
New Brunswick, Camden, and Newark, New Jersey, and London

Library of Congress Cataloging-in-Publication Data

Names: Malin, Stephanie A., 1981– author. | Kallman, Meghan Elizabeth, author.
Title: Building something better : environmental crises & the promise of community change / Stephanie A. Malin, Meghan Elizabeth Kallman.
Description: New Brunswick, New Jersey : Rutgers University Press, [2022] | Includes bibliographical references and index.
Identifiers: LCCN 2021032978 | ISBN 9781978823686 (paperback) | ISBN 9781978823693 (hardback) | ISBN 9781978823709 (epub) | ISBN 9781978823716 (mobi) | ISBN 9781978823723 (pdf)
Subjects: LCSH: Environmental sociology—United States. | Democracy and environmentalism—United States. | Environmental justice—United States—Citizen participation. | Sustainable development—United States—Citizen participation. | Political participation—United States.
Classification: LCC GE197 .M26 2022 | DDC 304.2/80973—dc23/eng/20211014
LC record available at https://lccn.loc.gov/2021032978

A British Cataloging-in-Publication record for this book is available from the British Library.

♾ The paper used in this publication meets the requirements of the American National Standard for Information Sciences—Permanence of Paper for Printed Library Materials, ANSI Z39.48-1992.

www.rutgersuniversitypress.org

Manufactured in the United States of America

SAM: To Logan and Matt, my daily inspirations for building a better world. And to all the communities already doing this work

MEK: To my niblings: Charlotte, Faith, Mekhi, Gaelle, Gael, Gaettan, Elliott, Oscar, and Jack

CONTENTS

BUILDING SOMETHING BETTER

PART 1 # WHERE WE'RE AT
AND WHY

1 · INTRODUCTION

The world is at a crossroads.

We finished our first draft of this book during the fall of 2020. It was seven months into the global pandemic caused by COVID-19, and over 200,000 Americans had died of the virus. The United States was in convulsions, shaken to the core by the murders of George Floyd and Breonna Taylor, after so many other deaths of Black and Indigenous men and women at the hands of law enforcement. The administration of Donald Trump had just gutted the U.S. Postal Service, breaking down democratic and voting systems as it did so. Meanwhile, it had been the hottest summer on record and wildfires consumed California, Oregon, and Colorado, while much of the East Coast withered in an historic drought.

We revised the book in the late spring and early summer of 2021. Joe Biden had been elected president and inaugurated, following a terrifying insurgent attack on the U.S. Capitol. Globally, three million people had died of COVID-19, which, if not entirely unchecked, was still rocketing across the world; India was suffering a particularly terrible surge. Rollout of vaccinations continued to happen selectively, with the United States and western Europe getting the lion's share of the supply. The country watched the trial of Derek Chauvin as climate change became a presidential focus and federal and state politicians debated variations on climate policy. Meanwhile, Georgia launched a frontal attack on voting rights on the heels of Democratic victories in the U.S. Senate.

And so, in very real ways, this book was written within the throes of intersecting crises. It emerged amid a series of political moments that painfully exposed the existing—and widening—fissures in the social fabric. It was written in a moment of urgency.

The planet and the United States are here, at this moment, for many reasons. Environmental degradation, biodiversity loss, and climate crises represent some of the most serious existential threats and drive much of the anxiety and uncertainty people feel, especially the youngest generations. These experiences are patterned by gender, class, age, and race, among other things. At the same time, sociologists face crossroads and crises in scholarship—and bigger crises in knowledge, even debates about what constitutes "truth"—that delay collective responses to these problems. Anti-science cultures and politics deride social sciences, while, internally, the racist and colonial histories of sociology have been dealt with only partially.[1]

The origins of these problems are as interlocking and complex as the problems themselves. One thing is quite certain, though: the economic, political, and social choices we make here, now, will have outsized consequences for generations to come.

As the turmoil of these linked crises has unfolded across the nation and world, social scientists are called upon explain what is happening and why. However, sociologists have not typically distinguished themselves in this regard. It may seem odd to begin a sociology book by describing sociology's deficits or the times when it has failed to live up to its promise, but we do it to (1) outline some of what needs to be fixed within our scholarship and our discipline and (2) gain some insight into how to fix it. Sociology failed to predict the U.S. civil rights movement of the 1950s and 1960s,[2] and it has often pushed aside scholars who were not white, or male, or both. But for us, the measure of a valuable discipline is not entirely in its mistakes—it is also in how the discipline *corrects* its mistakes and how it uses its potential to become better as a result of them. It is in this growth—how it responds to past and present failures—that sociology can inform equitable social growth and change.

We are two sociologists writing this book, two women with intersectional and uneven experiences of scholarship and professional life. We are both white, living with the privilege that whiteness confers upon us; we have lived with it our whole lives. We are both women, living with the oppression that sexism has imposed upon us; this, too, we have lived with for our entire lives. One of us grew up in rural New Hampshire with a working-class background, the other outside Chicago in a middle-class family; both of us now have terminal degrees and hold tenure-line positions in public universities. As sociologists, we have both been trained within "structures of colonial education which underpin knowledge production."[3] In other words, we earned our PhDs within coursework, canon, and a discipline that bore the stamp of highly exclusionary and restrictive kinds of knowledge, namely, white, male, and Judeo-Christian, developed primarily within the cultural and intellectual contexts of North America and Europe. As Australian sociologist Raewyn Connell reminds us, "sociology was formed within the culture of imperialism and embodied a cultural response to the colonized world."[4] We are part of a system of knowledge that holds, as many systems do, parallel possibilities: of oppression and emancipation; of innovation and inclusion; and of stagnation, exclusion, and, correspondingly, of irrelevance. Sociology is full of transformative power and promise when it is inclusive and advances through our colonial history; it is at its least helpful and most irrelevant when it fails to do this.

Sociology, like many kinds of knowledge, contains the seeds of both. Like *all* kinds of knowledge, it is by definition incomplete and emergent. And so it is also true that, within the world of research, the choices we make now will also affect generations to come—how we study, how we understand the world around us, and what kinds of solutions we seek.

While calls to stretch, expand, and rethink sociology have gained momentum in recent years, these efforts build on earlier work of many scholars who were relegated to the sidelines because of their race, their gender, or some combination thereof. For instance, Aldon Morris's 2015 book *The Scholar Denied* challenges dominant discourses in sociology and shows that, ever since the U.S. inception of the discipline at the University of Chicago in 1892, sociology not only has dismissed the groundbreaking contributions of Black sociologists but also has offered a tacit disciplinary endorsement of racial hierarchy.[5] In other words, one of the core assumptions of the sociological canon was that both international and domestic colonialism are part of a global march toward progress, "whereby peoples at a lower plane of civilization are incorporated into the culture and institutions of groups that have innate superiority over the peoples they dominate."[6] Or, as Charles W. Mills puts it, "white misunderstanding, misrepresentation, evasion, and self-deception on matters related to race are among the most pervasive mental phenomena of the past few hundred years, a cognitive and moral economy psychically required for conquest, colonization, and enslavement."[7] To grow beyond its roots, then, sociology needs to acknowledge and take responsibility for these shortcomings—and honor and elevate the contributions of marginalized scholars.

Feminist sociology as well, starting nearly a hundred years ago, developed the general line of criticism that women are absent from the social analyses and world of classical sociology. Simone de Beauvoir, in an early attempt to confront social science from a feminist perspective, argued in 1947 that men fundamentally oppress women by characterizing them, on every level, as the "other"— while men themselves are considered the "default." This insight has informed a great deal of feminist theory for the past eighty years. The language and analyses of classical sociologists are those of (white, heterosexual) men, (white, Western) male activities and experiences, and the parts of society that (white) men dominate (including, historically, the formal economy). Karl Marx, Max Weber, and Émile Durkheim—who are tellingly considered the discipline's founding fathers—were typical of nineteenth-century European writers who assumed that the social world was primarily one of white male activities.

Here, too, even the reformers were incomplete. For instance, early feminist sociology was often racialized, its critiques premised on the experiences of white women with little regard to how women's perspectives varied by race, class, religion, and sexual orientation (among other things). This did not make the content of those critiques wrong, but it did make them limited, narrow, and exclusionary.[8] Recent work by intersectional feminists in sociology and related disciplines expands and stretches the collective understanding, documenting and analyzing the richness and variation of women's experiences and creating frameworks for understanding that variation.[9] Intersectional perspectives recognize the combined impacts of multiple social variables (like how race and gender interact in someone's life, for instance) and explore the broad range of women's experiences.[10] Intersectional research has emerged much more prominently in contexts of environmental injustice, work and migration, and economic inequity, for example.[11]

These patterns of exclusive knowledge production are not only sociology's problems. This sort of history is present in most social and natural sciences—social power shaped each of the disciplines that emerged and gained status as global dynamics ushered in the industrial age. And the first step in moving through this history of intellectual exclusion is recognizing that these patterns exist and asking what the effects have been. As Stephen Steinberg writes, this all raises a question:

> How do we explain intellectual hegemony and the process by which certain ideas achieve hegemonic status? This requires that we do more than examine the subtle ways that sociologists consciously and unconsciously reproduce social inequalities in our departments, universities, and even within the American Sociological Association. These issues are important, but the larger issue regards the structures and dynamics of knowledge production. We need to examine the machinery of hegemony, the precise mechanisms through which ideas become ensconced and canons are formed.[12]

Much sociological research fails to respond actively to a world that desperately needs it, then, *in large part because of whose views and experiences it has excluded*.[13] When a discipline is built on assumptions of homogeneity, it misses a lot. Social location (the position that someone occupies in society, influenced by things like gender, sexuality, religion, and class) affects how people make meaning and "define grievances, opportunities, and collective identities."[14] Scholars with privileges of whiteness, economic security, and/or maleness have frequently behaved as if their own identities and positionalities did not matter—which has made their own biases harder to see. These unrecognized biases have also created significant weaknesses in scholarly disciplines' predictive powers, sociology included.[15] After all, how can a field predict the emergence of something like #MeToo when so many sociologists think patriarchally?

In addition, and although sociologists live and breathe rigorous analyses of many issues relevant to this moment—racism, gender, climate crises, organizing—as a discipline, we often struggle to convey our findings, or even the basics of our scholarship, in ways that invite understanding or action. Sociology is built on critique—critique of existing structures, of all the ways in which the world as we inhabit it is unjust. This can, in our experience, make it hard to engage in the messy stuff of organizing, because no real-world social change is ever clear-cut or without contradictions. Sociologists are not the only scientists falling into this trap: the disconnect between the state of knowledge and public discourse emerges in planetary and biological sciences, research enterprises, our legislatures, and other spaces where vital decisions are made and institutionalized. We are in good company—but that is no excuse. The big questions become: Why and how are some knowledge systems privileged while others are systematically excluded? How are those patterns reproduced, and how can we interrupt them? How does this affect the relevance and usefulness of knowledge? How do we use what we know, even when it is imperfect? And how are some groups building something better at keenly important ecological and historical moments?

This last question is perhaps the most important for the most people. Our main concern here is not only about how sociology as a discipline can become better and more inclusive. For most people reading this book, *it is also about what sociology can do to help build better systems.* Inclusion remains central to that concern. As sociology expands to include more intersectional scholarly voices, it must also learn from real-world examples of how people organize, how they resist, and how they build better systems at multiple scales. Sociologists may be experts in social science, but most people have expertise in their own communities, their daily lives, and the way systems can be improved in those contexts.

This is *not* to say that scholars should neglect or negate the scientific method, the value of peer-reviewed research, or ignore the need for deep knowledge formation over time. These are valuable practices that research can give us. And given that many disciplines currently experience what has been dubbed a crisis of expertise—where "post-truth" thinking encourages dismissal of academic inquiry, scientific processes, and facts—scholars must walk the tightrope of becoming more inclusive while upholding the rigor of scientific inquiry. So this *is* to say that sociology's canon and methods need to thoughtfully incorporate knowledge systems of communities—especially those living at the margins. After all, people's lives offer them tools to organize in new and effective ways—and sociology has much to learn from this.

We argue, in this book, that *solving humanity's ecological, economic, and political problems and solving humanity's knowledge creation and epistemological problems are connected projects.* To have better understandings of the world and its problems requires better and more inclusive knowledge. The macro-crises of the world and the meso-level "crisis of expertise" seen across disciplines, in fact, have important similarities. In both cases, scholars and organizers are faced with a clear mandate—to be more inclusive, more justice focused, more clearheaded about the implications of what we do and to build systems that support these goals. Sociology can either prioritize our collective well-being or return to the well-trodden road of insularity and groupthink.

We hope to participate in the former—which, to be clear, is a *collective* process that requires a lot of listening, funding, pushing, pulling, visioning, experimenting, grunt work, and time. Our book is designed around this premise, and we are not the only ones doing this work. We write sociologically—using the tools of our discipline to explore, understand, and synthesize how groups, mostly based in the United States, are building better and more inclusive futures. We hope to lift up and contribute to scholarship and organizing that advances and prioritizes collective well-being.

At the same time, we are pushing our own discipline, alongside many other scholars.[16] Sociology has a mixed history. Disciplines can change and be reimagined—here we will use the language of "decolonized" and "feminized" and otherwise made more inclusive—but that requires a concerted effort from both within and outside of them. We will propose that environmental sociology—as a relatively new subfield within sociology—has unique potential to help reimagine sociology as a whole. Environmental sociology began by questioning sociology's habit of ignoring the biophysical world and the ways that social inequalities manifest in relationship to the environment.[17] It has pushed the discipline to engage with environmental racism and injustice, climate justice, the role of community-based knowledge in addressing socio-environmental problems, and the vital roles that marginalized people and places play in disaster recovery.[18] Environmental sociology can advance in key ways while also setting an example for the rest of the discipline.

BUILDING SOMETHING BETTER THROUGH SOCIOLOGY, MOVEMENTS, AND DEMOCRACY

Womanist and activist Audre Lorde once said, "There is no such thing as a single-issue struggle because we do not live single-issue lives."[19] What she meant was that our problems are connected and that solving any of them means addressing the systemic inputs that create those problems. Indeed, her use of the word "womanism" (a term actually coined by novelist Alice Walker) is meant to distinguish her standpoint from white feminism, acknowledging that experiences of being women differ by race.

We will cover a lot of ground together in this book. For some of you, it will be new ground. And for some, we will be traversing familiar territory. We want to begin with a few thoughts about the nature of what we are up against, and the tools that people are already using to shape the world into something better.

Bear in mind that the premise of sociology is that systems and structures that are bigger than individuals shape our lives, even as individuals have agency and can exercise their will to some extent. Individuals, in turn, shape society and social systems through our actions and beliefs. This is reflected in the idea of a *sociological imagination*, a concept articulated by C. Wright Mills, who observed that "the first fruit of this [sociological] imagination—and the first lesson of the social science that embodies it"[20] is that people can recognize how their own individual, personal troubles are really part of and created by collective, public issues. Our individual biographies are shaped by the time periods, communities, systems, and cultures in which we are embedded. That is, the sociological imagination asks us to realize that individual experiences can be rightly understood *only* in their social contexts. Society is greater than the sum of its (individual) parts.

For us, understanding neoliberalism—and its core ideologies and policy measures—is a significant first step in reimagining systems that have helped accelerate global crises. Providing a sophisticated but clear overview of neoliberalism and its discontents is thus a core component of this book. The political, social, and climate threats that we face are logical conclusions of this fundamentalist form of capitalism. The tenets of neoliberalism utilize and encourage consumption and individualization as main mechanisms of social change: they valorize market-based approaches to all aspects of life, and, in doing so, they devalue all the non-market-based, unquantifiable, noneconomic parts of our lives. They dismiss misogyny and racism as fictions and make ecological systems invisible, preferring to externalize harms and to pretend that all people have equal opportunities to "pull themselves up by their bootstraps." Specifically, the tenets of neoliberalism include the following:

- Commodification: understanding people, animals, places, and ecosystems as goods to be bought or sold in a property-based market system
- Privatization: the taking of communal or public resources (like water, land, or public utilities) and enclosing them, making them available for private ownership via the market system
- Deregulation and reregulation: removing or changing regulations, or taking away budgets for enforcement of regulations, that often protect environment, labor, children, and other potentially vulnerable groups, in order to facilitate corporate access to people and resources
- Dismantling of social safety nets: diminishing the state's ability or mandates to provide services that ensure the well-being of the community, such as health care, higher education, housing, and childcare—and redirecting those assets toward markets

These ideologies have powerfully but stealthily shaped daily life around the world. Indeed, neoliberalism is the water most people swim in but do not see. Many people can hardly imagine any other way of living or being.

But imagine we must.

The point of this book is to explore how people and communities actively counter neoliberal prescriptions. We make specific and concrete recommendations, based both in existing scholarship and in the organizing that we describe here. Two forms of data inform this book, each designed to do something slightly different. They are (1) sociological data designed and collected according to social scientific methods and systematically analyzed and (2) narrative explorations drawn from contemporary movements that illustrate new systems and approaches and offer provocative avenues for exploration. In other words, we prioritize concrete examples of how varied communities do social change work and experiment with solutions. To talk about this in a meaningful, grounded way, we give examples of what *has* worked—but also of what *is working right now*, and why. These illustrations are emergent, happening in real time and on the ground. We use them to open inquiry rather than to say something generalizable about social processes.

What Seems to Be Working?

We spend much of the book sharing examples of how people build something better out of the crises we face. There are a few similarities across the work being done, which we want to outline up front.

First, we show how these groups and organizations work to *explicitly address and resist neoliberal capitalism*. In other words, they very deliberately confront the fundamental tensions and inconsistencies that capitalism generates. While some are semi-professionalized or professionalized, all of these organizations take seriously how neoliberal approaches necessarily subordinate human and non-human species to profit, and they talk about it openly as they counter these effects, making explicit links between their on-the-ground organizing and the larger systems shaping the lives of their communities. They do not avoid talking about it, and they do not pretend it away. Each of our cases highlights this in its own way.

More than that, though, these movements explore the intimate relationships between capitalism, class struggles, sexism and racism, colonialism, and ecological destruction—and make those relationships a core part of their work. This, as well, requires an explicit conversation about systems. Scholars have looked at these relationships for a long time, exploring how capitalism builds upon intersecting radicalized, racialized, and gendered sets of exploitation.[21] Real organizing, given this, must mean acknowledging the different effects that neoliberal capitalism has had on people of different races, classes, and genders. The organizations and communities we highlight here take on this challenging, iterative, and complex work—even while building on-the-ground alternatives.

In all of this, identity matters. It always has, and it always will. Identity politics are frequently dismissed outright as divisive (and often that is because they challenge patriarchal and neoliberal dogma). But individual identities also take on meaning in the *collective and historical* sense; they mean something because of the systems and structures in which those identities are embedded and through which they are given meaning, context, and power—or not. The cases here acknowledge those multi-scalar links and work with them.

For instance (to preview some of our case studies), Indigenized Energy showcases how to build community-based and community-owned energy systems in the midst of extractive landscapes and histories—and how to do this with intergenerational needs as central priorities. The Hemp and Heritage Farm builds nonextractive, regenerative economies that draw on Indigenous knowledge systems, rooted in the Ojibwe practices of its founder. Thunder Valley Community Development Corporation (Thunder Valley CDC), on Lakota land now referred to as Pine Ridge, South Dakota, also exemplifies how to build interwoven regenerative systems that allow equitable access to housing, food, education, and spiritual and other supports for communities dealing with systemic poverty. The Havasupai Tribal Nation's fight against uranium mining's encroachment on water systems vital to their ancestral and current home showcases how noneconomic values can be prioritized.

Each case, then, can be described as "intersectional"—as recognizing the interactive ways that different aspects of people's identities matter. As discussed earlier, an intersectional framework (in both organizing and research) is premised on the idea that different systems of oppression are coproduced by, and productive of, unequal realities.[22] While Kimberlé Crenshaw is credited for the term "intersectionality" and Patricia Hill Collins popularized it, the idea drew upon decades of work by other feminists.[23] This included work by the Combahee River Collective, a Black women's group that articulated a version of intersectionality in 1977, emphasizing "the development of integrated analysis and practice based upon the fact that the major systems of oppression are interlocking."[24] Rather than examining gender, race, class, spatial location, sexuality, age, historical era, and nation (to name just a few) as separate systems, an intersectional approach looks at how these systems comprise and complicate one another and the effects that those combined experiences produce in people's lives.[25]

An example illustrates these patterns and relates to our cases: the history of American environmentalism, as presented by many authors until quite recently, was a history of white, upper-middle-class, male environmental activism. Yet, as Dorceta Taylor has argued for years,[26] this perspective has deprived scholarship of deeper understandings of how environmental experiences are different for different people and how those experiences have varied over time. This dominant construction of "the environment" emerged from imagery of wilderness, wildlife, and themes of recreation, themselves influenced by Romanticism and transcendentalism.

This narrow, exclusionary account rendered invisible countless other perspectives and normalized one view as *the* view of environmental movements.[27] Romantic understandings of "the environment" differed greatly from, for instance, a history of sharecropping that shaped many Black Americans' experiences. Black scholars and activists began to write and speak about environmental issues explicitly in the 1970s by linking them with race and social inequality[28]—and Taylor's work has repeatedly made such connections. This narrow view of the environment also failed to recognize—given its emphasis on ideas like "unspoiled" wilderness—that Indigenous and tribal people and nations in settler colonies were forcibly and violently removed from their ancestral homelands to make room for white settlers and wilderness designations, which also depended on perpetual treaty violations by the U.S. state.[29] Indeed, as other scholars have observed, the violent losses rendered by settler colonialism necessitate an Indigenous Environmental Justice that recognizes how ongoing inequities extend from more than 500 years of environmental injustices that Native nations have endured.[30] Additionally, many people's experiences of the environment were and are frequently mediated through farm labor. For instance, the United Farm Workers movement (whose better-known organizers included Cesar Chavez, Dolores Huerta, and Jessie Lopez) had its own way of engaging the environment.[31] The mainstream environmental movement also largely failed to recognize or represent how gender shaped environmental experiences[32], as people of different genders were frequently separated spatially and occupationally.

Each case study presented here, then, reminds us of the power of intersectional perspectives. Indeed, the communities and organizations we highlight all clearly demonstrate that good organizing is intersectional because neoliberalism and ecological destruction do not affect all people in the same ways. Any sustainable path to healing must acknowledge this. And the organizations whose work we explore also value this as an important sociological reality. Diversity of experience can *enrich* collective efforts to build something better. Each case's intersectional approaches to community-building inform their more distributive and regenerative efforts.

Related, there are clear distinctions in the cases we highlight between *organizations* and *organizing*. The groups shared here deliberate explicitly about the trade-offs they make (or do not make) between creating organizations as stable institutions that pay people salaries, and organizing on specific issue campaigns. A great deal of work has shown that formal organizations can have deleterious effects on the orientation and demands of civil society,[33] even as they can also become consistent foundations for community work. In other words, the pressures of the nonprofit industrial complex can muffle the breadth of the demands, even while offering stable bases for community-focused work. The case studies we share focus on spaces of organizing that (while sometimes formalized) are clearly not only businesses. Soul Fire Farm, for instance, complements its agricultural work with speaking and educational engagement and land rematriation strategies, where Indigenous land is returned to Indigenous people and nations. Thunder Valley CDC focuses on spiritually guided community development and healing work, alongside the building of affordable housing designed in traditional Lakota layouts. This dynamic *organizing* (as opposed to formal organization-building) also opens space *to build coalitions.* Each case study illustrates how organizing work can inform and strengthen organizations by making them more malleable, adaptable, and open to the infusion of new members, partnerships across causes, and changes in course if necessary.

Because of this, *organizing work* (as opposed to *organizational* work) *is often emotive, or affective labor.* Across these case studies, we see examples of organizing that are creative and spiritual, based in the evolving needs of diverse communities—and sometimes even funny. Much of this organizing resists the norms of hierarchically organized institutions, which often exacerbate inequalities along the lines of gender, class, race, and ethnicity.[34] There are spaces for different kinds of people and knowledge in these cases—and different kinds of expression.

As part of this deep engagement with the stuff of humanity and life, *these groups also typically work with well-developed understandings of the synergies between humans and more-than-humans—between humans and environment, broadly defined.* Among them, "natural resources" are often understood as relations. One of the groups, Soul Fire Farm, counts the land it farms as a voting member of its decision-making process, for example. And other groups we write about, like the Hemp and Heritage Farm, were founded by Indigenous Water Protectors who fiercely defend the Rights of Nature. In other words, these groups elevate that which is most human and which we can aspire to become as human beings, while honoring humanity's relationships with more-than-humans.

Across cases, groups strive to see humanity's potential while acknowledging its faults. As discriminatory systems have become institutionalized, the ugliness of inequality, poverty, state-led violence, "power-over" thinking, and ecological disaster can seem all too real and permanent. *The groups we focus on highlight both where humanity is flourishing and where it needs to grow.* They call *out* the systems and the thinking at fault. They call *in* potential participants, allies, and accomplices. They highlight how systems of white supremacy, sexism, colonialism and capitalism, extractivism, and speciesism have created current sociological and ecological disasters. They talk about why these systems need to be dismantled—and soon—if people are to build other systems that can contend with climate crises, massive economic inequality, and the disastrous outcomes of racialized capitalism and patriarchal systems. And just as importantly, they underscore that these sad systems are not the only fruits of humankind, that there can be richness, humility, cooperation, connection, respect, and love in what people do and create.

Each of these groups also works to heal the deep social wounds inflicted by *patriarchal systems—systems where men hold power, privilege, respect, and often control over property and lineage.* Like racism, patriarchy and sexism are deeply embedded, and they show up in the very blueprints of polity, organizing, schools, and jobs.[35] Patriarchy, capitalism, and colonial regimes have often intersected, and they have tended to erase and subsume other systems. For instance, the matrilineal approaches of some of the cultures we examine in our case studies were all but decimated by patriarchal systems, which, like racial hierarchies, tend to overtake other ways of being—right down to the language that people use to describe daily experiences.[36] The groups we highlight here acknowledge this and shape their organizing around resisting it.

Because of their clearheaded perspectives about what humans are and can be, and what they are not, *these groups also have a serious engagement with context—social and environmental.* Whether that context is a city, a neighborhood, a university, an industry, the land they cultivate, or even just a street, the groups in our case studies are deeply connected to, and intentional about, place. They strive to be grounded in the needs and experiences of their environment, including humans, more-than-humans, and land and water. And while they include abstract critiques (of capitalism, for instance), those critiques get their weight from the lived, grounded experiences of people themselves.

A great many of these organizations are also intergenerational, which matters conceptually as well as practically. When you think about the future, you have to reflect on who you expect will be alive and what they will need; this can change calculations in the present. The movements we highlight in some of our cases, from youth-led campus divestment organizations to the Society of Fearless Grandmothers, explicitly adhere to intergenerational ethics. These groups see humanity in a complex web of more-than-humans, ecosystems, and countless generations before and after those currently here—and model how to take the long view, with well-being as the central goal.

Finally, all of these groups have an active recognition of both the structural and the personal. Some of them—like Soul Fire Farm—explicitly talk about the link between structure and agency. Groups have systemic views on big social issues, understanding their historical roots and their institutional forces. But they also offer lessons in how to use individual and community agency to actively change these systems. Systems can feel so daunting—because they are often so hard to see—and individual people within them can feel powerless, small, and inept. But once we recognize structure—once we see the systems that hold power-over—we gain insights into how to change them.

LOOKING FORWARD: THINGS TO CONSIDER WHEN IMAGINING A "PUBLIC" IN A DEMOCRACY

We focus on emergent solutions in this book, which is intentional. But we need to be clear—there is resistance to these emergent solutions, and it comes from all corners. This work is not straightforward or easy, and it involves constant reckoning. Changing systems is hard.

First, there are institutional barriers to effective community organizing. Those, in conventional words, are the systems that govern the world: forms of political representation, organizational structures, financial and economic systems, educational settings, ideologies, and the other powerful institutions that govern our shared lives and that are set up to empower and elevate some values while repressing others. These are embodied in the systems of capitalism, colonialism, and inequality that we will discuss more throughout this book.

An extended illustration may be helpful here: in the spring and early summer of 2020, groups across the United States sought to end law enforcement's systemic abuse of Black Americans under the rallying cry of "Defund the Police!" In the aftermath of George Floyd's murder at the hands of Minneapolis police, protesters in many cities gave up on trying to change police behavior and instead advanced a more radical idea: to "defund the police" by cutting their budgets and shifting police functions to other municipal departments or community groups.

Their argument for doing so was that the institution of policing itself was unsalvageable, built as it is on racist and classist principles, building on legacies of slave patrols, enforcement of Jim Crow laws, and repression of the civil rights movement. Slave patrols (called patrollers, patterrollers, pattyrollers, or paddy rollers by enslaved people), were organized groups of armed white men who monitored and enforced discipline upon enslaved Black people in the antebellum United States.[37] Members of slave patrols could forcefully enter anyone's home, regardless of the occupants' race or ethnicity, on the basis of suspicion that they were sheltering people who had escaped bondage. The trajectory from such patrols to the contemporary police state is well documented.[38]

The structure of policing also typically protects the interests of the ruling class, while criminalizing poverty. Another foundation of modern law enforcement was the centralized municipal police departments that began to form in the early nineteenth century, beginning in Boston and emerging as well in New York, Albany, Chicago, Philadelphia, and elsewhere, which were formally mandated to control a "dangerous underclass."[39] In other words, racism and classism constitute the very DNA of the institution of policing.

The question then becomes: What could alternative forms of community safety look like? How might communities structure safety to be supportive, antiracist, and consistent? These questions stretch our collective imagination, and they require huge amounts of work. Community organizing is the work of time, coalition-building, and effort.

But there are other barriers, too. One is the role of the state. These examples—as well as many throughout the book—mean that we, as both scholars and activists, must consider relationships between communities and the state and government. The state is fraught. It can be an important ally at times—a beacon of public representation and protection—but it can also be the source of powerful, violent oppression. Throughout this book, we will advocate frequently for state or public regulation; we do that because we believe that regulations should be universal (since that is when they are most effective). There should not, we believe, be loopholes to allow freehanded polluting, or norms for one company that do not extend across an industry. System-wide regulations make the most sense. Further, communities pay taxes as part of their contribution to protective structures.

But in order to make that argument with integrity, we need to seriously grapple with the fact that the state has often been an arm of, and an apologist for, elite-centered capitalism and tremendous violence toward and oppression of women, people of color, and religious and ethnic minorities. Even as we, the authors, argue "for" community ownership and use of public space (and we do), we have to reckon with the reality that the "public" is, in itself, contested because of our very history. Put differently: many states, including the United States, were built upon a series of violent expropriations of both land and people. The U.S. state is at the root of ongoing violent oppression of Indigenous nations and Black Americans, and it still relies on the sexual and reproductive labor of women of all races. How, then, do we imagine a "public" space in this context? What does it mean to recognize that the streets of Boston were built on the homelands of the Massachuset people, even as radical street bands resist neoliberal capitalism by making music for free upon them?

The state, in turn, produces another set of questions about how to engage and decide on shared standards of life. Any government entity enshrines certain expectations and opinions about how the world is and how it should be. The U.S. model of democracy is structured around very specific assumptions; the idea of democracy itself has a specific (Western) history, which excludes other forms of social organization. This does not mean that it is necessarily *bad* or that we advocate against it (we do not). But it *does* mean that we must consider how the format of U.S. government includes some people and excludes many others, in a variety of ways. For instance, white men represent 30 percent of the population but 62 percent of officeholders, dominating both chambers of the United States Congress, forty-two state legislatures, and statewide roles across the nation; women of all races and people of color constitute 51 percent and 40 percent of the U.S. population, respectively, but just 31 percent and 13 percent of officeholders.[40] And systems that are reliant upon a majority vote (like the ones throughout most of the United States) bypass values of consensus, even though there are other systems of voting—such as proportional and ranked choice—that are more supportive and sensitive to the needs of different constituencies.

Further, even if people have a good idea of how democracy and the state could be better, organizers and politicians alike must be realistic about the low levels of trust in that democracy, because the U.S. state has been violent. It has always been tied to capitalism—which has depended, in turn, on the subjuga-tion of women's bodies and the bodies of Black and Indigenous people and other people of color of all genders. So part of the bold vision of "strengthening democracy" is *envisioning what a healthy government could look like*. It is unrea-sonable to advocate for state regulation and then simply expect it to be fairly enforced, given the trajectory of U.S. history.

So the cases we highlight also begin to illustrate what smaller-scale gover-nance might look like and how community-centered organizing—connected with the larger systems in which communities are embedded—might make sense in addressing the local-global issues of climate crises. It is equally impor-tant to recognize that smaller-scale governance and local solutions are not neces-sarily more representative, more just, or more likely to be sites of progress or transformation—indeed, part of the role of governments is to offer protections that communities alone cannot offer. There are many potential solutions and interlinkages; part of the work is exploring the breadth of possibilities.

Correspondingly, we feel compelled to underscore that organizing is inter personally hard. Building community is hard, especially in a world where people are bound by underpaid jobs, where housing is unstable, where human and envi-ronmental health is so precarious, where institutional barriers are so great, and where pandemics can roll unmitigated across the globe. Communities are the building blocks of institutional change at any level. Strong communities are those that can figure out how to disagree and resolve conflict, recognize power, examine biases and privileges and orientations, and explore how institutions do (or do not) reflect their professed values. We do not think that communities should be glorified as universal salves for social problems; the state can some-times be a more neutral arbiter of protections, for example. But local communi-ties' geographic scales make them powerful: they offer meso-level spaces of social interaction and institution-building that can be more accessible and gen-erate more trust than larger-scale systems like states.

Given all this, we are not suggesting, either, that before us is a straightfor-ward march toward a common utopia. Communities have extremely disparate visions of what "the good life" even is, given the extremely disparate experi-ences they have had of social and environmental problems. However, to address some of the bigger existential problems like climate crises, people and societies have to move at an unprecedented pace. Doing work that acknowledges these differences—the tensions between the long, slow work of community-building and the need to move swiftly, between the different experiences of the past and the varied visions of the future—is part of the challenge.

This is where the examples lent by the cases in upcoming chapters can offer wisdom and model alternatives. For every case we include in the book, there are hundreds of others that utilize similar principles but look just a little different, embedded in their own time and place. Lorde's words are helpful here: "We are not perfect, but we are stronger and wiser than the sum of our errors."[41]

MOTHERHOOD AND WILDFIRES—STEPHANIE'S NOTE ON POSITIONALITY

As we worked on this book, I felt like the world fell apart. All those predictions from climate scientists and social scientists were coming to bear. I witnessed basic norms of democracy and science crumble under an authoritarian American president. I panicked as environmental regulations were scaled back every day—even as climate crises became increasingly apparent. I felt dread in the pit of my stomach as the economy crumbled, mostly because it is not built to serve everyone. And I felt enraged as my rights as a woman came under attack to a degree that I did not want to acknowledge was possible.

In all of this, I became a mother for the first time. My partner and I had debated about having children for years. Were we really going to bring another human being into this world? Into this chaos? The morning after Trump was elected, my husband and I woke up in a depressed haze, and I remember him saying, "How can we have kids now?" I wondered, too. But we did it anyway. The strong desire to raise a good human took over, and we just could not overthink it any longer.

But this motherhood thing is raw and emotional in the best of times. And now . . . my goodness. Being a mother means incredible stress, uncertainty, and existential crises. It certainly always has—but somehow the stakes feel higher at this moment. What will the world look like for my son when he is twenty? Or forty? Or what does it look like even now? I was pregnant and gave birth in the midst of a global pandemic. My child was surrounded by people in masks for the first days of his life. He has been almost completely isolated since then. As we brought our new son home, ash rained down on us, and the sky had an eerie orange glow from historic wildfires burning up Colorado. Two months later, as we finished our first draft of this book, those fires were still charring some of the places my family finds sacred, which we had so desperately wanted to share with our new child. On the morning I first penned this section, I woke up to a house that smelled like campfire and an air quality index that meant I could not take my son outside—not that inside was much better. As we edited this chapter months later, the fires had stopped and winter had come and gone—but snowpack was low and historic drought meant that a similarly hellacious fire season could lie ahead. It is almost too much to bear sometimes—and I am privileged in many ways that make this easier for me than for so many people.

All of this is to say—the social and environmental problems we write about here are deeply real to me. As a new mother, that realness is amplified in ways I did not expect. My new role intersects with a time that is unprecedented in too many ways. As a white, middle-class social scientist in the United States, I had been able to skate along the surface too much of the time—as embarrassed as I am to admit that. I have known for years that our systems create stark, catastrophic problems—and I have worked to change those. I knew—and taught others about—the environmental inequities that industrial, capitalist systems create and the horrific violence used to colonize places like the United States. As a woman, I had my share of run-ins with discrimination and structural violence. Compared with Black and Brown women, though, I had immense privilege. I could feel safe most of the time, even as I fought for environmental justice. But now that has changed in important ways. Yes, climate crises hit those most marginalized and those least responsible for greenhouse gas emissions first and worst, and I am deeply aware that these impacts are multiplied and even more amplified now for people less privileged than me. But Risk Society theorist and social scientist Ulrich Beck was spot-on: the expanding risks and scale of climate crises meant "my" backyard was burning, too.

In a way, I am trying to see this as a blessing in disguise. Motherhood changes the stakes—and when combined with climate crises, it generates vulnerability and uncertainty that have made me want to fight harder than ever. The problems we analyze in this book no longer represent an intellectual puzzle; giving these stories a platform has taken on a new urgency for me as I have become more viscerally linked to future generations. I have loved and practiced sociology for years, but it has left me feeling hopeless at times because I am trained to see structural deficits. This is why I wanted to write this book: if sociology is done well and inclusively, it can serve humanity and give people the hope and skills to change the world.

The cases we present here give me hope that *maybe* that can actually happen. They have helped me hold back the feelings of despair as all these problems swirl around me and my son, around all of us. These cases help me feel that perhaps humanity can chart restorative paths forward, *if* things change quickly—*and* in the direction suggested by the communities we highlight. I feel lucky to have had the opportunity to learn from and then share these stories. I must admit, I have wondered whether I, as a white woman, was the right one to tell these stories. But I have decided that people shared them with me because they trusted me to tell them, and for that I am deeply grateful. Using this space to tell these stories is one of the ways I can best utilize the privileges I do have in this lifetime. I hope they give you the same sense of hope they have given me.

POLITICS, COVID-19, CRISES, DIVORCES—MEGHAN'S NOTE ON POSITIONALITY

The same summer that Stephanie and I wrote this book, and as so many crises unspooled at once, I ran for election to the Rhode Island State Senate and won.

I had been a city councilor representing the western part of the city of Pawtucket for two terms before that. I ran because the moment of political urgency was unparalleled in my life, although I had been a community organizer for many years—even before going to graduate school. My community was already getting walloped by COVID-19 as I finished my second term on the city council; we were especially hard-hit economically, and we are economically poor to begin with. Specifically, the coronavirus brutally exposed us to how much we rely on people who earn the least and who have the fewest protections—at the grocery register, driving the bus, caring for the elderly, cleaning hospitals. If there were ever an argument for universal health care, a pandemic is it: stopping the pandemic requires care for *everyone*, not just those with insurance. Our health-care system—built on profit rather than on people's well-being—was unprepared to face COVID-19, and Black and Latinx community members bore the greatest burden in Rhode Island. Some estimates put up to 5 percent of Rhode Islanders at risk of losing their home as a direct or indirect consequence of the pandemic. Protestors across the country were clashing with the police over murders of Black people; parents, and mothers especially, were in untenable situations as they juggled childcare and job responsibilities while working from home; my students were struggling to write dissertations or even to do their coursework as COVID-19 claimed lives of their family members and upended research plans. The University of Massachusetts system tightened its belt, worried about the pandemic's economic fallout, as we all pivoted on a dime to remote teaching and learning. In the middle of all this, I got divorced—my own personal crises entwining with the daily tragedies of 2020.

I was both a scholar and a politician before the pandemic, and I hope to be a scholar and a politician for at least some time after it. The two roles combine in ways that are both instructive and awkward. First as a community organizer and then as a politician, I have spent a lot of time in the metaphorical trenches, where experiences are messy and conflicting and where nothing is ever clean or perfect. As a sociologist, I am trained to look critically at policy, and process, and political decisions—trained to see their systemic influences and impacts. I am also trained to pick holes in things, to critique until I am blue in the face. Critique is a way of life in academia. Critique is a useful skill to have, and I am glad I have it.

But it has become very clear to me that critique alone is a limited and limiting way to engage with the world, and that imperfect things are still worth having. Problem-solving requires risking failure, risking mistakes—and indeed, *making* mistakes and experiencing failure, owning it, learning from it, and trying again. I am *not* saying that we should use the existence of those inevitable imperfections to avoid growing, as individual people or as communities. I am not saying that those imperfections are excuses to indulge our lesser natures or ignore our biases or absolve ourselves of accountability. I *am* saying, though, as the quaint adage goes, the perfect is the enemy of the good. It is straightforward to point out systemic challenges; sociologists are great at that. Creating systemic solutions, on the other hand, is the work of time, effort, humility, deliberation, and a goodly amount of trial and error. It requires a willingness to get one's hands dirty and a willingness to be wrong.

This political conviction—the conviction that we have to try—is linked with my identity as a sociologist. And as we seek to solve our entwined epistemological and political crises, I find myself moved by what writer Peter Elbow calls "the believing game." Generally speaking, the kind of thinking most widely taught within sociology is critical—it is a disciplined practice of trying to be as skeptical and analytical as possible with everything we encounter. The idea is that through doubt, we can discover contradictions, bad reasoning, and the like. In this critical perspective, we are taught to use doubt as a tool for scrutiny of ideas. Believing, by contrast, is just as disciplined: it is a practice of trying to be as accepting as possible of every idea we encounter, of not just listening to different views differently but *actually trying to believe them.* The believing game uses belief rather than criticism as a tool for scrutiny of ideas, looking instead for hidden virtues. It can be just as valuable a check on our own biases. For instance, one hope for finding invisible flaws in *our own* thinking is to enter into different ways of thinking—those that carry different assumptions. Only from this new perspective can we see our point of view from the outside and thereby notice assumptions that our customary point of view keeps hidden. This idea is, to me, an invitation to see knowledge on its own terms—to explore new paradigms and new ways of thinking. Surely we need this very badly, in sociology and beyond.

A WORD ABOUT OUR CASE STUDIES

A goal of this book is to look at how people are doing actionable work in the midst of wicked problems. The reader will doubtless note that we refrain in some important ways from engaging a critical perspective as we explore our case studies. In organizing our book this way, we are diverging a bit from the conventional format of sociology, which is designed primarily around critique. We are choosing instead to engage in the believing game, in which we take as a premise the idea that we are going to believe what we see—as fully as possible and with the idea that by stepping into a range of different realities, experiences, and belief systems, we in the fields of sociological study and community organizing can learn a lot about our own weak spots.

We are not suspending critique entirely; we have both been too deeply socialized as sociologists to forgo it. But what we *have* done is use our critical and sociological training to scan the field of community organizations pretty carefully—based on existing critiques within (environmental) sociology, social change scholarship, and related research—and we selected our cases purposively. We are aware that ways of organizing can reproduce and even deepen existing social inequalities and problems. So we have carefully chosen cases that are intersectional, that often have women of color at the helm, and that actively engage with social problems and ecological realities. These organizations are not perfect. But they *are* bravely modeling how to build different systems; dismantling current neoliberal, racist, misogynist, and ecocidal tropes; and being incredibly self-reflective at the same time. Exploring their work is an opportunity to see into possibility.

WHAT LIES AHEAD

Chapter 2, which we titled "A People's Sociology," highlights the premises of environmental sociology and digs into the ways that sociology can learn from past mistakes to become a more inclusive and transformative social science. Chapter 3 explores neoliberalism in depth—its color-blindness, its history, its consequences, and its political, social, and ecological implications. Chapter 4 leads with a simple prescription: think of yourself as a human being within a vibrant human society rather than as an individual whose only voice is through consumption. Here, we examine organizations recentering *collective* action and systemic changes. Chapter 5 argues that we must reclaim public space as social space: a commons dedicated to building relationships with others and creating communities. Here, we explore the implications of privatization and showcase radically different approaches to stewarding land and water and building communities. Chapter 6 argues that we must embed the economy in our daily lives and environments—building systems (including economies) that work for everyone. Here, we examine how people fight de- and reregulation and fortify social protections through regenerative systems-building. In chapters 4 through 6, we highlight case studies showing how people are actually *doing* social change and building better, more inclusive, distributive, and regenerative systems and communities. Our conclusion, in chapter 7, reconsiders and synthesizes the insights and patterns from our case studies, rethinking our relationships with one another, the planet, and the economy—and how inclusive sociology can help guide those processes and policies toward more emancipatory futures.

2 · A PEOPLE'S SOCIOLOGY

Climate change is a problem that cuts across all aspects of how we live. This is true of many environmental crises, from plummeting biodiversity to environmental racism, to health effects of contamination and pollution. Later in this book, we hear from people who build capacity and community to counteract the negative effects of these crises in distributive and regenerative ways: from building sustainable and climate-aware economies based on hemp cultivation, to rematriating land, to mobilizing youth-led action toward new economies and renewable, nonextractive energy systems. Before we can get to productive solutions, though, we need to take a look at the social and historical aspects of environmental problems. Here, we use the tools of environmental sociology to illustrate how environmental issues relate to systemic social inequities—and how, then, problematic systems can be dismantled and rebuilt. Sociology, as many have argued, is embedded in its own legacies of white supremacy, sexism, and colonialism.[1] But it, too, can be reshaped. We aim here to build on the innovative work within sociology to assist in this process of rebuilding the discipline so that it might aid us in building equitable social systems.

The social, economic, and political systems of industrial capitalism are unsustainable—for people, for more-than-humans, and for the planet. We face challenges of survival and existential crises in the most literal sense. The best science says people have about a decade to avert worst-case climate scenarios[2] like catastrophic weather changes and natural disasters, alongside the unpredictable social and economic effects of climate meltdown. The choice (even if it is forced) of 1, 2, 3, or 5 degrees Celsius of global warming was never a scientific one. Rather, it is a social and political choice, extrapolated from the science, of what people want the future to look like, weighed against what humanity can transform and sacrifice—and how quickly we can mobilize to get there.

Sociologists often think about social change as happening in response to an *exogenous shock*—a problem that occurs outside the boundaries of a social institution or even an entire society. But climate change and other existential environmental crises muddle that distinction. They are exogenous in the sense that humans cannot directly control these crises in real time—but particular human systems have caused them and continue to shape them. In other words, humans cannot "cause" a superstorm in the immediate term, but increased superstorms come as a result of runaway carbon emissions caused by industrialization, and the human tolls that such crises take are worsened by bad policies, as in the case of Hurricanes Katrina and Maria.

The word often given to this idea is the "Anthropocene," which refers to a new "age of man" (yes, we mean to say "man") that has drastically shifted the Earth's systems and threatens the viability of human life on this planet. "Capitalocene" riffs on Anthropocene, and we prefer this term. Capitalocene refers to the idea that current environmental crises were created *not* by all human beings or by something defective in human nature—but by specific capitalist, industrial, and oppressive systems of power and relations among humans and nature. So, as with most environmental crises, responsibilities—and burdens—are not experienced evenly. Western nations driving dependence on fossil fuels have been the most responsible; further, researchers can name and identify about one hundred corporations that have been responsible for about 71 percent of all global emissions in the past forty years. Indeed, "since 1751 . . . a mere ninety corporations, primarily oil and coal companies, have generated two-thirds of humanity's CO_2 emissions."[3] This perspective locates responsibility with certain industries and corporations, while also recognizing vital distinctions in culpability between nations—and within them, too. Within settler states, for instance, Indigenous and Native people, other communities of color, and poor communities have dealt with the dystopian impacts of industrialization for centuries, with climate crises as the pinnacle of those tragedies.[4]

As frequently happens in times of crisis, our imaginations become stunted; we can barely imagine what we need, much less how we might get there. So often, the solutions we *do* imagine consist of variations on market-based thinking—in other words, variations of the deeply flawed systems we already have. Yet, this high-stakes situation means that institutions, patterns, and habits all need to shift drastically and rapidly. Those shifts need to center justice and inclusion. Incredibly, groups and communities all over the world have lived, worked, and organized themselves to both shift the terms of the debate and combat the crises at the same time—groups ranging from MOVE (a Black liberation group with strong environmentalist and naturalist principles) to campus divestment organizations.

None of this is new. But mainstream political and institutional, even sociological, realities need to catch up to the community-based work.

The urgency of systems change has taken on a qualitatively different focus since the mid-2010s, however. To focus on justice in such a radical way means reconsidering most things about social systems: rules and norms, framing of and relationships to nature, systems and institutions, and indeed, the values that underwrite everything. This obviously must be a collective endeavor in societies, assisted by disciplines like sociology—where each grows beyond its history to help build better systems. This book aims to help with a piece of that work. Considering how different communities react to different pieces of climate crisis, we hope, can offer new ways to think about entwined problems confronting humanity.

Environmental crises intersect with, and emerge from, a host of social and economic problems: inequality; extractivism and unsustainable industrial systems; white supremacy and other forms of fascism; widespread confusion around social media and the onslaught of "fake news" and conspiratorial thinking; deep social and cultural divides and disputes over values; widespread professionalization of the nonprofit sector; and multi-scalar complexities of globalization processes, to name a few. All of this makes clear that many people badly need some new ways to live with one another and on the planet. But no discipline, no community, no scholar can fully move forward without understanding, acknowledging, and working through the past.

This process is known to some as decolonizing—here, specifically, it is decolonizing *sociology* to better tell the stories of communities and organizations that actively decolonize *society*. We note up front that the term "decolonizing" itself is contested: Eve Tuck and K. Wayne Yang argue that decolonization without the formal repatriation or rematriation of Indigenous land to Indigenous people is not the work of decolonization; it is social justice work but not decolonizing work.[5] However, given the widespread use of the word to refer to a more generalized process of justice-seeking,[6] we also utilize it here in that way. For University of Cambridge social scientist Ali Meghji, decolonizing sociology is at once a recognition of what have been "exploitative and excluded sociological knowledges"—a fundamental reassessment of the thinking and people that currently count as canonical within the field—and, indeed, a reexamination of what constitutes sociological thought at all.[7]

A vital first step is to understand and recognize the privileging of certain types of knowledge—whose knowledge is considered valuable, correct, objective, or rigorous. Sociologists in the nineteenth century were connected by their desire to show that the European "race" was morally and scientifically superior to other racial groups. And those initial imprints are persistent: more than a century later, the way that sociology is taught still focuses on straight, white male theorists from Europe and the United States. These orientations also shape dominant approaches to how sociologists conduct research, how they design studies, and what sorts of experiences and knowledge systems are seen as legitimate representations of the empirical world. For instance, even as environmental health has become a central focus of environmental justice researchers, poor or minoritized communities' firsthand experiences of illness are not always accepted as accurate representations of public health.[8] These knowledge hierarchies reproduce colonial systems.

Sociology is "part of the global economy of knowledge that grew out of the imperial traffic in knowledge."[9] As philosopher Paulin Hountondji puts it,[10] empires created a division of intellectual labor between "periphery"—the marginalized parts of the world, from which sociologists collected their data—and "metropole," a standpoint where sociologists typically perched to study society. In other words, it emerged from a divide between those who "researched" and those who were "researched on." This division is still deeply embedded in modern knowledge formation, and it shows up in theories that sociologists hold dear and use regularly, without acknowledging the positionality, origins, or orientation of those ideas. We also must recognize that this research "embeds perspectives on the world that arise from the social formations of the global North, because of their historical position in imperialism and their current core position in the neoliberal world economy."[11]

As this reckoning gets more fully underway, sociology must reassess who and what is understood as contributing to valuable, correct, and rigorous sociological thought. Ultimately, decolonizing sociology requires a reimagining of what makes sociology in the first place, understanding how power works and how the field has evolved differently in different places. A significant piece of this reassessment is also *what* we study and how. As Raewyn Connell writes:

> It's hard to get worked up about reflexive modernity or shifting subjectivities when you are facing starvation in a drought, rampant pollution in a mega-city, a grey economy embracing half the population, rape and femicide committed with impunity, military dictatorship, forced migration, climate disaster, or other such conveniences of modern life. If social science is to be relevant, it has to be a different social science.[12]

We assert that environmental sociology has the potential to help people address some of these pressing crises, given its attention to climate crises, pollution, and environmental inequities. But for that to happen well, it has to better reflect the breadth of knowledge that exists among many different groups of people and their different lived experiences, identities, and positions. Specifically, this means expanding the canon to include more diverse perspectives on how race and ethnicity, class, gender, age, geographic location, and other variables impact sociology *and* societies. Environmental justice scholars provide a strong example of where to start, as well as how to move more decisively toward decolonizing sociology by adopting intersectional analytical lenses—ways to understand how different aspects of people shape their experiences in the world.[13] Contemporary scholars like Kishi Animashaun Ducre, David Pellow, Kyle Powys Whyte, and many others cited here lead sociology in this direction, demonstrating what it might look like to convey more intersectional sociology with historical honesty.[14]

Our goal in this *book* builds on this last point: that sociology needs to be bolder and more inclusive, especially if we want it to be a useful guide for building more equitable systems. Our goal in this particular *chapter* is more straightforward: we will discuss some of the precepts of sociology that help us understand what humanity faces currently and what we are up against as a global community.

But we want to be clear about one thing first: our case for sociology insists on nature.

FRAMING THE CONVERSATION: THE NATURE OF NATURE

Western cultural and intellectual orientations tend to see *nature, culture,* and *society* as three different concepts and three different realms of experience. But the problem with this view is that nature, culture, and society are intrinsically interwoven. We cannot separate them in our lives—and trying to do so has resulted in shortsightedness.

Misunderstanding Nature, Misapprehending Human Nature

Nature, ecological systems, and society are inseparable, as environmental sociologists have observed—and as other forms of knowledge (particularly Indigenous knowledges) have always insisted. Ideas about nature are social constructions—by which we mean that the idea of "nature" says more about human beings and how society is arranged than it necessarily does about the biophysical world. Nature and the environment are not just things "out there"—wilderness without people, for instance, the type of thing we might see in Sierra Club ads—but rather *include* people and the built environment along with the biophysical one. Nature as people experience it consists of a set of power relations and a way to understand ourselves and our surroundings. In other words, *human* thinking about power and identity has shaped various cultures' ideas about what nature is.

Since sociology emerged from nineteenth-century European thinking, it contains many of the assumptions, myths, and values of that time and place. Much sociology has seen nature, or ecological systems, as appendages to the human endeavor (something extra or outside the human experience) rather than as constitutive parts of (human) life. European sociologists throughout the nineteenth and twentieth centuries focused on "social facts"—on ideologies and norms viewed through cultural and religious lenses.[15] Sociology's anthropocentrism mirrored other Western social sciences, natural sciences, and philosophies of the time, which also characterized the natural world as a passive set of resources to be controlled, industrialized, and managed by human systems and institutions. Until the recent founding of environmental sociology, the discipline overall remained taken with ideas of human exceptionalism.[16]

More broadly, Western society has tried to distance itself from nature through an array of other social constructions, including cities (building walls around people and businesses to separate them from nature) and industrial infrastructures, technologies, political systems, and economies (which consider environmental impacts "external" to processes of trade). So, on the one hand, Western society has seen nature as something *external* to humans, and on the other, it has consistently tried to put more distance between itself and that which it defines as nature, mostly by trying to control it.

Voices that pointed out capitalism's deep links to racial exploitation were subjugated or ignored, too. As production and labor systems industrialized through the nineteenth century, Western cultural and ideological systems began to normalize the extraction, colonialism, human rights abuses, and fundamental ecological shifts that industrialization introduced, and all of this was also tied to gendered ideas about dominance and ownership.[17] Because of that, and instead of seeing current ecological, environmental health, or contamination crises—and especially climate crises—as products of a specific historical era of industrial capitalism and Western domination, the overwhelming tendency became to see them as outcomes of "human nature."

Yet, this inherited narrow, mechanistic thinking about nature has continued to obscure the extent to which people are *interdependent* with nature and ecological systems, including more-than-humans (a more inclusive and less anthropocentric and binary way of conceptualizing non-human species and relations).[18] Further, many cultures have continued to think of human nature as somehow deficient, selfish, and programmed to defile our environments.[19] But this thinking, rather perversely, pulled us deeper into the industrial, political, and economic *systems* that have caused many of the problems we blame on *human* nature.

These ideas have had serious staying power. It is now commonplace to suggest that people cannot even be trusted to manage resources communally; instead, we have been encouraged to privatize those collective spaces to keep selfish, noncommunicative humans from ruining our own backyards.

Such assumptions about human nature have affected generations of Western discourse and policy making, including among resource planners, managers, and social scientists—even though there is abundant evidence from sociology, economics, and anthropology that communal management and public goods can *encourage* cooperation, sustainable labor and production systems, and deeper knowledge of ecological systems.[20] For instance, the Quechua concept of *sumak kawsay* (roughly translated to *buen vivir* in Spanish or *wellbeing* in English) is actually bigger than that: it describes living in harmony within communities, ourselves, and, most importantly, nature. The term is an illustration of how cooperation is embedded into human nature. Yet competition is an idea that is core to capitalist and neoliberal thinking—which, in turn, has shaped Western thinking about how humans are. Solidarity and cooperation are not, in fact, inimical to human nature. Yet, most Western thought treats them as such.

Ideas of human nature become particularly treacherous around conceptions of ethnicity, gender, and race. This is a kind of naturalistic just-so fallacy that is not quite the same as walling ourselves off from nature, but it has similar roots. As an example: if part of the goal of a phrase like "human nature" is to character-ize that which is universal about humanity,[21] then it should come as no surprise that such thinking has also created essentialized definitions of women. In doing so, it has privileged certain ways of being a woman. For instance, that female bodies can reproduce is understood to be the universal factor that separates sexes in terms of authority and power. If the view that female people reproduce is seen as "natural"—and what is natural is subjugated and controlled under Western views of nature—there also emerge "natural" explanations and justifica-tions for enforced divisions of labor, subordination of women to men, and era-sure of the existence of trans women altogether. The idea that biological differences produce dichotomized sex relationships turns on the idea that such a dichotomy is natural. It is therefore (socially) much harder to question.[22] In other words, perceptions of that which is natural have been used to justify dra-matic power inequities—we need look no further than recent debates about marriage equality and trans inclusivity for telling examples.

Perhaps most important, thinking of human nature as inherently selfish obscures all the ways communities act generously and constrains our imagina-tions about what human behavior *could* be. Arguments about "essential human nature" stunt conversations; they do not let people envision any other way of being. If selfishness or destructiveness are seen as parts of human nature, then trying to behave differently feels futile. If, however, we can develop the habit of thinking about human nature as shaped by and adaptive to physical and social systems—as responding to the crises before us, as emerging in conversation with our communities, social and ecological—many more possibilities appear.

But what material conditions encouraged this powerful notion of human nature as separated from, destructive to, and antithetical to all other nature? We address this question by turning to the idea of metabolic rift.

Metabolic Rift and Industrial Systems

Some social science has long observed the inextricable relations between eco-logical and human systems, alongside the adaptability of human nature within those systems. For instance, Karl Marx began analyzing capitalist production and its relationships to socio-ecological problems amid the Industrial Revolu-tion.[23] Marx relied on the concept of the "universal metabolism of nature"—capturing how extensively human systems are embedded in and part of nature. Human social systems (especially production systems, including factories and farms) represent key ways that humanity mediates and transforms the rest of nature. But they also show how humanity is a *part of* nature; after all, even these activities do not emerge randomly—farming is done, for instance, in places where soil quality is good and water is accessible. Farms, in turn, alter the landscapes in which they sit—perhaps someone has cleared a field from what used to be forest, or perhaps dams have been built to control the water supply, which then changed the rivers upstream and downstream. In other words, humans and the rest of nature coevolve, shaping each other materially. Practically speaking, this has meant that, as humanity's production systems became more industrialized under capitalist expansion and trade—and as humans started altering the physical environment more—people's social systems and daily lives have become increasingly alienated from nature. Even at the beginning of the Industrial Revolution, this was exemplified through increasing reliance on large-scale, industrialized agricultural production that had early detrimental effects on soil quality and its ability to reliably sustain food systems.

In these early analyses, we see some of the first explanations of metabolic rift, a central (if debated) concept articulated by Marx and later resurrected by environmental sociologists such as John Bellamy Foster, Brett Clark, Stefano B. Longo, and Rebecca Clausen.[24] The concept of metabolic rift can help us understand the political-economic and cultural drivers behind unprecedented ecological destruction and humans' alienation from the rest of nature as industrialization separated the daily lives of people from ecological systems and created an "irreparable rift in the interdependent process of social metabolism [or social life and processes]."[25]

Once industrial scales of production began to fundamentally alter ecological systems, people experienced these changes through their own labor, which can be understood as a form of "metabolism between humanity and nature."[26] Labor connects the (so-called) social with the (so-called) natural. Capitalism altered that relationship. On one hand, people worked directly with the land less and less frequently, becoming increasingly dependent on technological, urbanized systems predicated upon an industrialized environment; and on the other, extractive economic activities started migrating to other naturally rich geographies as a result of the incentives of globalization. Industrialization, urbanization, and the steady separation of people from the land and from their own creative labor continued to expand metabolic rift. As sites of extraction and production and of disposal and waste became more physically separated from sites of consumption, the rift got bigger still.[27] Most people's sense of connection to nature, of environmental degradation, and of human consumption's consequences became lost, more easily ignored, or pushed onto others.[28]

This rift still impacts people's daily lives and larger social systems—perhaps now more than ever. As economic historian Karl Polanyi[29] predicted, dis-embedded, self-regulating, capitalist systems of production and trade would cause irreparable ecological destruction, alongside their unsustainable socioeconomic outcomes. It is almost impossible to escape the examples of metabolic rift under capitalist industrialization: overarching climate crises, changes in air and water quality, rampant and unprecedented loss of biodiversity and ecosystems, depletion and collapse of fisheries,[30] and the beginning of large-scale changes to ice sheets, ocean currents, and jet streams—and denial that many of these outcomes are even happening, according to some anti-science and post-truth narratives.

Indeed, even as these problems become more palpable in the twenty-first century's neoliberal system, that very system encourages many people to deny or ignore these crises; this is the logical conclusion of an ever-intensifying rift. Even in sociology, it was not until environmental sociologists resurrected Marx's concept that the discipline meaningfully incorporated this concept of rift as an important part of that which is "social."

Metabolic rift, though, has *enormous* sociological consequences. In the context of this rift, contemporary Western constructions of nature—in people's daily thinking, in most scientific disciplines, and in political and economic thinking— are increasingly separated from people and subordinated to global capitalism. The economy has become more real than nature for many people—and it certainly takes priority in most contemporary policy. For instance, as people work to address and mitigate climate crises, many popular political approaches are premised on capitalist, Western, market-based systems. Proposed solutions, such as cap-and-trade systems, carbon offsets, and consumer choices, exemplify how notions of nature have become inextricably linked to market-based systems of production and extraction. Instead of healing our rift with the rest of nature, this approach encourages and perpetuates commodification of nature and people, weakening accountability and mutual respect (analyzed in depth in chapter 4). Even as we recognize climate crisis as one of the gravest existential threats to humanity's existence, market-based principles still dominate discourse and policy; global nature is "increasingly remade in the image of the commodity,"[31] and most proposed solutions adhere to this norm.

We aim to help repair and address these omissions. We explore ways that communities work to actively heal this rift, acknowledging that humanity has always been an intrinsic part of nature. And in so doing, we aim to show that human nature can be wonderfully adaptable, constructive, and cooperative—if and when it is embedded in systems that encourage adaptation and cooperation. Our goal, then—shared with many other environmental sociologists—is to build critical perspectives focusing on how social natures are transformed, by whom, for whose benefit, and with what consequences. Later, we focus specifically on organizations and communities working to heal metabolic rift, recenter nature in human relations, and build realities outside neoliberal norms. As we show in chapters 4–6, these organizations and communities challenge rift-making premises of hyper-marketization, privatization, and environmental deregulation as they build alternatives.

Reconnecting Nature and Human Nature through Environmental Sociology

The idea of nature has many different meanings. The word can refer to the object of natural science (for instance, the material reality of something); nature as it is protected by laws (for instance, wild animals, plants, landscapes); nature as it is experienced and dealt with in everyday life (including weather); and nature as human bodies (for instance, exposed to negative impacts of pollution).[32] We proceed, then, with one of the central premises of environmental sociology in hand—that people and the rest of nature are fundamentally inseparable and always affecting each other, and that how nature is defined often reflects understandings of power and human relationships more than any physical reality.

We turn next to a series of key concepts from environmental sociology, ideas to which we will return throughout the book, that help us both understand and move the needle on efforts to realize environmental justice. These key concepts, which we describe and analyze in the discussion that follows, are capitalism, colonialism, inequality, civil society, social movements, the state, extractivism, climate crises, development, and the need to recognize social and ecological interdependence. Here, we explicitly consider these ideas through a lens of nature, using them to understand how nature and culture are linked and shaped via institutions and social structures. These concepts and observations are intended to elevate some of the big thinking in environmental sociology, in service of the rest of our book. They illustrate how some societies have gone to great lengths to pretend humans are separate from and superior to other living beings and ecological systems. But they also offer ways to begin healing industrial humanity's metabolic rifts. In describing them, we also consider whether, how, and to what extent these big ideas incorporate an understanding of nature and what questions arise when thinking about them in concert.

CORE CONCEPTS IN ENVIRONMENTAL SOCIOLOGY

Capitalism. An orienting concept in this book is **capitalism**. Capitalism's central tenets have, in many ways, laid foundations for the crises humanity faces—and for the rest of the sociological concepts we explore. Capitalism is defined by private or corporate ownership of land and goods, and relies on myths of unending market growth and infinite resources to fuel that growth. Markets determine values, and expectations of unending growth shape behaviors. At its core, capitalism is an economic system, but it is also a conceptual framework, a way of life, a social system, and a set of values, as Polanyi[33] famously argued. To amplify this, we add that it is an ideology: a set of values unto itself that structure many Western political, social, and civic systems and ways of thinking. The values that capitalism offers shape what many people believe and have perceived as natural and correct—centered around the naturalization of private property and ownership of resources (or relations) like land. Its basic premise is that competition over resources creates efficient outcomes and innovation, which accompanies the ideas that markets should regulate states and that markets are the appropriate (and, for neoliberalism, the ultimate) arbiters of social life.

These notions of markets as a supreme social authority have only intensified as capitalism has transformed and spread across the globe. We must therefore note that capitalism has a number of variations and looks different depending on where in the world you are, when in history you are living, and in what body you happen to be living. In the United States from about the 1970s on—and in other places impacted by U.S. policies and trade regimes—capitalism most commonly emerged in its neoliberal variant. (We will take a closer look at neoliberalism in chapter 3). In places like Scandinavia and even China, the state plays a much stronger role in shaping market outcomes, though market-based competition, growth, and industrial production are still standard principles.

Capitalism, as a system, has a number of by-products; it causes ripple effects. For instance, economic and social inequality are structural features of it because capitalism requires reproducing relationships of domination and exploitation to accumulate profit at the expense of a mass class of racialized and colonized poor.[34] David Harvey[35] has observed that, beyond primitive accumulation of land via colonization, accumulation by dispossession has been a central feature of industrial capitalism, especially since the 1970s. Accumulation by dispossession describes capitalist policies that centralize wealth in the hands of a few people or corporations by dispossessing poorer people, or the public, of their wealth or land. In the neoliberal variety of capitalism (again, analyzed in the next chapter), this practice has accelerated a massive consolidation of wealth and power globally since the 1970s. Accumulation by dispossession has been a last hurrah of sorts for industrial capitalism as market-based logics spread globally via development agencies and trade regimes—and as increasingly financialized systems of capital co-opted and privatized the commons, be they social or ecological, in order to commodify and sell the "goods" available.[36]

Through practices like accumulation by dispossession, some central contradictions and ecological problems of capitalism become apparent. Capitalist systems and logics increasingly attempt to dis-embed market systems from their social, political, economic, and ecological realities, pretending that markets operate independently from human societies and well-being; policies that dis-embed the market from ecological contexts pretend that markets are independent of ecological well-being. Profits can thus accumulate regardless of social and environmental harms. In fact, profits are maximized by making the public pay for those harms, directly or indirectly: *by privatizing profit and socializing risks.* People can no longer rely on systems of social protection or regulations, principles of ecological concern or stewardship, or longer-term reciprocal social and communal relationships to balance the effects of market systems. Instead, industrial capitalist systems constantly attempt to separate market systems from all other aspects of life, an artificial, wholly ideological attempt that results in experiences of volatility, instability, vulnerability, powerlessness, and uncertainty for most people—not to mention more-than-humans and ecological systems.[37]

One of environmental sociology's central theories about capitalism and nature—known as the Treadmill of Production[38]—sees capitalist approaches as creating socially and ecologically unsustainable production systems. These systems simply take as much as possible from land, labor, and institutions while adding back little more than toxic waste to ecosystems, and inequality for those laboring to keep the treadmill running. The treadmill usurps all institutions, requisitioning them to work in the service of ecologically devastating markets, while educational, political, and social institutions work to keep the treadmill running. Ecological modernization represents a different theory in environmental sociology,[39] essentially positing that more of the same (specifically super-industrialization and corporate engagement) will provide robust solutions needed to address environmental problems. This approach often mirrors neoliberal, market-based solutions, over-relies on technological solutions,[40] and is inadequate for reasons we continue to explore in this book.

When societies attempt to commodify land, money, or people's labor, Polanyi[41] contends, we end up with systems that are inherently unstable. Ironically, extreme commodification can make *markets* unstable as well—because society is so unequal that the market becomes highly distorted. This is the first contradiction of capitalism; when people's means are so low that they cannot consume goods and services (the basis of a market economy), then the market has destroyed the conditions of its own survival. In the second contradiction, capitalism's constant growth depends on treating finite resources as if they are infinite. Runaway capitalism, then, ruins the things that are the basis for stability: ecological systems, social institutions, and one another. Yet, capitalism encourages people to proceed—frantically—in this direction, and keep attempting more of the same. For human relationships with land and nature, this is especially problematic, as current climate crises so painfully illustrate. And as a variety of Indigenous thinkers,[42] Polanyi, and environmental sociologists have observed, commodifying nature ends up leading to destabilized, volatile, and unsustainable market systems that alienate the vast majority of people from the land and from one another while also creating untenable ecological outcomes.

Colonialism. Capitalism, particularly leading up to and since the Industrial Revolution, has begotten **colonization and colonialism**. Globally, this has unfolded for centuries as European nations sought to violently open up new markets and to extract natural resources and labor in places like sub-Saharan Africa, Southeast Asia, and North and South America. Scholars of Latin America have relied on theories of coloniality to account for the production of racialized power as a hegemonic and historical project.[43] Colonialism also relies on cognitive modes of power based on a "new perspective of knowledge within which non-Europe was the past, and because of that inferior, if not always primitive."[44] As Evelyn Nakano Glenn writes, colonialism is an "ongoing structure rather than a past historical event." In her analysis, the settler goal of

> seizing and establishing property rights over land and resources required the removal of indigenes, which was accomplished by various forms of direct and indirect violence, including militarized genocide. Settlers sought to control space, resources, and people not only by occupying land but also by establishing an exclusionary private property regime and coercive labor systems, including chattel slavery to work the land, extract resources, and build infrastructure.[45]

Colonialism, by this definition, is part of the ongoing social dynamics that shape knowledge, power, and legitimacy in former and settler colonies. Settler colonialism, too—where outside societies invade an area, seize the land by force, and try to take over the space using genocidal acts towards the Indigenous people already living there—flourished in places like the (now-called) United States and Canada, South Africa, New Zealand, and Australia.[46] It varies in its manifestation, then, but all forms of colonization "involve a cultural, political, and psychological assault on the colonized";[47] the word refers to the many ways by which powerful actors overtake and attempt to remake the less powerful.

In the United States, for instance, settler colonialism has been a multi-faceted, ongoing project consisting of labor exploitation and land dispossession, coupled with power hierarchies. Functionally, this began and continues as the elimination and displacement of Indigenous communities, reliance on slavery and then institutionalized racism, and the settlement of white communities in North America. And it continues as a series of institutional measures and social systems that privilege the colonizers. Similar patterns occur in Canada, Australia, and South Africa. In the (so-called) United States, this set of processes meant the literal genocide, forcible relocation, and disappearance of Native nations, which was an intentional consequence of the spread of industrial capitalism—and which was understood as fundamentally necessary to establish the contemporary United States.[48] Military forces killed and relocated people of Native nations; the state signed treaties that contained them in particular places; forced assimilation was attempted through boarding schools, the Dawes Act, and outright murder. Disappearance also happens discursively—through deliberate changes to or criminalization of Indigenous languages and cultural systems and systematic erasures from history, schooling, land, and political and social institutions.[49] These processes have certainly not stopped. Contemporarily, murder rates are *ten times higher* for Indigenous women than for any other ethnicity, and this is linked in compelling empirical ways to the presence of extractive industries in settler states.[50]

Colonialism also meant reliance on chattel slavery, which produced lasting racial inequality. These structures of inequality blocked Black Americans from accessing many U.S. institutions after emancipation, and they continue to be broadly economically, culturally, and socially consequential. They ranged from sharecropping to forced labor camps, Jim Crow laws, police violence and mass incarceration, and redlining.[51] Colonialism is ongoing, and its effects are persistent.

Colonization typically has both economic and social dimensions, and a colonial ethic emerges everywhere—from the Peace Corps to education.[52] But resistance to it emerges as well, particularly in settler states. For instance, we need look no further than the vast coalition of Indigenous people and allies that was built during the Standing Rock protests of the Dakota Access Pipeline to see how internally colonized populations have created a "matrix of resistance"[53] to counter industrial systems of resource extraction that endanger sacred Native sites and vital resources (or relations) such as water (more on this in chapter 6).

Sociology itself was integral in reproducing the colonial order as dominant sociologists constructed theories either assuming or proving the supposed barbarity and backwardness of colonized people.[54] It continues through less visible practices that pattern everything from structures of knowledge to university hierarchies. Beyond the specific sociological canon, universities themselves are "local instantiations of a dominant academic model based on a Eurocentric epistemic canon"[55]—which attribute truth to European modes of knowledge production and which make it difficult to imagine truths that exist beyond these ways of knowing.

Correspondingly, much of the programmatic discussion on decolonizing sociology has focused on the methodological framework of the discipline itself. As Linda Tuhiwai Smith and Raewyn Connell both argue, agendas of sociological change would (and should) focus on finding new conceptual frameworks (or rethinking familiar methods), to make them usable for the social groups that have been marginalized by empire.[56] U.S. land-grant universities, for instance, now face public derision for their continued role in land grabs and settler colonialism, given that each institution was founded on land taken from Native nations via the Morrill Act. According to recent investigations, about eleven million acres shifted from Indigenous stewardship by about 250 "tribes, bands, and communities," with that land redistributed to land-grant universities throughout the United States through about 160 "violence-backed concessions."[57] While many of these universities now have land acknowledgments and other symbols that gesture towards colonialism's ongoing injustices, more substantial actions are warranted, including universities actively working to recruit and support Native students and to facilitate Native nations reconnecting with and having reinstated rights to their ancestral lands.[58] On the research side, using community-based participatory methods driven by and useful for communities participating in research is just one way to democratize and decolonize sociology. Similarly, making paradigm shifts to environmental health perspectives, where communities' observations about environmental pollution and health are legitimated, is another potential pathway. Many more are needed.

Like capitalism, colonialism understands nature as a set of (seemingly infinite) commodities separate from and subordinate to humanity—commodities to be owned, dominated, and/or mobilized to serve markets, corporate firms, private owners, and states. Nature is to be extracted, used, and then dumped back "out there," defiled and often polluted irreparably by the extractive systems propelling global industrialization. Indeed, as neoliberal forms of capitalism and industrial production systems have again colonized the globe through imperialism—especially through global development regimes and lending agencies such as the World Bank[59]—colonizing and commodifying nature in service of human markets becomes not just the norm but rather the *requirement* for participation in a global economy. This ideology drives global development and helps amplify accumulation by dispossession. And colonialism is ideological: noncapitalist worldviews, systems, and structures are erased and subsumed under the goals of progress. Unfettered capitalism combined with colonialism has exacerbated humanity's growing rift with the rest of nature. Combined, colonialism and capitalism often exacerbate gendered forms of violence, too, as women, minoritized populations, and nature have been perceived as bodies to be dominated and exploited by markets and industrial processes.[60] The tragic circumstances of missing and murdered Indigenous women, noted earlier, gives just one compelling but often invisible example of how extraction of nature links to subjugation of and violence toward women.

Inequality. Capitalism, combined with colonialism, both produce and are shaped by multiple intersecting forms of inequality. This emerges both from contemporary political landscapes and the drastically uneven histories experienced by different groups since colonialism kick-started the Industrial Revolution. In the United States particularly, this inequality is often defined as economic—but it can also take the forms of racism and sexism, alongside classism or religious discrimination. Inequality is defined sociologically as unequal access to resources, though much of those resources are in practice understood to be material; the study of inequality is the study of "who gets what and why."[61] Race is a particularly important construction, meaning that at its core, it is an idea used to physically and symbolically differentiate between people's bodies; there is no biological basis for distinguishing people along racial lines. The construction, though, has been built up within many institutions such that racial differences are seen as "natural", and have been made real in the power they wield.[62] Racial capitalism has thrived within these institutionalized forms of inequality. Gendered inequality represents a third major intersecting prong of inequality.[63] Women are systemically devalued, while providing the vast majority of reproductive labor, even as they encounter significant structural barriers to raising the next generation of human beings.[64] Intersecting inequalities can of course multiply these effects.

Inequality lives in every feature of capitalist society, ranging from urban planning to systems of international aid.[65] Dramatic increases in global inequality coexist with dramatic decreases in absolute welfare; inequality has been widely documented in the twenty-first century as endangering social stability along many dimensions.[66] Arguments against inequality point not only to its inherently unjust nature but also to the devastating social, economic, and ecological consequences it engenders for many facets of society.[67] In addition to its moral dimensions, inequality can generate or amplify armed conflict, market slowdowns, poor health outcomes, and a host of other socially destabilizing effects.[68]

Very importantly for us, environmental inequality—not to mention how nature is understood and experienced—is heavily shaped by the intersectional effects of class, gender, racial, and even spatial inequities. For instance, Diane Sicotte[69] offers historical and institutional analyses of how environmental injustices and inequalities emerged in Philadelphia, Pennsylvania, outcomes of industrial pollution mapped onto race and class formation over several decades. Or, for example, we see how exposure to risks from unconventional oil and gas production and uranium extraction and production affect certain communities of color or poor communities much more than wealthier, whiter communities.[70]

Women, and especially women of color, have frequently led movements against environmental inequality, and they often experience its outcomes first and worst.[71] Women may lead these movements largely because their socialization into caretaker roles makes them some of the first observers of health impacts from exposures to toxicants and pollutants (which often manifest in children and elderly populations).[72] Women often face structural environmental inequities, such as less economic and social power, which can lead to procedural inequities and exclusion from decision-making.[73] Or their relationships to dominant polluting industries (like coal production) may make them *less* at risk of losing employment if they speak out about environmental injustices.[74] Across modes of activism and engagement, intersectional analyses are crucially important, encouraging analyses of the many ways that different groups of women experience injustices and how they resist them.[75]

Civil Society. When justice is achieved in cases of inequality, it is typically brought about by civil society. Civil society is the array of nonstate and nonmarket forces that shape our lives, ranging from book clubs to labor unions to the #BlackLives-Matter movement. In other words, civil society is made up of groups of people working together, formally or informally. Some of these efforts work to solidify the institutions and communities that already exist, helping them cohere and sustain their support systems for daily life—like, for instance, religious communities that see to the needs of their members in tough times. But much of civil society also brings about *changes* in the systems that govern people's lives, through an array of different approaches.

Civil society remains an important site of potential resistance to the alienating forces of neoliberal capitalism and an important place for people to enact positive visions of the world they want. Sometimes these actions take the form of social movements that target corporations. At other times, however, they target the state and regulatory institutions that are mandated to protect health, ecosystems, and economic stability. One example of civil society's environmental action helps illustrate this point. By the 1960s, unregulated industrial development in the United States had led to rampant pollution that people found difficult to ignore. American civil society organized for system-wide change—urging the creation of the U.S. Environmental Protection Agency and a suite of federal environmental regulations such as the Clean Water Act and the Safe Drinking Water Act.[76]

While this kind of environmental activism represents a success for collective power—targeting the state for regulation and environmental protections across economic sectors or industries—social justice activists justly critique it for its racial homogeneity and narrow definitions of environmental health.[77] These critiques inspired movements for *environmental justice*. Environmental justice (EJ) advocates observe that exposures to environmental risks (ranging from contamination to the effects of climate change) and that access to seats of decision-making participation and power are unequally distributed by race and class. The term "EJ" describes civil society's efforts to create systemic changes addressing inequitable exposures of poor communities and communities of color to environmental hazards, pollutants, and risks—and the lack of meaningful opportunities for these communities to make decisions about land uses and other policies. More critical, Indigenous and intersectional definitions of EJ, often utilized by activists and some scholars, also see EJ as working to dismantle the very settler state and industrial capitalist systems that perpetuate distributive, procedural, recognition, or restorative injustices.[78] For many, it is not just about "poisoning people equally"; instead, EJ means "stop poisoning people, period." The movement seeks not simply "to redistribute environmental harms, but to abolish them."[79]

Social Movements. As we have seen, one way that civil society emerges is through social movements. Social movements are, in brief, collectives of people trying to attain some sort of change in the systems and institutions that govern their lives. Groups—and *collective* action—are vital to these processes. In that sense, individuals buying Priuses to decrease their individual carbon footprint does not count as a social movement, but a *community* of people organizing to institute citywide public transit systems or solar installations does. Environmental social movements in the West have shifted over time from focusing on preservation and conservation starting in the late 1800s—concerns privileged by upper-class, Western, white, and male populations—to more radical and reformist environmental concerns, including environmental justice and climate justice.[80] These latter movements have often been led by and have better represented the concerns of poorer people, women, and communities of color.[81]

Social movements are constituted by either formal or informal organizations, networks, or coalitions of people or groups. In recent years, social movement organizations have begun to target nonstate institutions, which has meant corporations gain new power over movement logics and can solidify corporate control over social movements in a variety of settings.[82] This can look like, for instance, a recent campaign against Trader Joe's that led the chain grocery store to phase out single-use plastics.[83] While some social movements are exceptions to this rule (for instance, groups working to eliminate flame retardants have formed "multisector alliances" that simultaneously target a wide range of institutional, policy, and social and cultural spaces[84]), social movement now often target corporations instead of the state. This has happened because state authority and its perceived policy-making capacity is weak;[85] the idea here is that social movements must reckon with nonstate sources of power to achieve change (more on this in chapter 4). While boycotts and "buycotts" can affect markets and corporate behaviors, they typically do not have the same industry- or sector-wide impacts as regulations achieved when social movements demand *state* regulations; though conscious consumption can certainly lead to positive political change *if* it is channeled collectively and used to impact institutional change.[86]

Even with important exceptions and encouraging progress toward coalitions and alliances, we contend in this book that, overall, mainstream U.S. social movements have overwhelmingly failed to resist neoliberalism's social effects— effects we will explore more in the next two chapters. Many of them have repeatedly (and rather uncritically) sought out capitalist, market-based solutions or persuaded people to "vote with their dollar." And right alongside that, movement scholars have largely failed to systematically interrogate this shift to narrower, market-centered social movement goals that are constrained by the very perspectives that produce their problems. We align with scholars who advocate a clearheaded approach to civil society rather than romanticizing it.[87] Michael McQuarrie,[88] for example, describes the transformation of civil society into a "political technology" that dissolves conflicts and creates a "civic monoculture" operating in service of the state and for-profit corporations. This dynamic has weakened organizations' potential as agents of change in civil society, the consequences of which we explore in subsequent chapters.

Additionally, and until recently, research on social movements and civil society failed to see the rest of nature as a constitutive part of human experience—ecological systems were instead understood as external to social and political life. In recent years, environmental sociology has dedicated substantial attention to environmental social movements particularly, and it is within this body of work that new ways of thinking about the relationships between civil society and nature has emerged. To highlight but a few examples: Dorceta Taylor has done important work on how certain threads of civil society can amplify racial capitalism in showing how mainstream U.S. environmental movements have historically excluded communities of color, women, and environmental concerns specific to those communities.[89] Cody Ferguson has examined the promise of civil society and citizen-led initiatives that propelled significant progress in grassroots environmental activism.[90] Phil Brown captured the power and political prowess of civic scientists and health social movements, which have played key roles in linking environmental exposures to embodied health outcomes.[91] Alissa Cordner has analyzed the roles that civil society, alongside regulatory and scientific institutions, can play in shaping environmental health policy, especially as related to chemicals such as flame retardants.[92] The richness of this relatively new work is particularly visible given multiple and ambient risks that characterize industrial societies. Environmental concerns, in their present forms, seem to reflect growing uncertainties and anxieties related to the changing character of late modern society, including political anxieties, state-sanctioned violence, disease, and climate crises.[93] The cases we highlight in chapters 4–6 represent these kinds of intersectional, non-neoliberalized organizations, too.

The State. Civil society, social movements, and other forms of organizing happen in conversation with the **state**. When sociologists say "the state," we typically mean the government, usually at the federal level. States are some of the most important institutions of governance that have shaped modernity, particularly in the Western world. And in the West especially, it is important to note that the government has an extremely active role in managing economic and social life, despite the myth of free markets that prevails.[94] Under neoliberal policy measures, the state often becomes part of the apparatus of business.[95] This is a profound shift from understanding the state as a relatively neutral third party governing daily life or providing people with a safe, clean, and fairly predictable space in which to live.[96] The state can still balloon as its regulatory capacities are minimized and as its capacity to provide social safety nets is diminished—even as its power and reach in support of corporate expansion and privatization are enhanced.

The state's relationship to the public is fraught at best.[97] Settler states—including the United States—typically create profound ruptures between modes of governance, community needs, and natural processes by their very existence. Indeed, the state is an ideological formation that sees itself as something distinct from ecological systems, rather than entwined with and codependent on them. In other words, "nature" has been used by states to demarcate the edge of human social life.[98] The modern capitalist state also holds itself to be superior to the Indigenous cultures and governments suffocated under settler colonialism.[99] The idea of the state as a geographically bounded territory—a political arrangement with borders—already suggests a certain understanding of ecological systems, and of communities, as fixed and unmoving. While the idea of state boundaries may seem intuitive, these are precisely the types of relationships that need to be explored and at least denaturalized. If the United States lays legal claim to certain parts of the world but not others, how does that shape its approach to climate and environmental health? To, for instance, nomadic communities? To Native nations whose ancestral lands transcend those borders (as with the Tohono O'odham, whose nation extends from southern Arizona to Mexico)? To more-than-humans and ecosystems like the Sonoran Desert? And to problems that extend beyond states themselves?

Modern states are also almost entirely capitalist, meaning that Iceland was an outlier when it explored putting human well-being ahead of gross domestic product in its budget in late 2019.[100] The U.S. state's tepid approach to climate crisis is, obviously, partly driven by lackluster attitudes among many members of its public. But it is also a telling example of the inertia and/or priorities of the state itself, and the very ideologies inherent within it, based on a set of territorial boundaries and assumptions about how people live. In no other context, perhaps, than climate emergency can we see as clearly the ways in which the state has become (at best) an apologist for, and (at worst) an active arm of, neoliberal industrial development.[101]

Climate Crises. Both the potential and the shortcomings of the state are readily apparent in the response to the many climate crises unfolding worldwide. We know by this point that the world is warming, spurred by runaway carbon emissions and trapped greenhouse gases that cause the atmosphere to heat up.[102] And a sociological perspective on climate change demands that we think about how social and environmental systems are co-shaped and how climate change and human societies interact.

Our position in this book, as we indicated at the outset of this chapter, is that climate crises are, above all, a question of political and social systems and an experience of power, even as they are also a question of meteorological and natural systems. As sociologist Rebecca Elliott[103] puts it, climate change involves human societies in problems of loss: depletion, disappearance, and collapse. The climate changes and all other aspects of life also change, in specifically destructive ways. As with any type of social transformation, we must understand it. But seeing climate change as a question of loss also demands that we reckon with feeling that loss and the ways that losses are experienced unevenly across the United States and the world. What is more, policy makers' manifest failure to consider the human experiences and emotions inherent in these losses are part of what, in our analysis, has stalled more decisive action. Our case studies in subsequent chapters show how emotional reckoning often drives the social mobilization behind doing the tough work of building better systems and responding with sufficient urgency to climate crises.

Climate crises arrive on the intertwined natural, social, and political landscape that we have been describing—that is, climate change is also a social phenomenon reflected in weather systems, human societies, colonial legacies, and experiences of power. Climate crises simultaneously map onto social deprivations and inequities, in which the short-term thinking of powerful and profit-driven fossil fuel corporations will continue to impact the poorest and most vulnerable among us first and worst.[104] These corporations receive substantial state support as well, with recent studies estimating the fossil fuel industry receives what amount to hundreds of billions in subsidies annually, in the form of direct payments, tax breaks, reduced costs, and other publicly funded economic supports.[105] Yet, one of the most powerful barriers to rapid change has been the sham debate over whether humans, and especially capitalist systems, caused climate crises—as if human activity were somehow not part of nature, and as if the two could be separated. What's more, this distracting climate denial narrative has been funded by fossil fuel corporations, their supporting foundations, and ultra–free market think tanks and nongovernmental organizations.[106]

Extractivism. Climate crisis is one instance of the metabolic rift amplified by intensifying industrialization and extractivism. While we extensively reviewed the idea of the metabolic rift earlier, we link it here to industrial and racial capitalism's push to colonize, commodify, and ultimately extract wealth from all corners of the globe through a process called extractivism—which is itself an economic process but also an ideology about humanity's relationship with ecological systems.[107] Extraction of coal, oil and gas, uranium, and rare earth elements and even extraction of nutrients from soil have been a constant of industrialization, and extractivism has been a guiding logic of capitalism, of colonialism, and of continued imperialism. Communities that are particularly touched by displacement and gendered violence related to extractive industries (see the earlier discussion) live at the nexus of these links.

Extractivism as a *process* is enabled by extractivism as an *ideology*: the ideology centers on the notion of the inert, lifeless Earth as an infinite cache of goods to be exploited for global production and market systems, with the labor to be done by minoritized populations. As we explained, these approaches lead to powerful metabolic rifts between people, socioeconomic systems, and ecological systems. Further, these practices of endless extraction create some of the most significant conditions for environmental inequities to flourish, in which entire human and more-than-human communities and natural systems may be sacrificed to get at the last deposit of oil or gas or the deposit of uranium, all to solidify a nation's political and economic power.[108] As extractivism has spread, metabolic rifts have become more common across places and cultures—alienating people from environments and assisting rapid accumulation by dispossession. In this way, metabolic rift has allowed industrial systems and the states that support them to continue pretending as if human industrial activity could somehow be divorced from impacts to the ecological world and, ultimately, human health and well-being.

Development. The word "development" has been marshaled to capture a host of ideas about how to improve the human condition. The concept of development links inherently to racial capitalism and colonialism; though military, charitable, and political interventions have combined in what can generally be called "development" for centuries, contemporary iterations of international development began in earnest after the Second World War, with the establishment of the International Monetary Fund, the World Bank, and the U.S. Agency for International Development. "International development" typically refers to the combined spread of modern industrial capitalism and Western democratic ideals: an historical process in which states' economies become more productive and competitive, political systems come to more or less represent aggregated citizen preferences, certain categories of rights and opportunities are extended to additional social groups, and "organizations function according to meritocratic standards and professional norms."[109] The practice of development is now understood, explicitly or implicitly, to denote professional intervention in other countries' systems and affairs at some level.[110]

Development, both as an ideology and as a practice, resonates with other dominant Western ideologies and practices. Like the state, any concept of development presupposes the existence of a certain type of nature—that is, an objective reality divorced from more-than-humans, people, and their histories. International relations and international development especially "emerged as a global alibi for the imperial extension of specifically Western modes of economy, spatiality and being. This event occurred when European colonial practices called for capitalism to take up its ontological attachment with development—essentially soliciting capitalism to become development."[111] The concept of international development shares some similarities with ideas of community development, but the biggest difference is basically that international development as it is defined by the field and the state almost always means *economic* development, premised upon capitalist intervention and free market frameworks. *Community* development, on the other hand, sometimes offers a bit more room for different value systems and includes noneconomic concerns and the opportunity for human development to occur as a stated goal.[112]

Most types and measures of development, however, are explicitly or implicitly linked to industrialization, capitalism, and, by extension, the metabolic rift. Although this extractivist and industrial bias is well documented in the critical development literature,[113] most contemporary development entails projects that explicitly commodify both people and ecological systems, centralize and accumulate wealth by forcible dispossession, and seek to export these norms. Sustainable development, even as it is used with the Sustainable Development Goals of the United Nations, has also been critiqued as a market-centric, nonfeminist, and nebulous concept that fails to progress the well-being of many groups, including women as well as Indigenous and other marginalized communities.[114]

Interdependence. Finally, our understanding of all of these forces is shaped by an understanding of systemic social and ecological **interdependence**, the last idea that forms the foundation of our analyses. In many ways, the ideas that environmental sociology offers all propose different ways to think about the basic fact that life is a network of linkages among humans and their environments—and requires cooperation. Like it or not, we all need and depend on one another (as well as more-than-humans and other living beings) to survive; humanity is inherently dependent upon functioning, intact, somewhat predictable ecological systems. Alongside this, the current conjoined crises of climate change and inequality demand that we find new ways to organize ourselves and structure our (especially Western) market-based societies. Frances Fox Piven[115] has argued that community-based organizing has never been more important and will ultimately determine whether another world is indeed possible. (Importantly, Piven thinks that globalization actually *increases* the potential for this kind of popular power.) The international, intercultural, and multigenerational solidarity represented by global climate strikes illustrates powerfully how unity can be generated across seemingly vast global divides. In later chapters, we will review examples of these sorts of movements and attempts at change, using real-world examples to explore how communities embrace interdependence. We must grapple with coming together and leveraging our collective power, as well as with the stark reality that the cultivation of such solidarity is a challenging task.

A NOTE ON THE DOUGHNUT

One promising model for thinking through ecologically and socially balanced communities lies in Kate Raworth's model of Doughnut Economics,[116] which resonates with many of environmental sociology's insights. We utilize this model throughout this book, to analyze our case studies and to look toward solutions.

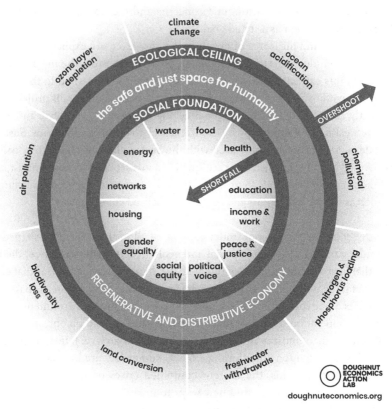

FIGURE 1. An illustration of the Doughnut Economics model, with social foundations in the center and ecological overshoots outside the perimeter. Regenerative and distributive systems make up the "doughnut." (Created by Kate Raworth.)

We draw especially on two central concepts in this model—*distributive* and *regenerative* economies. These terms refer to two types of economies that, rather than relying on constant growth and distributing wealth upward, for instance, aim to support as many people as possible without defiling more-than-human relations or ecological systems. Distributive economies shift concepts of ownership and property to be more collectively defined, while regenerative systems enhance and enrich environments and ecosystems.

As we will review in chapter 6, and as figure 1 illustrates, the centerpiece of the model is a doughnut-shaped space Raworth calls "the safe and just space for humanity."[117] This is the "sweet spot" where we can live within socially sustainable arrangements but also not overshoot some critically important ecological measures. Raworth's doughnut is applicable at multiple scales and offers a model for embedding economic systems in social, ecological, and environmentally just contexts. We find it a useful touchstone, offering some signposts and options for assessing projects, policies, and community organizing.

CONCLUSION

In highlighting these themes, then, we show how environmental sociology— and the evolution of sociological thinking—can help people draw maps toward the beginnings of just civic engagement that is so urgently needed. Clearly, societies depend upon nature or ecological systems, and useful sociology depends on the explicit recognition of that. Yet, social sciences like anthropology and sociology emerged as tools for colonial power—and so social scientists have spent much of our collective past ignoring those interdependences, the noneconomic aspects of life, and the inherent value of non-Western systems of thinking and relating to more-than-humans and ecosystems. These disciplines are in a process of reckoning—as are we, as sociologists ourselves. Reckoning does not happen overnight, nor does it happen once and for all. It must be a process of growth. But we have to be bold—and bravely acknowledge that we will make mistakes in transforming and rebuilding sociology, and social systems, as quickly as we need to, given the immense stakes.

Here, we focus on the ways that environmental sociology can help inform and shape solutions that are more holistic and sustainable than those offered by dominant market-privileging approaches. We show how each of these ideas has figured into community organizing or social movements in recent years— offering powerful evidence that people are hungry to move beyond strictly economic approaches to social change and to life and that the creative approaches to building a better world are both new and old at once. They are both innovative and ancient.

3 · FAILING PEOPLE AND THE PLANET

Neoliberalism and the Erasure of Difference

We reviewed environmental sociology in the previous chapter partly because so few people know what sociology is or what sociologists do—and so the field remains somewhat obscure, despite its promise. In this chapter we look at the economy, and its effect on our social and political lives. We focus on neoliberal capitalism as a driver of many social and ecological crises (and, perhaps, a driver of the spaces of resistance we highlight in chapters 4–6). Following political theorist Wendy Brown[1] and the insights of many scholars over the past several decades, we argue in this chapter that neoliberalism builds an anti-democratic culture from the ground up while encouraging anti-democratic forms of state power from above. And we show how that works.

One of the core tenets of neoliberalism is the idea that free market business models should guide governance, too. In fact, Jared Kushner, Donald Trump's son-in-law, argued for this explicitly: "The government," he said, "should be run like a great American company. Our hope is that we can achieve successes and efficiencies for our customers, who are the citizens."[2] The problem, of course, is that it is the *companies* (rather than the customers) who achieve these successes and efficiencies—and this has consequences that we will explore in depth in the rest of this book. People are also much more than customers. This one-dimensional, business-first thinking has a lot of public traction, though, and that is partly because superficial economic platitudes have been popularized in nations like the United States and have tremendous cultural and institutional support. Bromides about the needs of the market, alongside limited understanding of economics, permeate daily life in late-stage capitalisms, and they have become part of how societies have internalized neoliberal values.

Many people, especially those of us entrenched in neoliberal systems, unconsciously use the language of economics to describe everything from our households to our love lives; we participate in "growing the economy" as if this were our collective religion, or we casually talk about people's "net worth" as though they were bank accounts rather than human beings. The language of market value permeates popular thinking so thoroughly, it becomes hard to even identify. Neoliberalism has become hegemonic, so dominant that many people consider it a normal—and thus unremarkable—part of daily life.

This is a problem. Not seeing neoliberalism, not critically engaging with it, not seeing how it permeates people's realities—all help disguise how this stark variety of capitalism has created guilt and paralysis for many communities, all headed toward multiple existential crises. It disguises its own role in *creating* today's most pressing problems—climate crises, ongoing financial collapse, public health crises and pandemic, and the epidemic of loneliness. Here, we begin to undo this normalization of neoliberalism and, in subsequent chapters, show how various communities counter it, too.

CONTEXTUALIZING NEOLIBERAL IDEOLOGIES AND THEIR MATERIAL CONSEQUENCES

First, Some Definitions

Neoliberalism has been analyzed and explained through a wide variety of academic writing[3] and other media. It is omnipresent, yet the word "neoliberalism" itself can mean everything and nothing at once. This has happened in a process of *semantic bleaching*—a word is used so often that its meaning gets muddied and changes depending on who uses it. So we offer a quick overview of what neoliberalism means as we use it in this book.

The term neoliberalism actually originated long before neoliberalism itself took such a strong hold of political and cultural systems and institutions. Combining "neo," meaning "new," and "liberalism," the term formally refers to a "new liberalism"—a new version of liberal *economic* attitudes—referring to freeing or liberating *markets*. In fact, the word first emerged at a meeting in Paris in 1938. Among the delegates were Ludwig von Mises and Friedrich Hayek, two thinkers who came to define the idea. Both were exiles from Austria and committed free market advocates.[4] Published in 1944, Hayek's book *The Road to Serfdom*[5] argued that government planning would crush individualism and lead to totalitarian control. The book piqued the interest of some wealthy people, who saw in its philosophy an opportunity to free themselves from regulation and taxation using the discourse of "freedom". When Hayek founded the Mont Pelerin Society in 1947, he received financial support from millionaires and their foundations to do so. Since its inception, then, neoliberalism has been a program that has benefited the rich—and the rich know it.

Neoliberalism's history is characterized by a few important themes: idealizing economies and markets and seeing competition as the defining feature of human relationships.[6] At its core it is a set of market-oriented ideas that, in addition to shaping economic life, shape social life.[7] In other words, the principles that have come to govern economies globally also shape how many people see ourselves and one another. We describe these principles in depth in the sections that follow, but they include privileging of private property, free trade, and free markets; privatization, especially of natural resources; de- and reregulation of things like labor and environmental laws; financialization; and shrinking of the state's capacity (and will) to provide people with social safety nets like health care and affordable housing. Hyper-individualism is a central cultural characteristic, too.

As neoliberalism has been normalized and naturalized, the dominant discourse of our (increasingly global and interconnected) world is one that claims that markets are the sources of pure and perfect social order, that they could and should be trusted to regulate and ensure human well-being. Neoliberalism defines people first and foremost as consumers, whose democratic choices are most appropriately exercised by buying and selling. Neoliberal ideology holds that "the market" offers benefits that planning and cooperation—or, indeed, democracy—could never achieve.

Neoliberalism also focuses on competition as a tool for social progress. Yet, "nature is a collaborative act," writes media theorist and professor Douglas Rushkoff in *Team Human*. "If humans are the most evolved species, it is only because we have developed the most advanced ways of working and playing together. We have been conditioned to believe in the myth that evolution is about competition: the survival of the fittest."[8] But evolution, he argues, is about cooperation as much as it is about competition—and even more so. People and other species flourish when we support one another. "Survival of the fittest," he concludes, "is a convenient way to justify the cutthroat ethos of a competitive marketplace, political landscape, and culture. But this perspective misconstrues the theories of Darwin as well as his successors. By viewing evolution through a strictly competitive lens, we miss the bigger story of our own social development and have trouble understanding humanity as one big, interconnected team."[9]

But neoliberalism feeds on an entire subfield of evolutionary psychology that views individualized freedom as creating vitality and resilience in people. There is incredible institutional legitimacy afforded to some such positions (including chaired professorships in what is basically glorified race science). Often representing an erroneous reading of Charles Darwin, this perspective is a pseudoscientific justification for present-day political positions, including racism and sexism. Yet Darwin's work, among that of others, focused on the ways that species act collectively to enhance their survival chances; more and more recent research on trees[10] and other organisms teaches us that interspecies collaboration is frequent and prevalent as well. Sociologists, too, have interrogated these ideas of individual freedom, showing how this view is deeply and problematically reductionistic[11]—and fails to acknowledge all the ways that social structures (ranging from financial institutions to drug laws) are set up to privilege some groups and oppress others.

Therefore, we also use this chapter to address the elephant in the room: there is no such thing as a free market. Human values and preferences permeate all human systems, including markets, and neoliberalism depends in fundamental ways on systems of power and privilege that began with colonialism—even as it claims to be outside those systems.

A Minuscule History of Neoliberalism

David Harvey wrote a masterful history of neoliberalism, available elsewhere.[12] Here, for the sake of orientation, we offer a shorter background before describing neoliberalism's politics, tenets, and cultural power. Neoliberal policies enacted neoliberal ideologies, and they began in earnest as an upper-class project during the 1970s.[13] Members of the corporate class of the time organized their efforts to consolidate wealth after the 1950s and 1960s, during which time there was more support for social welfare and a general embrace of Keynesian economics. Based on the work of British economist John Maynard Keynes, Keynesianism focuses on the demand side of economies. Keynes, who advised multiple presidents during the postwar period, believed in strong state spending, government programs to build up infrastructure and alleviate unemployment, and the importance of building a strong middle class. These approaches would, he believed, keep the economy growing—because demand would also be growing. In other words, Keynesian economics put much less faith in the free market to correct for problems like unemployment and instead created policies to fortify social safety nets and benefits to keep workers and people healthy. In this period, nations like the United States and the United Kingdom saw a growing middle class, a "welfare state" meant to support the public, and a concerted effort to redistribute wealth across societies rather than to its top tiers. As the 1970s led to global stagnation in economic growth and inflation, as well as the entry of major Middle Eastern oil economies into global markets via OPEC, the Organization of Petroleum Exporting Companies, the corporate class moved to reestablish its dominance.[14]

Neoliberal ideologies and policy measures gained popularity starting in the late 1970s. They took firm hold through the 1990s in political-economic powerhouses like the United States, the United Kingdom, Japan, Australia, and parts of continental Europe. At this time, U.S. neoliberalism became established not as a Republican, conservative, or right-wing project but as one that Democratic politics also firmly represented and imposed; its emergence dovetailed with a Democratic Party that bolstered technocratic liberalism over working classes. *Neoliberalism became explicitly nonpartisan*, and this wide-ranging support helped establish its hegemonic grip on much of America and the global North.

One of the first intentional experiments in neoliberalism took place, in fact, before this in Chile, during the 1970s. At that time, a cadre of University of Chicago economists (some of them from Chile) known as the Chicago Boys partnered with and advised the U.S. Central Intelligence Agency to overthrow Chile's president, Salvador Allende, in a violent military coup that installed General Augusto Pinochet in his place. Allende's leftist policies went with him; inserted instead were some of the starkest examples of neoliberalism to date. Chile's state-owned assets and natural resources were captured and sold to the nation's elite; environmental and other regulations were cut and at times completely abolished; austerity measures were put in place; and those who protested or fought this imposition and drastic set of measures met the might of the new military regime. The state forcefully imposed such policies by disappearing people who objected.

In the global North, the rollout of neoliberal policies was subtler but no less malignant. The goal was to consolidate corporate class power by reducing the power of people and of organized labor and by redistributing wealth upward toward the elite and corporate stockholders. In the 1980s, U.S. president Ronald Reagan began to break down unions and push deregulation, free markets, and private property dominance—swinging forcefully away from Keynesian economics. The same occurred in the United Kingdom, where Prime Minister Margaret Thatcher became famous for her assertions that "there is no alternative" (TINA) to market-based, neoliberal capitalism. TINA continues to hold cultural sway today, as we establish later in this chapter, and pushes neoliberal ideologies into all corners of public life.

And these ideas have serious staying power—but it is useful to learn how to discuss them with precision and nuance. Every semester, we both teach our students to recognize neoliberalism in the world around them. Once they learn about it, though, it becomes tempting for them to see neoliberalism everywhere and to blame all manner of ecological, social, and economic problems on it. While neoliberalism may be ubiquitous, being precise with concepts and definitions helps distill specific challenges and make them easier to identify. To that end, we cover three dimensions of neoliberalism in the remainder of the chapter: its political ideologies, policies, and its cultural dimension. In the latter section, we also examine how neoliberalism has linked to white supremacy in important ways.

IDEOLOGIES AND POLITICAL ORGANIZATION OF NEOLIBERALISM: A VARIETY OF CAPITALISM?

Before examining neoliberalism's unique political ideologies, we first offer a caveat: neoliberalism is not identical to capitalism. It is a *variety of capitalism that includes (but is not limited to) late capitalism*. It is on the same spectrum as social democratic capitalism, laissez-faire capitalism, and even Keynesian capitalism—but it is different in being an austere, stripped-down version of capitalism that sees self-regulating markets as the ultimate social good.[15] Unlike Keynesian capitalism, for instance, neoliberal capitalism deprioritizes safety nets like health care, housing, childcare, and state regulations to protect the environment and labor. Neoliberalism also varies across times and spaces, as it is a political *process* that has been imposed in countless places, social contexts, and economic systems.[16]

All types of capitalism are premised on markets and the idea of expansion, but the neoliberal version of capitalism sees no role for the state in making life better for most people or more-than-humans. Neoliberalism understands market systems as regulators of states (rather than vice versa); when the state and market are at odds, the market is seen as the superior arbiter. The role of the state here is instead explicitly *in service of* the market—protecting investors and their interests *from* civil society and democratic processes. The function of governance is not protecting public well-being (of whoever is designated worthy of protections); it is protecting capital, including investors' property rights. The ultimate pattern, here, is that capital has greater weight and representation than people or democratic preferences, resulting in uneven and contested types of governance.[17]

A small state remains a core goal of neoliberal discourse and self-imagery. However, the small state is itself an ideological myth. The neoliberal state's functions simply change rather than disappear, and it can actually (stealthily) *grow* under neoliberal regimes.[18] Rather than getting smaller, the state ends up serving multinational corporations and property owners,[19] while becoming less visible in the lives of many people. Indeed, corporations are often given more substantial safety nets than humans, including tax breaks and bailouts. A clear example is the now-infamous U.S. bank bailout in 2008, in which the U.S. Treasury disbursed $440 billion to buy troubled mortgage-asset securities that were in danger of defaulting.[20] As geographer Manuel Aalbers notes, "neoliberal practice was never about total withdrawal of the state; it was about a qualitative restructuring of the state, involving not so much less state intervention as a different kind of state intervention, not aimed at the benefit of the population at large but at the benefit of a few. Neoliberal practice was all about redistribution, but not from the rich to the poor, but rather *to* the elites from everyone else."[21]

There are two ways in which the state does visibly shrink, however. The first is in relation to universal protections for *people*. The part of the state that provides safety nets for the public, protects public spaces, and stewards these rights and resources does indeed typically get smaller as lawmakers cut funding to it. Because wealthy people are "freed" from paying taxes under this scenario, the state has less money to spend on people's well-being. Social protections do not fit with the competitive premises of neoliberal ideology; health care, affordable or state-provided childcare, housing, subsidized or state-provided higher education, and other policies that support baseline well-being frequently get cut or are constantly threatened.

The United States has some of the starkest austerity policies compared with other industrialized nations. For instance, most people lack paid parental leave, and most people have meager unemployment protection. Further, the expensive U.S. health-care system is tightly bound to full-time and salaried employment. A national system of publicly available health care remains the centerpiece of contentious U.S. political debates. People who suggest public options are seen as radicals, even though these sorts of social safety nets exist in socialist democratic capitalist systems and even in places like the United Kingdom—places that have been bastions of neoliberalism since the 1980s.

The lack of social safety nets has significant implications for social justice in the United States, in large part because of *who* can access private systems. We must underscore that some members of the U.S. public have long been abandoned and victimized by the state, a problem mirrored in other settler states.[22] For instance, Native American and Alaskan Native people in the United States have the highest rates of being uninsured, followed closely by Latinx populations; white people have among the lowest. So the lack of a public option for health care hits minoritized communities the hardest—because they are more likely to be without health care in the first place.[23] Similarly, the lack of accessible and affordable childcare hits women's careers the hardest, meaning that the burden of this system is unequally distributed. In both examples, the unequal burden is at least partially masked under neoliberal language of individualism and choice in health care and childcare (explained more later in this chapter).

The second way that the state shrinks is in its democratic apparatus, affecting the tools that enable all people to participate in governance. Here lies one of the most crucial, dangerous outcomes of neoliberalism: the political crises that it provokes. As the visible domain of the state gets smaller and smaller, people's abilities to change the system through voting and democratic participation are also reduced. Neoliberal doctrine asserts that people can—and should—exercise their choices and make their preferences known through spending, not voting, as we explore in chapter 4. The landmark 2010 U.S. Supreme Court decision *Citizens United v. FEC* exemplified this ideology. The Court held that the free speech clause of the First Amendment meant that corporations, including nonprofit corporations, labor unions, and other associations, could make significant political expenditures in campaign finance. The ruling was based on the idea of "corporate personhood," the legal concept that a corporation may be legally recognized as an individual. And, as such, that "corporate person" is entitled to spend money to exercise its choice and make its preference known in politics as an element of free speech.

But the rub is that some persons have more to spend than others. And corporations have a *whole* lot more.

Votes are not equally distributed, then—it is not a one-person, one-vote system. Rather, in a system of "voting with your dollar," those with more dollars have more votes, even setting aside the troubling issue of corporate personhood. Consequently, minoritized, poor, and middle-class people—who have less money to spend on political influence and who are increasingly subjected to voter disenfranchisement via a range of suppressive policies[24]—are disempowered. As parties across the political spectrum embrace these policies, disempowerment becomes disenfranchisement for large swaths of the public.

NEOLIBERAL POLICY MEASURES— TRENDS AND CORE TENETS

Flowing from the political ideologies we described, neoliberalism's core policy measures have created consistently unsustainable outcomes for social and ecological systems.[25] These include shrinking state provision of social safety nets and democratic spaces (reviewed previously and included on the following pages); privileging of free trade and private property; privatization of public goods and ecological and communal spaces; de- and reregulation, and financialization.

Free Trade and Private Property

Neoliberalism, like capitalism generally, revolves around privileging market systems, private property rights, and "free" trade within regions and across borders (we use scare quotes around the word "free" because, as we will argue throughout, this type of trade relies on a very limited concept of freedom). Key to this is the claim that (certain) people *can* own the land, water, and mineral wealth of the natural world and that they *should*. The taken-for-granted assumption undergirding this idea is that it is the right of elites to enclose parts of the land and exclude anyone who does not own them from accessing those spaces.

Of course, property ownership (specifically landownership) remains the purview of a lucky few: those with the income, wealth, assets, credit, power, gender, and economic privilege to participate in buying land and developing real estate. Importantly, the idea of ownership is a Western social construction; other cultures and systems have long viewed people, land, and animals or more-than-humans not as commodities to be owned but as relatives—as alive and vibrant participants in ecological systems of which humans are but one part. In the United States, for instance, the idea that land is ownable helped justify the rampant settler colonialism that allowed westward expansion.[26] Today, these incommensurable views also lead to ongoing battles over water rights, water access, and other fundamental impasses over land and water as property.[27]

Property rights and ownership undergird the philosophy of free market superiority that defines neoliberalism—and that encourages privatization and deregulation, as detailed in the discussion that follows. Property ownership, free market superiority, and free trade align well with one another: if the idea is that land, water, and other natural systems can be commodified into market systems, and if the state or other entities should not limit the operation of free markets, then so-called free trade agreements represent the logical outcomes of that thinking. Since the 1990s, we have seen the North American Free Trade Agreement (NAFTA), the Central European Free Trade Agreement, the Pacific Alliance Free Trade Area, and a seemingly endless list of free trade agreements and areas that are either currently policy or under negotiation, alongside institutions like the World Trade Organization and the World Bank, which also enforce neoliberal policies as conditions of aid. These agreements involve opening borders to trade, rapidly expanding global industrialization, and taking down barriers to the movement of goods (but not people) across borders. Free trade agreements have helped globalize property ownership and increased consumption.[28]

While free trade has been central to neoliberal policy implementation, this has not meant that these agreements facilitate *democratic* freedom or increased participation for people. In other words, the money usually moves more freely than people do! A useful illustration of this is cross-border movement: while jobs move across borders, capital investment moves almost instantly between countries, and environmental contaminants flow freely via water and weather systems, people's own movement remains restricted through severe immigration policies.[29] Instead of expanded democracy and more self-determination, or truly "free trade," we see the rise of nationalist and protectionist movements and leadership, including in the United States, where the Trump administration focused on anti-immigration policies and even strong attempts to build an enormous border wall between the United States and Mexico. Not only does this block people from following economic opportunities, it also deeply disturbs Native nations and ecological systems that lie on both sides of these borders.[30]

Privatization of Public Spaces and Goods

While the idea of private property certainly predates neoliberalism, this era has changed how many people think of its relative importance. Neoliberal thinking sees markets as governing social life, rather than the other way around. It follows logically that this agenda advocates *privatization*—the transfer of publicly owned goods and services to private control. Public ownership of resources is seen as inefficient and unproductive,[31] and so neoliberal ideologies encourage *private* ownership and/or control of *public* goods or assets—everything from water supplies to utilities to prisons. Public utilities, nationalized sectors of the economy (like energy grids and electricity systems), roads, national parks, and other communal goods that are used by and accessible to the public—and even relations or resources like water and air—are seen as assets that should be commodified and marketized. This means that they are taken from the public sphere and sold to private buyers in market systems, who then charge rents to the public or the government for access.[32]

In places like the United States, the ongoing and fierce debate over public lands and access to protected ecological spaces provides one striking example of this push for privatization. In the American context, public lands refers to spaces such as national grasslands, forests, national parks, and wilderness areas or wildlife refuges that have been set aside and preserved, to various degrees, for public access and for enjoyment by future generations.[33]

We must first underscore that these debates all tend to ignore that Native and Tribal nations have been violently displaced, relocated, removed, forced into boarding schools, and faced with other cultural losses and travesties of settler colonialism in order for any of these lands to be considered "public," both historically and currently.[34] Further, access to these public lands has been shown to be skewed toward more privileged and whiter, wealthier populations.[35] Public lands especially have been the subject of political battles for over a century.[36] Nonetheless, discourse treats these lands *as if they belonged equally to every member of the public.* Additionally, although all public lands can theoretically encourage public management, ownership, access, and intergenerational stewardship, questions of power and access are still fundamental. Later in this book, we explore various community-led efforts to claim and reclaim these spaces.

As it stands now, then, about 75 percent of public lands remain federally controlled, with the rest controlled by states and cities.[37] As Steven Davis[38] observes, U.S. public lands remain precariously preserved "in the land where faith in private property approaches a civic religion." Constant attacks threaten their public accessibility and aim to privatize them. Especially since Garrett Hardin's *Tragedy of the Commons*[39] became common reading for conservation students, natural resource scholars, and future agency personnel, its assumptions about the superiority of privatization for managing natural resources have become gospel (the article has been cited over forty thousand times, according to Google Scholar). This assumption persists, as we detail in chapter 5, despite excellent empirical evidence that communal management of resources such as fisheries and water systems has been successful across cultures and spaces for millennia—and often achieves greater successes than privatization.[40] Further, there are some systems (like the climate, for instance) that can be protected *only* through collaboration—because pollution and superstorms do not observe national boundaries. Yet, free markets are assumed to offer the most efficient guarantees that land and resources will be productive, while the failure to develop them represents a "failure" of the "assets."[41]

Privatization advocates gained power after 2010[42], and a great deal more power during the Trump administration. We need not look further than the administration's assault on environmental protections and public lands for evidence: it oversaw extensive reductions in public lands holdings at sites like Bears Ears and Grand Staircase-Escalante National Monuments, which are sacred places for various Indigenous and Tribal nations; the appointment of land transfer advocates to prominent positions within federal agencies; and the opening of even more public lands to oil and gas production and other extraction.[43] As we revised this book, though, the Joe Biden administration had signaled a reversal or pause on most of these policies, had reached out to Tribal nations for more meaningful consultation, and in 2021 confirmed Laguna Pueblo Tribal member Deb Haaland as secretary of the interior—first steps toward addressing some of the most flagrant problems of ongoing privatization and settler colonialism.

Globally, privatization has accelerated rapidly since the 1990s, driven in large part by global trade policies and by international development regimes and agencies like the World Bank and the International Monetary Fund (IMF). These agencies frequently require, as a condition of development and aid, that countries privatize natural resources, nationalize utilities and public systems like water treatment and allocation systems, and open up to foreign direct investment. Since international lending agencies started this practice, states have been forced to restructure their domestic economies, political systems, and governance of public assets like lands and water.[44] Additionally, privatization is typically associated with layoffs and pay cuts for workers in privatized sectors. Hand in hand with formal privatization, many IMF and World Bank loans call for the imposition of "user fees"—charges for the use of government-provided services like schools or clean drinking water. For very poor people, even modest charges may result in being locked out of services. Having these structural adjustment programs imposed as conditions of aid packages often leaves poor countries feeling as though they cannot refuse privatization requirements. As such, privatization and all its environmental injustices become globalized and forcibly institutionalized neoliberal policies.

Deregulation and Reregulation

Neoliberalism normalizes a "jobs versus environment" rhetoric and relies on systematic removal or diminishment of regulations, particularly those that aim to protect the environment, labor, or noneconomic concerns. Rules are treated as barriers to economic success and wealth accumulation. Since the 1980s, we have witnessed concerted efforts to get rid of rules that may limit individual freedoms—even if they protect the collective. The results have been significant; we need look no further than the intense responses by some Americans against wearing masks in public during the COVID-19 pandemic and actual demonstrations against stay-at-home orders meant to protect public health.

Deregulation means reducing rules, whereas *reregulation* means changing rules or reducing support to enforce them. Deregulation also typically accompanies, or signals support for, market mechanisms to solve social and environmental problems, like cap-and-trade schemes. Reregulation involves the use of state policies—or lack thereof—to enhance privatization and free market systems;[45] even if rules remain on the books, if budgets to enforce them are cut, those rules might as well not exist. Both rely heavily on devolving governance to smaller political units, such as states or even state contractors.

Take, for instance, the Reagan-era assault on the U.S. Environmental Protection Agency (EPA). First, in a move now familiar in neoliberal administrations, a concerted effort was made to reduce regulations meant to protect the environment and communities from hazardous waste, air and water pollution, and industrial contamination. Reagan had been in office for just a few days when he announced the formation of the Task Force on Regulatory Relief, overseen by Vice President George Bush,[46] which reduced rules and regulations, or deregulated. Regulations had to be examined using a cost-benefit framework and risk assessment, with industry providing the data related to these measures.[47]

The administration also reregulated by using budgets and fiscal policies to undermine federal agencies' ability to enforce regulations. With the drastic reduction in the operating budget of the EPA—its budget for programs was cut by 30 percent during Reagan's two terms—state budgets required reductions of more than one-third for enforcement programs.[48] Yet, the responsibilities of the EPA were simultaneously increasing—as the industrial contamination and pollution brought on by decades of no environmental regulations had predictable, serious consequences. For instance, Love Canal in upstate New York became famous in this era as the site of an enormous environmental disaster; the working-class neighborhood had been built on top of thousands of tons of hazardous waste.[49] CERCLA (the Comprehensive Environmental Response, Compensation, and Liability Act), better known as the Superfund program administered by the EPA, resulted in part from this event in Love Canal—just one of thousands of contaminated American communities. Yet, this timing coincided with EPA budget cuts, making the federal agency less able to meet its own mandate to clean up this sort of contamination.

Here, then, we see reregulation, in which state budgets were diminished to truncate regulatory enforcement and where polluting corporations were effectively allowed to operate with less public oversight—even though the rules remained in place. Administrations like Reagan's and Trump's treated established regulatory institutions as suspect and disempowered them in an attempt to decrease their legitimacy, another long-term strategy aimed at weakening environmental protections. Further, the idea of "new federalism"[50] pushed administrations to devolve control of environmental (and other) rules and regulations to states. But federal budgets for states were reduced at the same time, meaning that state agencies absorbed responsibilities of enforcing regulations they could not afford to monitor.[51] Donald Trump, for instance, deregulated through his Office for Regulatory Rollback, after running on the promise to dismantle the EPA.[52]

Throughout his term, the EPA also dealt with reregulation as it weathered massive budget cuts. The administration also tried to institute historic assaults on environmental protections, including plans to dismantle the National Environmental Policy Act, a fifty-year-old centerpiece of U.S. environmental regulation.[53]

Under the Bill Clinton and Barack Obama administrations, environmental protections were somewhat strengthened—but only somewhat. For instance, though Clinton initiated an environmental justice executive order and increased the number of regulations enforced by the EPA, the EPA's budget did not really increase during that period. In fact, it decreased at times (by 2.7 percent in 1994, for instance).[54] Though Obama's administration increased EPA funding, for example, asking for $8.3 billion in EPA funding in 2017, compared with $8.1 billion in 2016,[55] it did so to pay for ambitious climate change and other regulatory programs that, arguably, needed even more funding than they got. In other words, administrations across the political spectrum deregulate and reregulate.

Financialization

Neoliberal policies have also been centered on financialization—trading in financial instruments rather than goods and services. Financialization is the expansion of the financial sector relative to the productive sector, in which financial services represent an increasing share of income, particularly for the wealthy. Some people use the word "financialization" to mean the rise of shareholder value as a mode of corporate governance. Others reflect on the growing dominance of capital market financial systems over bank-based financial systems. Still others use the term to refer to the increasing political and economic power of the "rentier class" or to the explosion of financial trading with myriad new financial instruments. For sociologist Greta Krippner, financialization means a "pattern of accumulation in which profit making occurs increasingly through financial channels rather than through trade and commodity production."[56]

We adopt political economist Gerald Epstein's[57] definition of financialization as "the increasing role of financial motives, financial markets, financial actors and financial institutions in the operation of the domestic and international economies." The argument here, of both sociologists and commentators, is that the wealth of the rich comes from manipulation of *money* rather than from exchanging *goods or services*—and thus often amounts to the extraction of value created by others.[58] If economics is about "how societies provide themselves with the wherewithal to live,"[59] then it necessarily involves the production of food and commodities, as well as the work of caring for and educating others. This "provisioning" can obviously occur within markets, but also occurs outside of them. From this perspective, there is often a difference between the usefulness of goods or services (their use value) and their market price (their exchange value).

This distinction is meaningful in practical terms.[60] Those who own and run privatized or semi-privatized services can make tremendous amounts of money by investing very little and charging a great deal. So financialization tends to facilitate income that is itself *premised on preexisting wealth*. As the poor get poorer and the rich richer, the rich then also consolidate their control over another asset: money itself. They do the investing; they decide what gets support. Regular people, meanwhile, take on debt to pay for college or cancer treatments. For social theorist and political economist Andrew Sayer,[61] the past nearly fifty years were marked by a transfer of wealth from the poor to the rich and also from productive to financial sectors. One distinguishing feature of the redistribution of wealth upward toward economic elites is that they can make much of their money by *controlling access to assets or services* and charging interest or rent (hence the term "rentier class").

This happened because the changing balance of power between classes in the past fifty years (from the working and middle classes to the rich) was accompanied by a real concern that a state run by elites would seem illegitimate in the context of global stagflation.[62] In order to avoid the loss of legitimacy that came with economic recession, a suite of new financial regulations was implemented; the unintended consequence of these reforms was financialization, which contributed to accelerating globalization and even the eventual 2008 Great Recession. Krippner sees three main drivers moving the global North (and especially U.S. markets) in this direction: the deregulation of financial markets in the 1970s; an "addiction" to new sources of global credit by the Reagan administration, which allowed it to maintain political legitimacy by cutting taxes without having to reel in spending; and a move by the same administration away from closely controlling financial markets, instead allowing markets to control the flow of credit and financing. These reregulations pushed the American economy toward financialization while also connecting it with transnational markets and sources of capital.

While trickle-down theory has been at the heart of neoliberal practice since the 1980s, we now have nearly forty years of evidence that it does not work: wealth gets distributed upward, not downward. This system instead allows for the enormous growth in inequality we discussed in chapter 2, while making upward mobility, especially to the very top 1 percent, almost impossible. This is why, for instance, Jeff Bezos, Bill Gates, and other billionaires topping the lists of the world's wealthiest were able to enhance their wealth by about $1.2 trillion in 2019 alone.

In ecological contexts, financialization means that natural resources such as water become increasingly marketized and commodified—which means financialization is linked to privatization in important ways.[63] For instance, as structural adjustments and other loan conditionalities require private investment in or ownership of public resources like water and water infrastructure, these can generate uneven outcomes related to water infrastructure and water quality, costs of water, and even access to water across households and water users.[64] In another example, increasing wildfire risk and water scarcity have combined to entice investors to speculate on water futures, while unprecedented wildfires ravage millions of acres globally and the future of public water access in the American West and other locations becomes even more precarious.[65] Financialization of food can increase metabolic rift (a concept we discussed in chapter 2), separating people from the systems that grow and distribute their food, while also creating extra complexity in the commodity chains related to food production—all of which aid inequality and accumulation by dispossession of global food systems.[66] Across all kinds of resources, then, financialization has allowed the rapid development and extraction of commodities from water to food to oil and gas, often to the detriment of producer communities, ecosystems, and people.[67]

THE CULTURAL POWER OF NEOLIBERALISM: DOMINANCE AND HEGEMONY

Perhaps one of the most unsettling and surprising aspects of neoliberalism relates to the support people have for the system, and its effects on individuals' self-images. As David Harvey[68] pointed out, (white) people in places like the United States support neoliberalism because it so clearly and cleanly maps onto foundational U.S. (settler) and Western values. Privileged classes within the United States frequently feel some resonance with values of individualism and bootstrapping and therefore have a strong allegiance to neoliberal policies. U.S. imaginaries deeply value individualism, and Horatio Alger's "bootstrap" stories (in which people achieve wealth against all odds) and ideas of freedom are especially related to the freedom to make money or not follow government rules. These resonate deeply with particular aspects of the U.S. self-image, which fails (or refuses) to see the communities, systems, and structures in which people are embedded as meaningful. It seems Thatcher's quip that "there is no such thing as society" has become perceived as reality in some spaces where neoliberalism has been the norm for decades.

While poor, Black, Indigenous, and Native people, women, and other minoritized groups can often see these systems for what they are—having experienced the weight of their oppression[69]—people most privileged by these systems are often most oblivious to them. It becomes difficult for people who have benefited from neoliberalism (even somewhat) to recognize that it is a coherent system of policies in which we are all embedded at different levels. In sociological terms, neoliberalism has become *hegemonic*—so much a part of daily life that many people do not even see it. People tend not to see the ways that free trade, property rights, privatization of communal and public goods, de- and reregulation, financialization, and frayed safety nets now shape nearly every aspect of daily life, as well as people's expectations of how the world should operate. Instead, these systems have become deeply internalized (again, more often by racially and economically privileged groups, for reasons we explore later in the chapter). They have become just a part of life.

This is the ultimate trick of neoliberalism—because (privileged) people do not see the system, they often blame themselves and other individuals for its failures. While the mortar around these beliefs has started to loosen since the mid-2010s, many people still tend not to see their own personal troubles as symptoms of larger public issues. Political and economic institutions have lacked the collective will to imagine alternatives, despite many calls from activists, women, Black, Indigenous, and other people of color, and organizers—and despite empirically documented and growing inequality.[70] This is politically consequential as well as being a kind of moral gaslighting: those who "win" the competition are taught to see themselves as superior, and those who "lose" are taught to either internalize failure or blame others.

More dangerously, this causes scapegoating, infighting, and divide-and-conquer approaches, with relatively more powerful groups blaming relatively less powerful groups for their instability and bad luck, rather than seeing those outcomes as consequences of the combined pressures of neoliberal globalization and climate crises.[71] This has shown up through increasing xenophobia and white nationalism in places like the United States, the United Kingdom, Poland, and Hungary, to name a few. And it explains, for people like political philosopher Michael Sandel, a good part of the right-wing U.S. populist movement, in which resentment against elites and people of color surged starting in the mid-2010s. "The notion that the system rewards talent and hard work encourages the winners to consider their success their own doing, a measure of their virtue—and to look down on those less fortunate than themselves," he writes.[72] Over time, these views become naturalized and internalized, even among the most minoritized people. For those who cannot find work or make ends meet, the failure comes to seem like their own doing, as if they were insufficient or lacked the talent or ambition to succeed. Often, this sentiment combines with scapegoating of minoritized groups. For instance, in the United States, loss of manufacturing and other jobs due to policies of deindustrialization and free trade, such as NAFTA, has caused loss of jobs in Rust Belt cities. Wealthy and powerful actors (the Trump administration was a particularly obvious example of this) have actively disseminated and pushed the rhetoric that "immigrants are stealing jobs," seeking to stoke political unrest and consolidate their own power. Indeed, white supremacy and neoliberal capitalism intertwine to a large extent; we turn to that now.

White Supremacy and Neoliberalism

If market-based language, loosely adopted, is one characteristic of neoliberal discourse, one of the core tenets of its free market logic is that the market is *color-blind*. The word color-blind is not a compliment here. The refusal to acknowledge race actually allows people and institutions—particularly privileged ones—to ignore manifestations of persistent, interpersonal, and systemic racism. In essence, neoliberalism fails to recognize that human agendas (agendas that privilege white people, men, and settler colonialism) *have all shaped how these markets operate.* Racism helped shape free markets, and it structures capitalism itself, as the concept of racial capitalism (the process of deriving economic value from others' racial identity) so brilliantly illustrates.[73] For instance, redlining policies in cities, which intentionally locked people of color out of property ownership through the 1960s, created segregated residential patterns that persist decades later. Boston, for instance, was and remains one of the most highly racially segregated cities in the United States.[74] Power inequities can survive some shifts (in this example, racism and segregation survived the formal end of redlining)[75]— precisely because they are *institutionalized*, because the actual social values and political-economic structures of neoliberal society continue to reflect the history of capitalism's white (male) domination. As another example, school segregation is no longer legal, nor is wage discrimination, but massive educational and pay disparities still exist, primarily along the lines of race and gender.[76]

Color-blind thinking is built on a racialized hierarchy; it simply allows those in power to pretend away the historical significance of how race has been constructed and deployed to cement social, political, and economic inequalities. Narratives of color-blindness suggest that race would not exist as a barrier if it was not named. In a color-blind analysis, race is seen as a matter of taste, lifestyle, or heritage—and is *not* seen as having anything to do with politics, legal rights, or access to education or economic opportunities.[77] The basic mechanism is this: in a market system designed to elevate the individual, differences between people (in this example, differences in race) are supposed to vanish under the guise of individualism and the color-blindness of the free market. This individualism— which refuses to see race and gender and many other group-based differences that meaningfully shape people's lives—undergirds neoliberal capitalism and ignores the racialized history of capitalism.

Partly because of this, neoliberalism strongly upholds a system of white supremacy. By "white supremacy," we mean a culture that elevates and prioritizes the white experience because what is white is perceived as normal, better, smarter, or more holy, in contrast to communities of color.[78] White supremacist culture is reproduced by virtually all U.S. institutions and many Western societies; the media, the education system, and the Christian church have played central roles. Western science especially has reinforced the idea of race as a biological truth, with the white race as the ideal top of the hierarchy. Neoliberalism has provided the globalized exclamation point to all of this, entrenching the racialized nature of capitalisms and making them especially stark and violent (alongside their devastating ecological impacts). This process builds on a number of other sacred American myths, all of which encourage (white) people to see themselves as rugged individuals rather than members of groups.

One of those myths, which is deeply entwined with racism, is meritocracy: basically, the idea that people advance according to their skill sets, and that they usually get what they deserve. The harder they work, the more they deserve. But meritocracy, like individualism, is a myth. Even though hope for upward mobility is at the heart of the American dream, capitalism continues to bestow its benefits unevenly. And globalization has amplified this inequality. The ideology of meritocracy fuels the neoliberal system and is central to racial, gender-based, and class oppression. In the political domain, it means that the common good is analogous to gross domestic product and that the value of people's contributions resides in the value of the goods or services they produce and sell. Governments, too, tend to equate value or merit with market performance and technical expertise.[79]

Perhaps most dangerous of all, meritocratic perspectives make systemic problems difficult to see for what they are—*problems within the social system itself.* Racism and sexism are understood as the bad behavior of a few bad apples, rather than the defining feature of political or social systems. These attitudes frame, for instance, systemic police violence against people of color as an idiosyncratic issue of individual personalities and a few bad cops rather than a reflection of institutionalized racism in U.S. policing; or they make promotion of men over women for tenure in sociology (and other disciplines) seem like individual issues of discrimination within universities rather than persistent problems with the design of the tenure system itself.[80] There is danger, then, that public demands for social justice and antiracism will get "privatized" by "removing the social significance" of systemic oppression—and by "substituting individual prejudice and psychological dispositions or expressions of 'hate' instead."[81] Neoliberalism replaces accountability in politics and organizations with "market rationalities" and reduces collective responsibility to individual characteristics.[82] In all these ways, neoliberalism extends white supremacy while claiming color-blindness.

Neoliberalism's Staying Power

Indeed, some of the most alienating, yet effective, parts of neoliberalism's power are its abilities to cross political boundaries—even as it encourages people to divide against one another. While daily consumption habits absolutely contribute to many of the issues we talk about here—especially climate crises—the real problem is that large, powerful systems have made it difficult, if not impossible, to live responsibly, well, and justly with one another. When policy-based or systematic solutions do present themselves, they face a great deal of cultural resistance in neoliberalized spaces. While this resistance can be seen markedly on the political right, the resistance is nonpartisan and bridges political divides.[83] In part, this is because environmental blackmail[84]—making people fearful that they will lose jobs or sacrifice economic growth for environmental protections—has been so successful in the United States, where most people have very few social safety nets on which to rely. The more left-leaning Democratic Party has been just as complicit in adopting broadly neoliberal policies as the right has; for example, President Clinton's policies in the 1990s, from passage of NAFTA to repeal of the Glass-Steagall Act of 1933, represented some of the most free market policy moves of any recent administration. In the United States, then, neoliberalism has become so normalized it is hegemonic *across* party lines.

Recall that neoliberalism has a strong moral valence, and this is part of what gives it its cultural power. Neoliberalism presents itself primarily as a moral intervention, extending "moral benefits of market society" and identifying "markets as a necessary condition for freedom in other aspects of life."[85] It trades on ideas of freedom, which makes it particularly appealing to people in the global North. Importantly, this is understood as the right to *freedom from government bureaucracy and freedom to consume,* rather than freedom from need. There is a cultural synergy here that makes it very attractive to (white) Americans particularly. Yet, it is also what makes systemic thinking so important to cultivate—to counter this obsession with individualism and instead to see collectively.

This remains an enormous cultural barrier to be overcome, since neoliberalism normalizes notions of individualism that were already so central to the U.S. settler narrative. Neoliberalism powerfully subordinates ideas of political or other collectives. Rather, the *individual person* is seen as the most powerful, most important, and most morally appropriate social unit. In this kind of thinking, groups (including professions, faiths, families, or even neighborhoods) do not—and should not—matter to people's democratic or political lives. As sociologist Pierre Bourdieu[86] observes, neoliberalism represents a "programme for destroying collective structures that may impede market logic." This project is accomplished across multiple scales of societies, including "the nation, whose space to maneuver continually decreases; work groups, for example through the individualization of salaries and of careers as a function of individual competences, with the consequent atomization of workers; collectives for the defense of the rights of workers, unions, associations, cooperatives; even the family, which loses part of its control over consumption through the constitution of markets by age groups."[87]

There are a few additional cultural reasons why neoliberalism continues to find such fertile ground in the United States particularly and in the global North more generally. For one, it feels secular; neoliberalism's ideology and policy measures offer ways to think about social goods and outcomes in terms of economic values and not religious views.[88] This avoids messy conversations about the different ways in which people value their lives. Partly because of its secular appeal, global North cultures have embraced neoliberalism such that it has become a quasi-religion of its own—a taken-for-granted economic and cultural foundation that shapes people's understandings of what is possible, what is desirable, and what is good. Neoliberalism is a framework that *does* inherently have values—moral valuations of the ways the world could or should work—while monetizing most aspects of life. In doing that, its ideologies and policies impoverish our ideas about who we are and what we value—and how change comes about.

Second, neoliberalism's cultural power also resides in markets being perceived as both scientific and quantifiable—and therefore (seemingly) measurable and objective. Neoliberal economics has mastered the ability to externalize messy variables, like social inequities and environmental damage. A related irony is that the kind of pervasive competition present in neoliberal systems relies upon quantification and comparison of both people and things. What this means in practice is that workers, students, job hunters, and all kinds of public services are subjected to a strict regime of assessment, evaluation, and monitoring, which is designed to control outcomes and ultimately identify the winners and punish the losers. The doctrine that Hayek's *Road to Serfdom* initially proposed as freeing people from a bureaucratic nightmare of democratic planning has created just such a nightmare—except all the benefits accumulate at the top.

Further, because of some particularly cherished American myths we have discussed here—especially notions of individualism and hard work—any attempt to limit competition in support of human well-being is treated as morally backward and *inimical* to liberty. If competition is equated with liberty, then any efforts to reshape it or build social cooperation are cast as oppressive. Attempts to create more equitable societies are perceived as morally questionable. Collective goals like organized labor (unions, but also minimum wage protections, for instance) are seen as market distortions that impede liberty, and inequality is understood as the morally appropriate outcome: the market will, of course, ensure that everyone gets what they deserve. But the opposite actually occurs. As political writer George Monbiot[89] observes, "Freedom from trade unions and collective bargaining means the freedom to suppress wages. Freedom from regulation means the freedom to poison rivers, endanger workers, charge iniquitous rates of interest and design exotic financial instruments. Freedom from tax means freedom from the distribution of wealth that lifts people out of poverty."

Neoliberalism's cultural power, then, derives from mainstream (white) Americans' active and often eager participation in the same system that disenfranchises and alienates so many who participate in the system. While this is clearly shifting in certain movements, like the efforts we highlight in the second half of this book—many people still largely assent to it, especially if they benefit from it (or hope to). In part, this is because neoliberalism manufactures consent as it offers concessions to multiple interest groups, making them feel like in-groups gathering benefits from the system.[90] It adapts to identity-based demands, such as demands for gay rights and marriage equality or some civil rights among racial and ethnic minorities, and other cases where certain segments of society can be appeased without shifting the overall neoliberal project.

With strong political ideologies and policy measures supporting it, and with cultural preferences so powerfully intact, neoliberalism has had fertile ground to become hegemonic—to become the lens through which many view the rest of social, political, and economic life and thus how thoroughly (or not) people value noneconomic entities such as ecological systems.

ADVOCATING FOR LIMITS, AND THE PROMISE OF A SOCIOLOGICAL IMAGINATION

The stubbornness of these neoliberal narratives relates in part to a prevalent disregard for any limits. Limits (on consumption, wealth, or contamination, for instance) are portrayed as an assault on individual liberties. Any shortcomings that exist are not seen as the fault of the system—there is no system, after all!—but are due to individual abilities and preferences. One's race, gender, and class are immaterial, and so limits or rules are seen as unnecessary.

But we would like to offer an alternative view, and one that has been the cornerstone of social organization for millennia: limits—whether in the form of rules, laws, or norms that protect people and the rest of nature or prevent excess wealth—are *protections* for spaces, communities, and other noneconomic entities that have inherent value, worth, and beauty. Limits are healthy. As adrienne maree brown says, "Your no makes the way for your yes. Boundaries create the container within which your yes is authentic. Being able to say no makes yes a choice."[91] Protections are at the core of sustainability, reciprocity, and cooperation; they ensure that resources can be available for future generations. Protections and limits also value people, more-than-humans, and land as relations that are part of interconnected webs of life to which all beings owe respect. Limits counter neoliberalism and laissez-faire approaches at their core. But this disdain for limits has created the twin failings of the neoliberal system—existential threats to people and the planet.

Classic neoliberal arguments deny this, of course, seeing markets as the world's contemporary savior. They will make the case that over the past forty to fifty years, humanity has seen global poverty rates drop dramatically.[92] "The poverty rate in the developing regions has plummeted, from 47% in 1990 to 14% in 2015," the *Millennium Development Goals Report 2015* crows, and the global extreme poverty rate fell to 10 percent in 2015 for the first time.[93]

These claims can be readily picked apart, though. For instance, most poverty reduction took place in China. That feat required massive population relocations away from rural areas with growing environmental risks (which were not solved but temporarily skirted) and losses of communities and traditional lifeways.[94] It has not solved massive and growing wealth inequality.[95] Perhaps most troubling from an environmental perspective, China's rural restructuring and poverty programs have created tremendous environmental injustices, where the majority of environmental risks and harms concentrate among poor, rural, and agricultural populations.[96] Further, the United Nations' definition of "extreme poverty" as an income of less than US$1.90 per day is likely not a fair indicator of quality of life. After increasing for nearly a century, life expectancy is now dropping,[97] and for most earners at the bottom of the income distribution, real wages have *declined* rather than increased. For instance, the "average" (male) worker in the United States made in 2020 approximately what he did in 1980 after controlling for inflation;[98] women, of course, face systemic wage gaps on top of this. So these claims of economic development are highly incomplete, with benefits accruing to a smaller and smaller sliver of the population; gains in wages have gone mostly to high-wage workers,[99] for instance. Additionally, the Millennium Development Goals used definitions of poverty and hunger that "dramatically underestimate the likely scale of these problems. In reality, around four billion people remain in poverty today, and around two billion remain hungry—more than ever before in history."[100] The Sustainable Development Goals have not, so far, substantially improved on these problems.

That is: claims of massive poverty reduction are premature at best.

What is more, these gains have come at the expense of an erosion of subsistence or sustenance living, non-wage-based economies, and non-neoliberal cultural systems and lifeways—erasing cultural, political, and economic richness and differences. They also encourage further dependence on markets (we continue to examine why this is potentially troubling in chapters 4–6). For instance, industrial monocropping policies destroyed the ability of Indian farmers to feed themselves and their families after the Green Revolution and have helped generate a suicide crisis among farmers in certain regions of India.[101] Even the International Monetary Fund—one of the key institutions spreading neoliberal policies through conditions attached to its loans—now acknowledges that neoliberalism has radically increased inequality, which ultimately weakens economic and social systems. In fact, the IMF calls neoliberalism "oversold."[102]

So even as neoliberal ideas have produced enormous benefits for some people, they have created multiple crises across societies, with costs paid disproportionately by those on the bottom. We are seeing the worst inequality since the Gilded Age.[103] The climate crisis is imminent and urgent. People's connections with one another are strained, loneliness and alienation are at all-time highs, and women and girls continue to bear the brunt of global inequality.[104] The market is not solving our problems; what is more, it may be creating more of them.

To solve these major crises, we advocate instead for limits and for other ways of knowing—critical, decolonized academic disciplines; community-based knowledge; stronger institutions; and new collaborations—that prioritize the needs of people and the planet and that reinvigorate everyone's curiosity, letting people engage with rich, imaginative alternatives.

We are certainly not the first to argue that limits can help communities progress beyond neoliberal hegemony when intersectional perspectives are integrated as key components of those imaginations.[105] In this way, environmental sociology offers an incomplete but promising tool kit for transforming a system that has caused and exacerbated so many deep-seated social and ecological problems.

Sociologists (who, at the genesis of the discipline, were actually called economic historians) have been thinking about the relationship of the economy and society for a long time. They were also some of the key critics of liberalism, although hamstrung by racist and sexist views. This, to us, is the promise of sociology—an ability to acknowledge intellectual and moral mistakes, to grow from them, and to build something better. As sociologists, we must acknowledge immensely important historical shortcomings of our discipline, and this is why we join so many others in calling for intersectional perspectives.[106]

We try to see the promise of the discipline moving forward and give credit for a couple of particularly insightful sociological critiques of liberalism. One of the best-known early thinkers was Karl Marx (of *Communist Manifesto* fame).[107] Most people who know Marx know him as a father of Communism, whose theories were raked across the coals as the Berlin Wall crumbled. But Marx was an astute observer of economic and social relations, and he developed many ways of describing the gradual progression through capitalism to Communism. For Marx, production was always the basis of social relations,[108] and production defined the struggle between classes. He had what we call a *materialist* view of history. But central to Marx's theories were also the spiritual, lived experiences of human beings and the inherent value and creativity that went along with *being* human. Capitalist production systems tend to devalue that experience, commodify most people's creativity and labor, and thus alienate people from their core selves (which Marx called "species being").[109]

Cedric Robinson's *Black Marxism: The Making of the Black Radical Tradition* aimed to correct some of the whiteness and Eurocentric tendencies of Marx's historical take. Robinson highlighted the radical movements that had mobilized outside of Europe in response to feudalism and capitalism, a strand of thinking that Claudia Jones also developed.[110] Robinson and sociologist Oliver Cox used this critical assessment to develop the concept of *racial capitalism*, in which white individuals and predominantly white institutions use non-white people to acquire social and economic value. They argued that the development of capitalism depended upon systems like feudalism, which were themselves already steeped in racial hierarchies. Out of that came a world system where capitalism could thrive on the violent foundations of slavery, genocide, and imperialism.[111]

Karl Polanyi, another central critic of liberalism, was a neo-Marxist economic historian. Writing in the mid-twentieth century, Polanyi utilized some of Marx's main ideas but also questioned the grand scale of them. Polanyi thought more of a society unto itself; he saw social *relations*, rather than economic production, as defining society. Polanyi did not deny the dominance of the economy in human history, but he did deny that the economy was the only appropriate lens.[112]

The fundamental difference between capitalism and other systems, for Polanyi, was that *markets* changed, as did the ways social systems (the state in modern times) oversaw them. These shifts acted as key mechanisms of social and environmental alienation. Importantly, Polanyi looked to Indigenous cultures in the South Pacific as examples of embedded socioeconomic relations, based on long-term reciprocity and more sustainable social and environmental relations—though not to the extent that Robinson examined non-European cultures. Whereas in these and mercantilist systems, economies were "embedded" within societies and accountable to them, capitalist markets were "dis-embedded" and no longer accountable to any aspect of society other than markets themselves.[113] Embedded markets respond to social signals like reciprocity and relationships in addition to profit, taking on the patterns of social organization that characterize that society. They acknowledge social relationships built over time, norms, agreements, expectations, and values that emerge from social spaces.

In self-regulating markets, however, everything—land, labor, people, space, and time—becomes a commodity. All production is offered for sale, and incomes are derived from those sales. Polanyi used the idea of a *commodity fiction* to describe inherent contradictions in these processes—of commodifying that which is fundamentally non-commodifiable. And commodification leads to people's daily experience of alienation, driving down prices of human labor and contributing to destruction of land, labor, and people. Neoliberalism represents a sort of hyper-manifestation of this kind of dis-embedded commodification. But employing an intersectional sociological imagination reminds people of how to see the collective, how to recognize the shortcomings of neoliberal policies, and how to transform a system that has devastated social and ecological systems. Rebuilding reciprocity in social and ecological relations becomes the goal—and the cases we highlight in later chapters exemplify this.

CONCLUSION

Terms such as "the market" summon visions of naturally occurring human systems that treat all people equally. But markets, as social interactions, are beset by power relations. Markets privatize, markets deny access to increasing numbers of people (and especially those with politics or skin colors they do not like), and at their core, markets are not democratic. We have given these markets a chance to dominate for over fifty years. We have given the ideologies of private property, free trade, deregulation, financialization, and individualism decades to show us that they are the ultimate arbiters of all aspects of life. They have failed, time and again. And they are bringing down the very web of life with them.

Neoliberalism has failed—it has failed people, the rest of nature, the linkages that hold us all together.[114] Its invisibility and its taken-for-grantedness, or hegemonic power, give neoliberal ideologies and policies incredible strength. But we want to be clear about something else: this invisibility is carefully cultivated, and these ideologies are promulgated intentionally by specific sets of powers with specific agendas in mind. Remember that this attraction to competition and markets is not just "human nature"—instead, humans act as adaptably as we can within a particularly austere, callous form of capitalism, which has brought the Capitalocene epoch (as we discussed in chapter 2). Recall that one hundred companies have created about 70 percent of all global emissions in the past forty years. These powerful institutions and companies have a lot to gain from neoliberal systems, and they have even more to lose should people start to see neoliberalism for what it is. Marginalized and minoritized communities have seen this the whole time. And many others *are* finally beginning to recognize this system for what it is and what it has done—fail people, fail the planet, and fail future generations.

Contrary to the thinking of some scholars,[115] we assert here that we have *not* entered a post-neoliberal era since the Great Recession, even as the Joe Biden–Kamala Harris administration makes more aggressive moves to institute social and environmental protections. Neoliberal ideologies have acquired a newer valence in some ways: policies have become more cleverly disguised as public-private partnerships, but privatization of public resources continues, as do losses of protections for ecological and social systems. In our view, it is a deeply dangerous assumption to make that we have somehow surpassed or cast aside neoliberalism. It is more entrenched than ever. And its shortcomings have been laid bare by global crises such as climate change, COVID-19, and the racial unrest rocking the United States into the 2020s.

What we have seen in the past decade or so, however, is growing awareness of and mobilization *against* the hegemony of neoliberalism. Neoliberalism may still hold power, but people increasingly challenge its dominance over daily life as ecological and social systems crumble. Recently, social movements against white supremacy and for climate justice have provided inspiring, meaningful indications that people are fed up with these market-based, often racist and ecocidal modes of social and economic organization.

In the following chapters, we explore how these movements work to dethrone neoliberalism. We explore some spaces where core neoliberal ideas and practices are challenged and dismantled as concerns like ecological survival, social sustainability, and community emerge as foundations for just and livable futures.

PART 2 BUILDING BETTER WORLDS

4 · HUMAN BEINGS, NOT HUMANS BUYING

Trends in Modern Environmentalism, and How Communities Are Reimagining Collectives

In this chapter, we focus on one of neoliberalism's most stark and successful pillars: hyper-individualism. We argue that for people and societies to move away from neoliberal ideologies and cultures, they must reject the hyper-individualism of consumption-based activism and instead reinvigorate collective action. And we explore how communities are doing this.

To understand hyper-individualism and its outcomes, we focus on practices of transforming goods, services, ideas, nature, and people into commodities or objects of trade, something sociologists call *commodification*. Commodification fuels a myopic focus on individualism as markets become central spaces in which people exercise their "freedoms" to buy, to consume, to act out their rights to spend money. It personifies the market and equates people's freedom with their ability to buy things. In other words, commodification has encouraged people to see themselves as individuals who locate power and freedom in pocketbooks and paychecks.

Related, and also central to neoliberalism's hyper-individualism and aligned with its market-centered approach, is the practice of *individualizing action and responsibility*. In the realm of environmental and ecological concerns, this has manifested through individualized activism—frequently by encouraging individuals to purchase an array of so-called green products on the premise that the more such products are consumed, the healthier Earth's ecology will be. Individualism has deep roots—the Enlightenment emphasized the moral worth of the individual, along with reason and skepticism, for instance.[1]

But particularly in the United States, which has been individualistic as a matter of culture and taste since settlers first arrived, neoliberal emphases on political and social individualism have found particularly fertile ground. The idea that a person's most effective role in society is as a consumer participating in the market (instead of, for instance, a community member participating in collective or democratic action) is especially strong here. "Voting with your dollar" has become a slogan of sorts. As mentioned, the landmark 2010 U.S. Supreme Court case *Citizens United v. FEC*, often known as the "corporate personhood" case (in which the Court declined to limit political spending and communications on the part of corporations) shows how this plays out. This fusing of individualism and commodification has been wildly successful; in fact, many of our students who are passionate about social change see consumption-based activism as one of their few legitimate avenues to social activism.

Here, though, we aim to demonstrate other possibilities. As human beings, we are more than our purchases, and our power is greater than our consumption. Each of us is but one of many participants in vibrant human societies and ecological collectives.

We begin this chapter by looking at neoliberalized activism and outlining some of the problems with it. Later, we examine different possibilities and examples of new kinds of nonmarket action popping up all over the place. Through our case studies and interviews with visionary groups, we examine counterprojects based in *de*commodification and *collective* environmental action. We use the tools of environmental sociology to show how powerfully transformative it can be to break the individualized, market-based thinking that helped create deep environmental, social, and economic ills.

ERAS OF ENVIRONMENTAL ACTIVISM: FROM COLLECTIVE TO INDIVIDUALIZED (AND BACK AGAIN)

Like all sociologists, we hold that social change requires actions by social *groups*. Social movements usually occur among organized groups of people, known as *social movement organizations* (SMOs). These organizations are typically civil society organizations that work within a social movement to help bring about changes in societies or in the institutions that govern their lives.[2] That is: they *organize*. They get people together. Social movements come about only when people build meaning and strategy and take action within groups. They employ specific tactics, different modes of organization, resource bases, and capacities for coalition-building.[3] They take many shapes. And they are certainly most powerful, effective, and sustained when they help build alliances across groups— building action and impact across sectors and geographies.

The contemporary U.S. environmental movement provides an important example of how social movements shift over time and are shaped by their material and cultural contexts. The environmental movement includes many branches—climate justice, pro-solar, anti-fracking, anti-pipelines, urban farming, river cleanups, conservation advocacy, and much more. It is also the largest and most complex movement in the United States.[4] Importantly, though, the movement has grown to embody neoliberalism in three key ways: (1) in individualized responsibility for enforcing regulations and solving market-based failures; (2) in individualized "green markets" that rely on class-based consumption; and (3) in activism that targets corporate actors rather than systems. These trends are troublesome and, we argue, have hampered the movement's progress significantly.

While the first modern era of U.S. environmentalism began in the 1960s and 1970s, preservationist and conservation movements began decades earlier—and had significant class-based and racial divides.[5] These movements represented mostly white, male, and upper-class concerns about preserving land for exclusive recreational access and animal populations for hunting. They helped spur some of the oldest environmental organizations in the United States, including the Sierra Club and The Nature Conservancy, and they ultimately helped lay the foundation for the mainstream U.S. environmental movement. But they reflected the goals and self-understandings of privileged groups—and relied on land grabs and co-optation to achieve their ends.[6] Later iterations of this movement would perpetuate the forcible relocation of Indigenous populations.[7] Hardly the stuff of social justice.

The environmental justice (EJ) movement mobilized in the late 1970s and 1980s—and built on community organizing work that had been occurring for decades before. This movement represented different environmental concerns, including the fact that poor communities and communities of color were often exposed to environmental pollutants at higher rates while they were also excluded from making decisions about land use and zoning that would affect them.[8] Factions of the EJ movement started to look directly at legacies of racialized segregation, slavery, and colonialism that had completely disregarded Black, Native, and Indigenous relationships to land and other relations, forced removal and family separations, and initiated other forms of trauma.[9] EJ researchers such as Dina Gilio-Whitaker emphasize that Indigenous Environmental Justice represents its own kind of EJ, recognizing that the initial devastating injustice for Native nations was being separated from ancestral homelands, from which all other environmental injustices have emerged.[10] Importantly, then, EJ movements need to be understood as distinct from the mainstream environmental movement's focus on market mechanisms as a major source of movement action. While EJ does have neoliberalized strains, its activists have more often worked to explicitly dismantle neoliberal policies.[11]

Bracketing EJ activism for a moment, then, we focus on mainstream environmental organizing that took place starting in the 1960s as a way to understand how the national conversation changed over time. In the 1960s—the era of Keynesian economic policies that strengthened the middle class—social movements often targeted government agencies for social change and regulation, seeing the government as the seat of power.[12] Congress passed expansive environmental regulations in part because of these movements, beginning with 1969's National Environmental Policy Act (NEPA). The U.S. Environmental Protection Agency (EPA) was established by President Richard Nixon in late 1970 (and Nixon was a Republican, representing an almost unfathomable difference from contemporary party politics!). The EPA combined all federal environmental research, regulatory, and enforcement efforts into one agency. The Clean Air Act of 1970, the Clean Water Act of 1972, the Endangered Species Act of 1973, and the Safe Drinking Water Act of 1974 were a substantial suite of environmental regulations enforced by the state. Collective action led to other legislative measures, including restrictions on lead-based paint in homes, pesticide product labels, and controls on toxic substances.[13] These were substantial national regulations enforced by the state. While they did not ameliorate racial capitalism's impacts and environmental injustices writ large, they did represent a public effort to broadly engage social and environmental protections.

By the 1980s, though, as neoliberal economic reforms began to unfold, multinational and U.S. corporations were challenging statewide environmental protections. These struggles ushered in a new era of environmental policy that continues today, centered on systematic de- and reregulation of environmental legislation,[14] as we explored in chapter 3. Environmental policies turned to efficient management of environmental "goods." Underfunded and overextended, NEPA and other regulatory mechanisms were constructed as bureaucratic barriers rather than state-mandated protections—and, collectively, the power and enforcement of these regulations changed dramatically. Even as EJ activism in the United States increased, then, the state was hamstrung by reduced budgets for enforcing environmental regulations, and burdens of proof were put in all the wrong places. For example, concerns over environmental health were increasingly contested and addressed as individualized troubles, rather than institutional ones.[15]

New social movements—like the LGBTQ+, environmental, and animal rights movements—sparked social, cultural, and economic changes but not necessarily *political* changes.[16] Increasingly, social movements did not target the state to instigate and regulate protections but instead set their sights on corporate self-regulation.[17] This weakened state authority and capacity to enact political change, and it persuaded SMOs to align their movement logics and their tactics with corporations.[18]

But targeting corporations remains a limited strategy.[19] Taking the animal rights movement as an example: we can see that, through this approach, consumer *culture* has certainly shifted, and practices like veganism are more common. Vegan food options have become another market niche in many grocery outlets, and organizations like People for the Ethical Treatment of Animals (PETA) lead countless campaigns boycotting companies or products. But increased *political* protections for animal welfare across economic sectors or enforced by the state have been almost nonexistent,[20] meaning that the extent to which ordinary people engage with animal protections remains largely a matter of personal preference. In another example, ongoing organizing in 2019–2020 resulted in a commitment from the grocery store chain Trader Joe's to reduce its plastic food packaging. Rather than advocating for federal rules to ban plastic packaging, activists singled out a specific single retailer. Here, SMOs treated the federal government as less legitimate and powerful—and Trader Joe's as more legitimate and more powerful—and focused social change efforts accordingly.[21] It is wonderful that Trader Joe's committed to reduce packaging—but it would be more wonderful if all grocery franchises did the same.

In some ways this shift makes obvious sense: actors aim for the targets that they perceive to be responsive and movable. But changing individual behavior and targeting individual corporations does not offer the scale of change needed to address climate crises, loss of biodiversity, or rampant plastic pollution. In fact, research shows that individualized approaches have consistently negative impacts on regulations that keep *everyone* healthy. For instance, as people's concerns grew over the safety of their tap water in the United States, they bought bottled water rather than demanding better regulations to protect overall water quality. Rather than mobilizing collectively for institutional changes, Americans had reacted individually—by buying bottled water and monitoring their *own* chemical exposures. And chemical exposure continued unabated.[22] Further, activists generally buy *more* stuff, not less, while simultaneously monitoring product safety for corporations. "Conscious consumerism" or "political consumption" has characterized U.S. environmental activism since the 1980s.[23] In this context, every purchase people make is cast as a moral act—an opportunity for people to vote with their dollar for the world they want to see. The culturally powerful narrative is that if we give consumers transparency and information, they will make the right choice. If people dislike what a company is doing, they will stop buying its products and force it to change.

But this is not how capitalism works.

Making a series of small purchasing decisions while ignoring the structural incentives for companies' unsustainable business models does not change the world for the better; it just makes consumers feel better for a little while. Case in point: A 2012 study compared ecological footprints of so-called green consumers with those of other consumers. It found no meaningful difference between the two.[24] But this kind of idea is attractive because it means that we can "have it all" (or, rather, buy it all)—fashion, beauty, comfort, style—while still being green.

The problem is that market-based, individualized activism produces a kind of political anesthesia in which (privileged) people adopt the modality of consumer rather than citizen.[25] They try to construct a moat of pristine, safe, healthy

products, separating themselves from environmental risks. This matters hugely—
and has historic consequences. Andrew Szasz explains the sociological outcomes:

> [This] changes people's *experience*. . . . Their sense of being at risk diminishes.
> The feeling, correct or not, that they have done something to protect themselves
> reduces the urgency to do something more about what, until then, felt threaten-
> ing to them. If many people experience such a reduction in urgency, that will have
> consequences in a democracy, in a society where mass sentiment affects what a
> government does.[26]

In other words, while conscious consumerism may *feel* effective and good, even
safer and transformative, it does not change the political economy. Importantly,
most U.S. consumers fail to see conscious consumerism for what it is—rather,
they characterize their consumption habits as transformative or as unique forms
of political activism that connect them with large-scale social change.[27] Conscious consumerism *can* draw the state's attention to aspects of the marketplace
that need greater regulatory enforcement, while often appealing to young, identity-
driven activists by offering spontaneous, informal opportunities to express one's
values through consumption.[28] But on the whole, evidence indicates that it does
little to engage people in democratic or political action.[29]

And while a consumption-based approach to specific market issues does not
often translate to political change, it virtually *never* produces changes that apply
equally to everyone. These actions are not "radical and disruptive"; instead, they
let companies set the agenda.[30] In a study of fair-trade coffee and third-party certification, sociologist Daniel Jaffee[31] shows how social movements with market
orientations are "co-opted and diluted." Jaffee's findings mirror sociologist Tim
Bartley's observations about forestry certification: "firms typically prefer weaker
commitments with minimal enforcement, while social movements prefer stronger, binding standards."[32] And here, the firms typically win.

Another major problem with individualized, market-based activism is that
who can participate, and *how*, is always defined by money and access. Targeting
companies does not typically produce an outcome in which everyone—regardless
of buying power—receives the same protections. The inequities of racial capitalism become amplified in this kind of consumer-centered action.[33]

These changes have occurred alongside massive shifts in the nonprofit sector,
too. Starting in the 1970s, nonprofit and community organizations—the civil
society groups that pushed social and environmental changes—began to profes-
sionalize, a process that became widespread throughout the nonprofit sector and
is now so common that it is unremarkable.[34] When organizations professional-
ize, their incentives change. For instance, when community groups depend on
big foundations for operating support, they are more apt to change their tactics.
They may even be less apt to advocate for systemic shifts, more likely to blunt

their political goals to satisfy their funders, and more likely to depoliticize their employees and volunteers.[35] In other words, community groups that could be vehicles for making system-wide demands are less likely to be radical when they are professionalized. Importantly, SMOs now frequently rely on professionalized nonprofits and foundations for most or all of their funding—further signaling how the retreat of the state impacts environmental action.

We want to emphasize that it is not necessarily negative or objectively bad that activism moved predominantly in this direction. In fact, it was to be expected as neoliberal ideologies and policy measures became hegemonic—and the pressures of the system shape all who operate within it to some degree. But it can be limiting. In the sections that follow, we will explore the work of some groups modeling how to make fundamental shifts within institutions while building alternative collective formats outside those institutions.

CASE STUDIES IN RENEWING COLLECTIVE ACTION: COMMUNITY BUILDING FOR NEW ENERGY AND ECONOMIC SYSTEMS

We have covered the limitations of individualized, market-based approaches to social change, and here we turn to examples of something different: collective action, based in community, which counters the individualizing, anti-collective ethos of neoliberal ideology. Here, we lift up examples in which people build spaces for collective action, demand environmental protections enforced by non-market, state, or global institutions, and nurture collective belonging. In many cases, these strategies have successfully contributed to positive institutional changes. And they are more deeply democratic—made of different stuff from the problem.

Utilizing three powerful case studies and interviews, we explore how this action can propel communities beyond neoliberalism.[36] First, we consider two cases related to youth-led climate activism, and then we turn to a Lakota community that is building and reclaiming traditional lifeways, fused with visionary plans for building better energy, economic, housing, and community-care systems. These efforts represent emerging patterns of activism and community-building that counter the individualized trend of activism in the past few decades.[37]

Primer on Youth-Led Activism

Young people in the early 2020s had a tremendous amount to lose. They came of age during rapidly intensifying globalization, inequality, and natural disasters; after the terrorist attacks of September 11, 2001; and in a culture of constant security crises and violence. They lived through a global pandemic, the wars in Iraq and Afghanistan, the Great Recession, and the slow, decade-long recovery that followed in its wake (which was promptly obliterated by COVID-19). They watched their parents lose jobs or met punishing job markets themselves. They have seen the growing wealth gap between income groups: from 2007 to 2016, the high-income group saw its income increase by 1,425 percent more than the low-income group and four times more than the middle-income cohort—and the gap is widening,[38] especially amid the pandemic's effects. A rise in basic expenses, such as housing, transportation, food, and health care, was part of their experience, making the world feel less affordable and stable. And they experienced a dramatic rise in higher education tuition and student debt; as of this writing, they are on track to be the most indebted generation to date, as well as the best educated.[39]

Globally, young people contend with urgent climate crises, the pandemic, destabilized political systems and economies, and the legacies of colonialism mapped onto imperialism through globalization. International inequality continues to grow, and there have been troubling tendencies toward more authoritarian regimes. Yet, as social and environmental problems intensify, leaders seem to either willfully ignore these problems or stick with slow-moving, status quo solutions to problems that demand rapid responses.

All of these influences mean that young people smell the rat. And a critical mass of them want to upend some of these norms, as we show here.

The global youth climate movement has risen in prominence since the 2010s. This kind of activism runs the gamut. Lawsuits have been one mechanism young people use to fight climate injustice. This tactic has been used everywhere from the Netherlands (a lawsuit that eventually involved plaintiffs of all age groups, showing the intergenerational power of collective activism) to Colombia, from New Zealand to Uganda and Australia, Ireland, Belgium, Canada, and Pakistan (where a young girl brought a lawsuit that set a precedent for youths' legal standing).[40] These lawsuits all use existing institutions in an effort to shift out of those institutions—a defining feature of significant youth climate activism. For instance, in the (as of 2021) unsuccessful case *Juliana v. United States*, plaintiffs cited the public trust doctrine, which asserts that governing bodies like federal governments have the responsibility to protect communal resources—such as air and water and the global atmosphere—for future generations. When states have failed to protect communal resources for future generations—as, for example, when they have continued to support fossil fuel companies despite evidence of their contributions to climate crises and air pollution—young people have filed lawsuits asserting that these institutions have violated the public trust, creating intergenerational inequities, uncertain futures, and existential threats. Not all cases are successful, of course, but they do highlight important legal concepts related to collective, intergenerational climate justice. Other groups (including two that we profile later in this chapter) pressure institutions to divest their endowments from fossil fuels, seeking to shift global financial norms and redefine ideas of financial responsibility.

Lawsuits and divestment campaigns are not the only approaches young activists take. Youth movements have also mobilized collective strikes and take-to-the-streets actions to agitate for state and global action to address climate crises, such as the Global Climate Strike held in the fall of 2020. Climate strikes include marches and other nonviolent forms of civil disobedience and direct action that demand quick, collective, and just transformations away from fossil fuel–based economies. Public figures such as Greta Thunberg have taken center stage as media have tried to make these collective strikes about individual celebrity. Yet, as Thunberg herself points out, *many* other young people—often young people who are Indigenous youths or people of color and more often go unrecognized by the media—have led and sustained these efforts.[41] So the work that we showcase here is not anomalous—these cases exemplify broader patterns and increasingly common actions led by young people who are agitating collectively for systemic political and economic changes.[42]

Case Study 1. Climate Justice in Uganda: The Rise Up Climate Movement and Vash Green Schools Project

The Rise Up Movement and the Vash Green Schools Project have become powerful organizers of young people on the African continent. We interviewed the founder of these organizations, Vanessa Nakate, who is from Kampala, Uganda.[43] At age twenty-three at the time of our interview, she works to create collective space for young voices from the global South—who are often excluded from climate negotiations and world media as compared with their global North counterparts—and wants her participation in global events to create more seats at the table for excluded groups.

Procedural equity can be hard-won in these spaces, and Nakate frequently encounters racism. In December 2019, Nakate participated in the United Nations Climate Change Conference COP 25, held in Madrid, Spain, and then she attended the World Economic Forum in Davos, Switzerland, alongside other youth climate activists. But treatment of Nakate was different. For instance, she was cropped out of photographs that were taken of her with white climate activists (including Greta Thunberg) at the 2020 World Economic Forum.[44] The Associated Press claimed the action was a "composition choice" and refused to acknowledge the consequences of its actions. The experience underscored how women of color are literally made invisible in these spaces. In our interview with Nakate, she commented: "The thing that really surprised me was when I was cropped out of that photo. . . . We are in 2020, and you don't expect things like that. . . . [But] I was also surprised by the support that came in and . . . people supporting and sending messages. It actually showed me . . . all the people who still face racism."

Structural challenges amid climate crises inspired her community-centered organizing. Nakate's Vash Green Schools Project (a new iteration of her initial

Youth for Future Africa organization) has worked to get solar panels on Uganda's rural schools and aims to get them on all Ugandan schools. It is now supported by the United Nations Educational, Scientific, and Cultural Organization (UNESCO) and their Green Citizens program.[45] The Rise Up Movement, an umbrella organization for Nakate's efforts, draws attention to climate crisis—especially the ways it already impacts global South communities and how the regular exclusion of global South voices further perpetuates power inequities. For instance, climate change has helped drive increasingly severe natural disasters in rural Uganda, where agricultural livelihoods and communities were recently wiped out by heavy rains and landslides. Nakate recalled one of the disasters that inspired her organizing work:

> The people in my country are heavily dependent on agriculture as a form of survival. For example, the people in the Mount Elgon area . . . they have been robbed of everything by climate change, through disasters like torrential rainfall that causes landslides and flooding, which is making them lose everything. . . . They've lost their houses, they've lost their farms, and some of them have lost their children in the occurrence of climate disaster. So . . . people in my country are suffering as a result of climate change. They are looking at climate change right now.

Nakate employed organizing strategies from other youth-led groups to mobilize collective action and bring visibility to activism outside of Europe and America. She explained, "I got to find out about the Fridays for Future movement started by Greta. . . . I saw that they'll go to the streets with placards and their messages to strike for climate. . . . So I literally got some of my siblings, they joined me, we struck in four locations. It was just really, really exciting. And it felt good doing the right thing. I do think that with our action, someone else would be helped."

The reach of Nakate's work has grown from there, strengthened by the organizations she formed. Rise Up communicates through social media campaigns about the millions of people in the global South already impacted by climate crises and intensified disasters. On the ground, they help fortify climate-resilient cultures and infrastructure by supporting public education, infrastructure, educational spaces, and evidence-based climate policy in African nations, especially through the Vash Green Schools Project. They mobilize unified, *collective* actions across Uganda and the African continent; they focus on organizing action in localized spaces and then scale up to connect with larger movements addressing climate injustices.

Nakate's organizing work has consistently aimed to inspire young Ugandans, and it continues to do so as she expands her influence. A central goal has consistently been to create a unified collective in which young people feel that they *belong*—and are empowered to counter climate crises by advocating for systemic changes. Nakate explained their vision:

It [organizing work] was mainly to make us [young people] feel like okay, you belong. . . . We are doing this *together* as young people. So you don't have to worry about feeling left out. In all the actions that we're working on, we are pushing for a more clean and healthier environment for people, sustainable cities. . . . This isn't just our home, it is home to animals, trees, plants, bugs, among others. . . . Through our activism, we hope to demand government leaders take action as soon as possible. . . . We all have the right to a clean and healthy environment. I see it in our . . . in the constitution of my country. So that means governments have to be held accountable if the environment is not healthy enough, because it is our right. . . . The main thing is about climate action, demanding action.

Rise Up fights climate crises alongside the systemic poverty that many of its rural participants experience, seeing the two as fundamentally interlinked. For instance, through the Vash Green Schools Project, Nakate's organizing work has focused on crowdsourcing funds to build solar installations on Ugandan schools—particularly rural schools without access to basic necessities such as electricity. Solar installations combine with climate education opportunities for students and their families, for instance, representing a juicy intersection of climate justice, community development, and the power of collective action. In its relatively short existence, the organization has successfully overseen the installation of solar panels at fifteen rural schools as of 2021—and now, as the Vash Project has grown and received support from UNECSO's Green Citizens program, it is working to expand these projects throughout Uganda. Nakate hopes that these infrastructure-building efforts will increase capacity for collective climate organizing in places like rural Uganda:

We started this project that involves installation of solar in schools. You know, we all talk about transition to renewable energy, but then there are people who actually do not have access to these things or who can't afford these things. This project . . . is fully financed by [crowdsourcing on] the internet, which helps bring solar energy and make it accessible to schools at no cost at all. . . . The schools that we worked on didn't have access to electricity. . . . So this project makes solar energy accessible to these schools . . . because we believe that everyone has a right to these basic needs. . . . The climate education in local communities—most [rural] communities don't have that. Most of the people in these communities, they don't have phones, access to internet, social media. Some of them don't have television. And they never get to learn about climate change. They never get to hear the news about climate change disasters. And then they're never pushed to that point of asking, "Why is this happening? Why are people suffering because of this?"

The Rise Up Movement belongs to a global network of similar organizations linking together young people (mostly women) from across the global South, aiming to connect with the global movement for climate justice. Rise Up specifically addresses structural racism and procedural inequities in climate negotiations. Nakate explained: "It helps amplify the voices of activists across Africa. [There is a] lack of representation of African activists, especially on the world stage or in media. . . . I really hope it can help give platforms to all African activists. Because this movement . . . creates opportunities to lend [our] voices, to add something with [our] voice, and be able to be heard and listened to as well." Nakate's early organizing work centered around organizing within communities, and Rise Up has broadened these climate justice efforts by connecting Nakate's organizing efforts to larger-scale climate justice networks.

By building solid platforms to give young Africans voice and representation in climate work, Nakate's organizing work has centered procedural equity in ways that can be scaled up to connect with other institutions and organizers. The Rise Up Movement has already spread to multiple African nations and collectively creates space for a wider array of African and global South voices during global climate negotiations. The international Rise Up umbrella group builds organizational nodes led by women and girls like Nakate, trained in organizing, gender equity, and economic justice. Nakate explained their focus on procedural equity:

> The issue of not having [African activists] at the table is not something that can help us get climate justice. This is because [we] are the frontlines of the climate crisis, suffering the impacts of climate change right now. We usually hear people saying we still have time. But, actually, when it comes to the African continent— there is no time. Time was lost the moment people started dying, people started starving to death, people's lives started getting destroyed. And that is what is happening in Africa. People are suffering as a result of climate change. That is why it is important to have African voices at the table to discuss because they themselves can easily explain what is happening in their specific countries and give the necessary solutions that are needed in order to make people's lives better.

Targeting government leaders and policy changes remain central goals of Rise Up, rather than boycotting companies or targeting industries. As Nakate sees it:

> What Rise Up hopes to achieve is for every activist in Africa to have their voices heard, at least through media or on an international stage. So that they can feel like they're doing something to influence the decisions of leaders. We've already seen under-representation of African activists when it comes to some of these climate-related conferences. . . . Sometimes people take Africa to be a country and yet Africa has 54 countries. It is [a] full continent with many countries. . . . So this is something that Rise Up hopes to change, so that we have a balanced representation from the Western community as well as from African communities.

The work is multi-scalar—focusing on localized efforts, such as the infrastructure-building just described, alongside global actions such as using social media networks and UNECSO's global audience to raise funds and highlight crises, solutions, and actions in the global South. Rise Up counters the neoliberalized trope of individual-centered action by encouraging collective thinking and scaffolding from local to global action. Nakate's training taught her how to unify her organizing work, to mobilize daily and weekly points of collective action spanning multiple related issues. Nakate continued:

> We do regular strikes for the Congo Rainforest. . . . And then weekly, we do the climate strikes going out to the streets every Friday. Now [during the COVID-19 pandemic], the strikes have moved online. . . . We started this daily demonstration [on social media], where we have many people who are saying the same message. And we have this run every day [to] create momentum. . . . I think there's ways to excite people regardless, even being in lockdown.

Rise Up's organizational philosophies rest on systemic critiques of market-based ideologies, especially neoliberalism, that accelerate climate crises. Its mission, then, envisions fighting climate crises by building more accessible, democratic economic and social systems that facilitate collective well-being. Explained Nakate:

> We wouldn't have a problem of less-privileged people if there wasn't an issue of everyone caring about themselves . . . and everyone trying to generate more wealth. The problem is that the rich want to get richer, at the expense of those who are already poor. And that's a very big problem. I believe that if we had communities where the government cared about everyone's well-being . . .

Nakate paused, considering. "For example," she continued,

> [we could make] school free and accessible for every child. Make health facilities free . . . even when we don't have money. We wouldn't have problems of people dying because they can't pay for hospital bills. . . . So I believe that we can live in a much better world where everything is accessible to everyone. . . . Equality would erase the problems of this world if we all . . . treated each other in a more fair way, in a more just way. . . . There is no need to accumulate lots of wealth. . . . At the end of it all, capitalism benefits the privileged and small populations, while leaving out the least privileged, who are the larger population. Capitalism isn't a system that will lead us to a sustainable future.

As this youth-centered organizing demonstrates, *collective actions* with distributive, non-market-based approaches become the goals for building more sustainable futures with community-wide and ecological benefits. By rejecting the norms of voting with your dollar, Rise Up models how to build fundamentally different systems, fueled by the vision and energy of youth activism. It represents one important node among many; Rise Up helps build global coalitions of social movement organizations creating spaces for procedural equity within climate justice action. Through this work, the organization combats inequities produced over several hundred years by systems of colonialism, imperialism, and racial capitalism.

Rise Up, then, helps build out an infrastructure in which more organizing can occur. It organizes communities for young people who otherwise feel alienated at the prospect of global climate catastrophe. It generates *collective* capacities for climate justice, while addressing economic and ecological inequities, especially by insisting on the global South's and young people's inclusion during climate negotiations. Rise Up and the Vash Green Schools Project also showcase how material changes can be accomplished at multiple levels simultaneously. As a vibrant node in a global network, this organizing enriches local educational spaces and communities, makes infrastructure more renewable, and then models how to scale up to global, youth-led action for climate justice.

Case Study 2. The U.S. Youth Divestment Movement

As Vanessa Nakate works to fortify the youth climate movement in Uganda, another node in this growing youth climate coalition has emerged in the United States. The fossil fuel divestment movement is a network of campaigns aimed at universities and other large organizations, urging divestment as a strategy to combat climate change. It is a bottom-up movement that is largely based in university student groups, although it has rapidly spread to other institutions.

Protest divestment is a form of dissent in which stockholders intentionally sell their assets from a corporation to express dissatisfaction with the company's behavior. The fossil fuel divestment movement had its roots in the anti-apartheid divestment movement of the 1970s and 1980s. Apartheid was a legal and political system of racial segregation in South Africa in which the National Party used racialized violence to uphold political and economic control of the Black majority by the white minority. Beginning in the 1970s, anti-apartheid campaigns in the United States and elsewhere began to gain momentum as violent repression of South African liberation movements grew worse. Across many sectors, there was a push to divest company holdings from South Africa to communicate that the global community objected to the actions of the South African government, thus forcing it to change its behavior.[46]

The same logic applies to fossil fuel divestment. In 2013, climate organizer and writer Bill McKibben argued that university students should convince administrations to sell off their investments in fossil fuel stocks.[47] The philosophy behind fossil fuel divestment campaigns is to use systems of stocks and investment portfolios to remove or reduce significant financial support for some of the most profitable corporations in human history—oil, gas, and coal. Divestment campaigners work within existing institutions to chisel away at the market share and power of fossil fuel companies, intending for their actions to hit those companies where they will feel it most keenly: in their financial solvency and relationships with shareholders. The purpose of this tactic is twofold: the first is to move political consensus away from the fossil fuel industry, and the second is to stop educational institutions from knowingly profiting from climate-related degradation.

Rather than the individualized approach of voting with one's dollar, though, *divestment activists mobilize collective action to change market dynamics.* They utilize strategies such as rallies, protests, and sit-ins to demand that administrations divest endowments from fossil fuel companies. While the goals remain market-centered, the means to those ends are collective, and designed to change the landscape of investments and to starve the oil and gas industry of its financial support. Activists use the corporations' economic well-being as a point of leverage.

The fossil fuel divestment campaign has been gathering steam in recent years; as of 2020, more than one hundred colleges and universities committed to partially or fully divesting holdings of fossil fuel stock from their endowments. We focus on campus divestment for this chapter, but it is important to note that an increasing array of institutions are being pushed toward divestment, including religious congregations and even whole cities, towns, and nations. While the direct impacts of divestment are still relatively small, the indirect impacts—in terms of public discourse shift, for instance—are significant. Divestment has put questions of finance and climate change on the agenda of fossil fuel shareholder meetings and convenings of boards of trustees; it has played a large part in changing discourse around the legitimacy, reputation, and viability of the fossil fuel industry. This cultural impact has contributed to changes in the finance industry through new demands by shareholders and investors and to changes in political discourse, such as rethinking the notion of fiduciary duty.[48] A fiduciary duty has typically been understood as the responsibility of a corporation to its shareholders; it requires *both* the obligation of prudence *and* a duty of impartiality. This means that companies must meet the needs of careful investors but also not favor one party over another. Fiduciaries must put the interests of all their beneficiaries above their own interests and protect the assets of their beneficiaries equally. By this logic, continuing to invest in unstable, unsustainable, and uncertain assets becomes problematic. Financial analyst Kathy Hipple has argued that the volatility of the fossil fuel industry and its contributions to climate change mean that (especially for young beneficiaries), "investments in oil and gas companies are almost impossible to defend," and divestment is a moral imperative.[49]

At the university level, these divestment campaigns are typically run by students, with faculty occasionally playing a limited supportive role.[50] Especially compared with many of our other case studies, this movement is largely mobilized by young people with educational and social privileges. Unlike the Rise Up Movement, for instance, the central divestment movements are heavily white, well connected, wealthy, and politically savvy and rely on a network of well-heeled workers and volunteers within universities themselves. This position informs their approach, which emphasizes pressuring relatively elite institutions for system-based changes. Campaigners use their understanding of the machinations of universities, their roles as students and stakeholders, and their understanding of public relations and social media as leverage to compel university boards and decision-makers to divest. In other words, their networks and institutional positions give most divestment groups opportunities to use public and political pressure to change financial norms.

More than most of our other cases, the divestment movement is a link between the prefigurative work of building something better and the experiences of institutions as they currently exist. This case highlights how people can work within the logics and norms of capitalism to create fundamental institutional changes; divestment organizers model how to build bridges between neoliberal capitalism—with its corporate- and market-centered policies—and newer approaches that move societies beyond fossil fuel consumption and extractivism.

For McKibben and others, the divestment campaign is also an opportunity to build collective power in the form of a national movement by forming multiple nodes in a network of mobilized campus groups. As a whole, this coordinated movement can push on many aspects of climate crises at once, including raising active climate awareness among college-age people, even as they force oil, gas, and coal companies to pay attention to the very real costs of climate change.[51] In this way, divestment groups may embody a scenario of working within the system to game the system, making the contradictions of capitalism more visible.

We spoke with representatives from two different divestment organizations at two prestigious northeastern institutions: Smith College and the Massachusetts Institute of Technology (MIT). Smith College, one of the elite "Seven Sisters," is formally designated as a women's school, although it has many trans and non-gender-conforming students. Smith also has a reputation for radical politics and strong feminist organizing. MIT is a preeminent Boston research institution with robust undergraduate and graduate programs in STEM fields (science, technology, engineering, and mathematics) but also in policy, social science, and science and technology studies.

We spoke with Jessica Brown and Emily Woo Kee from Smith College and Jessica Cohen from MIT, all organizers with their divestment groups. Each joined with, or started, their campus groups because they were moved to action by their concerns over climate crises and their desires to belong to organizations working for systemic changes. Divestment got them involved with *communities* working to address climate crises, and in both cases, this has helped them develop focused perspectives on systemwide shifts. Brown recounted:

> I joined Divest from [the] beginning of my first year.... And it was not my first experience organizing. I had taken part in some electoral work before then with the "Yes on 3" campaign in Massachusetts for transgender rights.... But Divest is really my first dip into real climate organizing. I had been feeling the fire about climate change for a long time, because I had worked a job where they talked a lot about climate change and taught us a lot.... And I was like, "I need to do something about this." And so I joined every environmental branded group on campus, and didn't stick with all of them because a lot of them were doing more individual-level work like, "Let's make compostable soaps!" and that kind of stuff. And I was like, "This is not what we need." So I joined Divest and stayed in Divest because I was like, "We can actually move millions of dollars away from the fossil fuel industry!" And that felt worthwhile. And also, it was just a very strong community that we had built of folks.

Woo Kee also described developing an understanding of the structure of fossil fuel investments and their relationships to organizations to which she belonged—showing her the places where institutional changes could be made. She went to a Divest Smith College meeting with a classmate the first time:

> So [my classmate] brought me to one of the meetings. And I think it was definitely my first time organizing. And I definitely started to ... it was my first time understanding how the fossil fuel industry worked, in terms of other larger institutions like colleges and churches and corporations and all this stuff.

Cohen of MIT outlined a similar trajectory, which motivated her to help start MIT Divest:

> I was originally focused more on the tech and research side of things when I was coming into college, but I was still very interested in policy and advocacy. I got involved with the MIT climate action team, which was more policy-focused, and we did phone banking and talking to representatives and state senators, et cetera.... And then out of the climate action team, the idea for MIT Divest sprang.... And from there basically we all thought it would be a really good idea, because divestment is a national and international movement. A lot of university students are using divestment as a way to push their universities in terms of climate action.

For all three young people, the pull of working on divestment issues was their interest in systems and processes (rather than, say, compostable soaps). All were drawn to the idea of joining a national movement focused on shifting institutional norms and moving money on a large scale.

The nature of this mobilization (here and in other cases like Rise Up) also represents something that is perhaps unique about Gen Z. This generation of young people was born just before or just after 9/11; they are more racially and ethnically diverse than any previous generation in the United States and likely to be the most educated. As a generation, they are progressive and pro-government; they are less likely than older generations to see the United States as superior to other nations.[52] They have come of age during the COVID-19 pandemic and several years of increased racial and political tension, which fundamentally changed the zeitgeist of their lives and may have fostered more structural takes on politics, generally, than was the case for generations just before them.

As the students explained, they feel motivated and excited to join organizations that involve collective goals and communities; they are able to clearly identify neoliberalism's individualistic tropes and cultural effects in their own organizing lives. Woo Kee, reflecting on collective action, explained:

> [There's] that instinctual thing to join in community with one another. First, . . . I think it is a tendency on the Smith Campus to join in community with one another. . . . The best professors I've had have encouraged us to work together, to seek mutual support, to seek community. So I think, to some extent, that's a by-product of Smith College campus. . . . But I do think with the rise of social media, with the rise of TikTok, there is so much more education around issues, period. . . . The joining community with others is, I think, easier to do now.

Brown made similar observations:

> For me, it was just more of a growing up thing and realizing that I couldn't solve problems on my own. And . . . realizing that in the places I worked and in the classes I took at Smith. . . . I also think for other folks, I'm guessing that a lot of the uprisings this past summer [referring to the #BlackLivesMatter protests of 2020] made it so that people saw how clearly community action and people showing up in multitudes would really push things forward.

Cohen, of MIT Divest, pointed to the potential for coalition-building around a tangible issue and a nationwide community as an argument for divestment as a movement goal. She said:

> I think part of the reason why divestment is so powerful is because: One, it's a *movement*. There are lots of other people and campaigns around us that are all working towards the same goal, and so there's community and power and solidar-

ity in that. Two: it is a really clear ask. It's very succinct—short, I guess, what we're asking for. There's not too much amorphousness to the demand. If our demand to MIT was push for a "just transition"—that's what we want, but that's also super amorphous—and it's hard to hold them accountable to anything. There's no tangibility in that. So divestment is something that's tangible and you can grasp it. And the third thing is: it's one way that these institutions can use all of this wealth and resources that they have to shift how society is moving and also give back to their own communities.

All three young women possess keen awareness about how divestment fits into their understanding of social change. For instance, Brown had worked with the youth-led Sunrise Movement, and she described her theory of change as emerging from that experience: "[Sunrise's] theories of change [were]: one, personal transformation; two, changing dominant institutions; and three, building alternative systems. And I think we [divestment] would be in the second category: mostly changing dominant institutions like Smith." She paused to consider, and observed: "Plus personal transformation, because we did have a lot of discussions about white supremacy culture within the group and how it was manifesting. And the fact that almost all of our organizers were white, and things like that. So there's been an element of personal transformation as well." Although climate crises and related divestment issues are Divest Smith College's main focus, other defining components of neoliberal capitalism (here, white supremacy) become part of the work as well.

Divest Smith College won divestment in 2019 when the college announced that it would be divesting its fossil fuel holdings (though the email announcing the divestment did not mention campus organizers, a rather striking omission). Since that time, the students have turned their collective efforts to local community organizing, supporting housing organizations and mutual aid and abolitionist groups. Brown said, "One thing that we have been in agreement about as a group is that we do want to support more radical means of change, like mutual aid, abolition, or things that are countering neoliberalism on the ground." She described a shift from working on "changing existing institutions" to "building alternatives" in post-divestment work. "Personally at least," she concluded, "I've worked with alternatives much more." Cohen of MIT Divest had a similar story, describing a shift toward working more directly with people:

> Through MIT Divest, I would say I've learned a lot more about organizing and community care and mutual aid. It's more people-centered, versus even nature-centered, than I was before, or even system-centered. And not the "change it from the inside" deal. I feel like there's a lot more power in communities and almost enforcing or making that change happen versus begging for it to happen.

This move to on-the-ground work focusing on the needs of people seems, in both groups, to be partly a reaction to the highly complex, multi-scalar, and ambiguous forms that institutional change takes—not to mention the length of time it requires. It also reflects the emotive appeal and cross-cutting nature of community-based work. Woo Kee said:

> I don't think that [divestment] registers in my brain [as a success] because for me, it doesn't feel like we won divestment. Because once we won, we realized—well, at least I realized, I should say—I realized how complicated and difficult divestment really is.... The UMass divestment for instance, that group just drifted apart.... After they won, they didn't really come back together, and they were unsure if UMass had actually moved the money.... So it was very, very sketchy how these colleges can just say that they've divested. It's very, very hard to look at financial stuff, it's inaccessible, it's hard to find.... The internal push was more about educating the student population, educating the people in my network, and basically pointing to the hypocrisy of the College and really shaming them.... Because when you're fighting within the system, you can only do so much before the system turns around and says, "We're still playing our game," before they moved their piece.

She continued, reflecting on why some small-scale wins at the community level (like housing) have been edifying: "So I think that that's why it's really satisfying... raising money for tasks.... We raised a little over $2,000. That money is going to go directly ... to the people that need it. It's very, very satisfying to do that work because the people are actually in control of those resources."

For all three, fighting from within to change the neoliberal structures that underlie fossil fuel and extractivist systems is incredibly challenging. Not only are the stakes enormous—the planet's climate and cascading effects!—but the stubborn ubiquity of neoliberal ideas and policy measures both require enormous amounts of work to shift. And even when divestment is won, the enormous problems related to climate crises persist. It is daunting work.

Divestment organizers at both institutions also describe an emergent understanding and apprehension of the interconnectedness of their climate work with other issues. They all credit these early organizing experiences with their coming to understand how different social problems are connected and mutually reinforcing. Woo Kee continued: "I feel like also something that we've changed [post-divestment] is our understanding that there are other types of politics besides environmental politics that need to be radical." Brown adds: "I think for me, it's just, I don't know a world without cops, and prisons, and borders, and the military, and all of the things contribute and have caused these systems that have, in turn, caused climate change."

Both outline their post-divestment work as being not specifically environmental but rather arising from different perspectives on the intersections among issues—in this case, borders, prisons, housing, *and* environment. But despite these emergent understandings of the intersectionality among issues, Divest Smith College is demographically very white, and it is grappling with the racial implications of organizing within elite systems and universities founded at a peak of racial capitalism. Woo Kee, a Mexican American woman who identifies as white, said:

> Divest is very, very white, and we have actively struggled to include people of color in our organization. And besides having to work within Smith College, I think one of the most disheartening things about Divest for me is that there aren't more people of color. . . . Divest is very close-knit, it's hard to recruit, period. And it's also just hard to hold onto people; so we might recruit people, but then as the year goes on, people will drop off. . . . And I think that people of color don't want to walk into a room with all white people and organize with all white people. Especially when there's . . . conversations about white supremacy, being like, "how is white supremacy manifested in this group?" And like, what can we do to fight it? Like, what is the one person of color supposed to say? It's very, very difficult. And I think that Divest has, inadvertently, has a reputation on campus for being white.

Brown added:

> I also think the financial institutions that we're fighting are meant to be inaccessible and we never, I don't think we ever succeeded in making it clear what we were doing. . . . And I don't think we ever made the case for how this work was liberatory. I still don't know if I'd consider it liberatory. I mean, I love the work, and I think we do good work. But I think it makes sense that cross-class, multi-racial organizing happens when the solutions we're fighting for are cross-class and multi-racial. When those solutions capture a base like that. I don't think divestment—divestment is just dealing with these financial institutions that make no sense.

This case highlights a few important themes. First, divestment organizers clearly recognized the need for a collective and institutional push; two of them specifically pointed out that coordinating community efforts is easier with a national divestment movement to link to. This format links smaller-scale (campus-wide, for instance) community organizing efforts with an attention to larger financial systems, building bridges from the system that currently exists to the system they would like to see. As a piece of this, these groups clearly value collective power and are openly critical of consumer-based and individually based solutions (the compostable soap).

Additionally, the divestment groups attend to the particulars of their community environment—in this case, their community environments are universities. Organizers are very clear that they have an inflection point in elite spaces (universities, in this case) and are intentional about using it.

They do, however, seem to feel ambivalent about their engagement with the financial and institutional mechanisms of investment and divestment. Members of the Divest Smith College group spoke openly about their disaffection with the structures that are themselves designed to be opaque and disempowering. But it is more than that, it seems: divestment organizers undertake their work in a university setting. They also desire inclusion and want to develop cross-class and multiracial coalitions—which makes the work much bigger than divestment alone. The challenges are much broader, much more deeply rooted, much more permanent, and not likely to feel finished even if they attain divestment. And these challenges also illustrate the ultimate gift of collective action and community organizing: the work is too much and the pressures too great for any individual person. Communities are the fundamental requisite to this work.

Case Study 3. Thunder Valley Community Development Corporation and Lakota Nation Approaches to Collective Community-Building

Here we move from youth-led activism to youth-focused community development within Indigenous and Native nations, part of a growing movement for Indigenous decolonization and self-determination.[53] The Thunder Valley Community Development Corporation (Thunder Valley CDC) began in 2007 in Porcupine, South Dakota, on the Pine Ridge Reservation. This nonprofit organization aims to build collective, regenerative, and non-capitalist systems informed by communities' needs.

Thunder Valley is Lakota-led and women-led: liberation, Lakota spirituality, multigenerational participation and youth inclusion, and a focus on wellness and community-generated solutions animate the Lakota Oyate Omniciye, or the Oglala Lakota Regional Plan. Thunder Valley CDC earned a Sustainable Communities Regional Planning Grant from the U.S. Department of Housing and Urban Development (HUD) to facilitate its innovative sustainable home construction and community engagement efforts. President Barack Obama's White House recognized it as a Promise Zone in 2015.

With the HUD grant's support, the Thunder Valley CDC's teams conducted over one hundred hours of community engagement sessions across Lakota lands, which constitute over 2.5 million acres. Their exhaustive efforts ensured that their Regenerative Community Development Master Plan was created *collectively* by their entire broader community, across multiple generations and vast spaces. The resulting goals have become what they call the Nine Pillars to achieving more social, ecological, and economic sustainability. Nine major principles hold up this vision and help community members heal individually and collectively.

We interviewed their executive director, Tatewin Means, a lawyer from the Sisseton Wahpeton Dakota, Oglala Lakota, and Inhanktonwan Nations. Means specializes in human rights law, with additional graduate degrees in Lakota leadership and management from the Oglala Lakota College. She served as attorney general of the Oglala Sioux Tribe on the Pine Ridge Reservation from 2012 to 2017 and now directs Thunder Valley CDC.

During Thunder Valley's community meetings, decolonization emerged as a collective goal. Decolonization here refers to the process of reclaiming a community's or Native nation's cultural values and systems and redefining and reasserting people's identities as distinct from colonialism. Returning land from settler to Native nations is often another centerpiece of decolonization efforts, and each community works to counteract settler and colonial influences in its own way. Here, the vehicles for these processes center on spiritual healing; (re)claiming of Lakota lifeways, language, and culture; wellness; and decolonization through building alternative systems. Thunder Valley sees opportunities for collective regeneration and community-building in the very existence of Lakota communities, which have survived despite generations of violent genocide. Means explained:

> The fact that we still exist as Lakota people—with our language, with our lifeways, with our spirituality—is an act of regeneration. The genocide that was committed here on this land—all of the acts of oppression and forced assimilation—the fact that we are still able to speak and acknowledge each other in our language, practice our spirituality, and have our teachings is regenerative. . . . Because, in our efforts and emphasis so much is on returning to . . . that Lakota thinking, that Lakota mindset. That ritual returning to who we are, is reconnecting to all values and principles of individual responsibility, responsibility you have as a relative, as a daughter, a son, a niece, a sister, a brother.

One lesson emerges right away: collective community development and decolonization begin with individual healing. This individual healing is relational, though—individual wellness happens only in relation to others—and becomes the root of collective healing and regenerative action. Means summoned the image of a tree on which all Nine Pillars connect to a central trunk:

> If you envision a tree, the root of that tree, what gives it life? What makes it grow? It is our lifeways and wellness equity. The branches and the leaves that grow from that, those are our Nine [Pillars or] initiatives. So you have regional equity, food

sovereignty, education, youth leadership, Lakota language revitalization, work-force development, housing and homeownership, our regenerative community development—which is the actual building of our community—and then social enterprise.

The intergenerational and contemporary traumas suffered by Lakota people must be healed first. In this view, if individuals are not healthy, the collective projects of decolonization and community development will not happen. As Means observed, individual healing ripples into community healing because people are part of, and responsible for, a collective:

> Every single [Pillar] is addressing some social determinant of health. . . . Lifeways and wellness equity are so important because that's how we will operationalize liberation . . . and pragmatically approach liberation and hope. . . . So you have to have first sovereignty and liberation of yourself, then that extends to your family, . . . to your extended family, your community, your nation. So a liberation ripple effect. And then we strongly believe at Thunder Valley, the first step of lib-eration is healing. All of the trauma that our people have experienced, that Indig-enous people have experienced, are clear there. . . . *A return to that mindset of: "if I don't fulfill responsibility to my community, my people will not live."*

Healing and well-being, achieved through collective efforts to preserve Lakota spirituality, language, and knowledge systems, involve the tough work of claim-ing community. As part of a commitment to intergenerational health, young people have been at the center of these efforts: an attempt to make good on these values of community well-being. Even when faced with immense exis-tential crises, *collective* imaginations and participation have been key to healing—working and being in community allows people both to extend care and to be cared for:

> It's nice to say . . . "Let's fight for liberation, we want healing. We have to heal from historical trauma. Let's do it." But how do you actually operationalize? . . . Because it seems so overwhelming. . . . Like how do you overcome 400 years of trauma? Like it's too much, and so I'm just gonna worry about myself?

Means paused, then resumed:

> We have to take a very systematized approach to this, that fits us. . . . This is our expression of sovereignty. . . . This isn't the only way to be a sovereign citizen. This isn't the only way to be liberated. It's just *our* way. And we hope that others will want to join in that. So we don't want to take the approach of the colonizer

and say, "You want to be liberated, join this movement!" [Rather], it's really trying to excite and galvanize that interest in the community to be a part of this movement.

Means described the focus on young people as a commitment to the future:

> Initially, it was "if we connect our young people back to our spirituality, back to our lifeways, back to our language—that will have downstream effects for future generations." . . . So a lot of time was spent in reaching as many people as possible, [with] a multi-generational approach to community engagement from the youngest relatives to the oldest and everyone in between. And the one thing that they were asked was, "What do [you] hope for in the future? What do you envision? If you can have your ideal community, what would be included?"

Doing this collective work of envisioning enabled community members to put forward a vision of what they wanted—together. As Means asserted, each Pillar strengthens their distributive, regenerative community design and builds decolonized systems, moving beyond capitalism:

> How do we build a regenerative economy that is in line with, culturally, who we are? That isn't just about profit and loss statements and the bottom line, but really is about building a better community and redefining what community wealth is. Right? That's a part of our social enterprise initiative. . . . You know, all of these initiatives tie into that: changing mindsets and changing systems. We should hashtag that. Changing mindsets, changing systems [laughter].

Thunder Valley, operating as a cooperative, forms a type of exchange predicated on the needs of community—and can in fact serve as an anchor for that community. It also represents a significant departure from money economies and a recognition of how people, especially young people, can enrich social systems. Means rejects the idea of money as power and, indeed, the idea of money as the goal:

> A spiritual leader in our community . . . once said that our two greatest resources are our young people and our spirituality. It wasn't "Oh, this mineral because we can make a profit off it" and it wasn't . . . money. And the heart of colonialism, colonial mindset, and capitalism is that money is the power, right? He who holds the money holds the power. So one part of that is in order to really shift your mind and heal from that, you have to value other things than money. And that might seem really simplistic, but when you really look at it, most people don't do that. Everything is based on money.

Thunder Valley's housing and community design has become one concrete representation of the community's vision for systemic change away from capitalism through collective, regenerative design. The Thunder Valley CDC has helped build neighborhoods oriented to community histories and the surrounding landscape itself. For instance, within the Regenerative Community Development initiative, the physical act of building and the social act of creating community are one. The architecture of these homes incorporates many Lakota components, and the houses are built in circles of seven—representative of the Lakota's position as a part of the greater Sioux confederacy of nations.

Thunder Valley's vision means that liberation—and the responsibility for healing—does not depend on individualized action but involves everyone, working at multiple levels. Healing requires work from everyone—including settler culture—in ways that are iterative and ongoing. Means observed:

> We have to decolonize. And decolonization isn't on the part of oppressed people. It's not only the responsibility of Lakota people or Indigenous people. Every single person that's a part of a colonial settler society in America has been colonized. This means white people have to decolonize. Everybody has to be willing to have a mindset shift to change the way they think, to completely obliterate every system, every narrative that we've come to know living here, right? Because it's so rooted in colonialism, colonization, and white supremacy. Our theory of change takes direct aim, as a fight against colonialism, as a fight against white supremacy. For our people to prosper, and for our people to persevere for generations to come, there has to be this massive healing across this land, across this country.

Means continued, focusing on the inherently *collective* action needed and the transformative hope it can bring: "And that's everybody. Everybody has to be a part. And now is a really exciting, exciting time . . . because this conversation is happening at a national level and international level around 'how do you be an anti-racist?' How do you address white supremacy and white supremacist systems? These are all things that especially some people have been talking about for generations."

This analysis also comes with a specific perspective of power—one that is rooted in the collective. For Means, erasing power inequities is not the goal, not exactly. *Flattening* the hierarchy, attaining balance and intergenerational equity, being quiet and listening to lessons of reciprocity—*these* are the goals. As Means shared, the Lakota word *wówašake* comes closest to "power" in the Lakota language and refers to having the ability to accomplish something together. The first part of the word refers to "collective," and the second part of the word refers to "strength." As Thunder Valley's materials observe, "In our language and in our lifeways, there is no strength of power without community." Means explained:

I sat in a lot of think tanks or working groups where they're saying "You have to shift the power. There's a power imbalance. There's a wealth imbalance. We have to shift those, and we have to reclaim power." It's power, power, power. And it's under those auspices, it's under that preconceived notion of what power meant, that our [Indigenous] communities were subjugated, that our communities were marginalized and nearly annihilated. So I refuse to use the language of the oppressor and think of things in terms of power. Because that's how the colonizer thinks, right? So we're not trying to reclaim any power. . . . We never lost that strength, right? Spiritual strength is different than power. . . . It's not power, it's *balance*. It's restoring the balance. Indigenous people have always lived in balance with everything with the earth, with the elements, with all living creatures. People like to stereotype that and make it all mystical. But it's really true, right? Everything was in balance. Everything had a place. And so it's really reclaiming a balance. Or we find a balance.

As Thunder Valley grows, community members continue to refine their model for how to achieve this balance. Here, many of us have an invaluable and distinct opportunity to listen and learn. Anyone living within a capitalist system can learn something about how to let go of the obsession with individualized efforts and material gains so often measured at that scale. Collective action—extending all the way to other generations and other beings—is a cornerstone of this approach. Means observed, "It's really important to us as an organization to have the foresight that our ancestors did. They always planned for seven generations. And so that's how we have to think."

The material changes accomplished by Thunder Valley community members involve embodying this collective understanding of power—*wówašʼake*, based on collective strength—and building their work in community development around it. They aim to build regenerative, healthy communities around the Nine Pillars based on multiple levels (and multiple generations) of well-being. From intentionally planning new home construction according to Lakota principles to reclaiming their spirituality and language—the work of Thunder Valley CDC continues to accomplish remarkable regenerative, decolonized community development, building alternative institutions that center on the well-being of people and the planet.

CONCLUSION

The collective actions we have highlighted here provide concrete models of community-based work aiming for something better: models that reject hyper-individualized solutions and instead focus on building collective capacities. They utilize visions of intergenerational equity to address climate crises and other socio-environmental problems we reviewed in previous chapters. These case studies show how people can organize to demand serious, rapid limits on fossil fuel emissions while also modeling how to build more sustainable systems powered by renewable energy and sustainable community development.

Countering corporate power remains a key goal of these organizations and coalitions, although they go about it in different ways. Although they are based in communities and typically advance noneconomic models of exchange, both those in the divestment movement and Thunder Valley CDC's network of communities still operate within the current capitalist market structure, advancing alternatives within the system. And in doing so, they demand fundamentally different systems centered on more equitable distributions of wealth and power.

What is more, these cases also demonstrate that, in many instances, power can be found *only* in collective action. At times, as with Thunder Valley and the Rise Up Movement, settler colonialism and global colonization are acknowledged and resisted—and the goals become even more relational and community based and move beyond the state. In a neoliberal market economy, maximizing profit is typically the major goal of large and small companies alike. The groups profiled here offer up alternative visions of major goals: ecological sustainability, reciprocity, and nurturing the social fabric of communities themselves. They do, as we noted, of course make use of the limited institutional legal structures to protect those goals—Thunder Valley CDC is a 501(c)3 nonprofit corporation, for instance—acknowledging the existing systems that contour their work even as they seek to move out of them.

Scholars such as Pierre Bourdieu have observed that neoliberalism can break down collective action[54]—and his observations seem to have been borne out in many ways. But here we see examples of groups purposefully building community and, in doing so, embodying material and institutional changes, moving away from hyper-individualism and toward different visions of collectives. Each seeks to build institutions that acknowledge the force and values of collectives.

Maybe this is just the beginning.

5 · DEMOCRATIZING THE COMMONS BY BUILDING COMMUNITIES

In this chapter we make two arguments, both about public space and both of which bear on neoliberalism's pillar of privatization. The first argument is that public space should be *public* space: all people need to be able to access it and utilize it to build relationships with one another, with ecosystems, and to create stronger communities. Our second argument flows from the first: that in order to claim public spaces and resist privatization, people must turn toward one another and more-than-human relations[1]—thinking of ourselves as parts of collective, relational communities (human and ecological) rather than as individual consumer-members of market systems.

Privatization, which is the transfer of something from public to private ownership, becomes possible only by commodifying it—assigning it a value intended for exchange. And, as we showed in chapter 3, in many places privatization now extends throughout social life: to education, public services, utilities, prisons, and health care. Privatization now permeates the political understanding of what is normal and desirable, aided by ideologies that have framed it as a pillar of so-called successful and developed societies.

This matters for many reasons. First, privatization has been a central mechanism through which a handful of elite corporations have drastically impacted the habitability of the planet and, with that, the futures and well-being of millions of species and future generations. These devastating outcomes have become very apparent through impacts to the global climate, to biodiversity and land's integrity, to degraded soils and polluted spaces, and to hydrologic systems.[2] Outcomes affect humans, more-than-humans, and all so-called resources (entities, like water, that some cultures treat as relations).[3] Privatization is a core part of neoliberal ideological hegemony—and that it has expanded so forcefully in such a short period of time while benefiting so few corporations and private actors speaks to an important pattern. Namely: taking public goods and making them private commodities to be bought and sold, or commons to be plundered and polluted for profit, has unsustainable, unjust, and inequitable consequences.[4]

Privatization is a problem because it redistributes profits upward toward an elite few, while spreading the costs out among the rest of us—especially environmental, public health, and social costs. In other words, profits are *privatized* as costs are *socialized*. The devastating outcomes show up in economic inequality, decreased life expectancy, and inequitable distribution of risks on one hand, and limited power to change them on the other.[5] Further, without the ability to privatize or pollute air and water or to access publicly funded resources like infrastructure, corporations would be unable to generate a profit. This makes privatization a double assault.

Here, we focus on how community groups are undoing those patterns and how they are building more distributive systems, where the goals are public access, public enrichment, and intergenerational and interspecies justice.

We are careful, though, to talk about people democratically *accessing* or *claiming*, rather than *re*claiming, public spaces. There is a tendency within U.S. political discourse to ignore the ongoing traumas and realities of inequality and to romanticize the past (we need look no further than Donald Trump's famous slogan "Make America Great Again" to see this in full force).[6] This ignores the fact that for some, America has never been great: what Americans consider so-called public space is space that was stolen from Indigenous nations, claimed and colonized by a public that excluded many (most?) people because of their race, class, gender, or religion—and that also relied on genocidal practices, slave labor, and the subjugation and exploitation of women and children.[7] Further, we must acknowledge that there are enormous differences between land as a commodity and land conceptualized as ancestral lands and territories of Indigenous communities or Native nations, to which people and communities *belong*. In this latter case, people often see land as a relation undergirding their material cultures and see life as composed of many relations among so-called resources, from the water to mountains and trees. In these contexts, the idea of owning those relations as commodities is unthinkable because land is alive and humans belong to those larger living systems.[8]

At any rate, your authors are not seeking a return to any imagined past—we are seeking to help claim collective futures that are more just and inclusive. The components of these futures need to account for past harms, and they need to be worked out collaboratively.

Here, we show organizations and communities doing this messy and meaningful work—and dismantling neoliberal norms of privatization by building systems of access and stewardship that surpass private ownership and model how to build something better. But first, we will look carefully at what we mean by communal space. We will do so by exploring the idea of the commons.

THE COMMONS—URBAN AND RURAL

The classic anthropological definition of the *commons* is about shared public space—literally, about land that is held in common. It is the idea that "property is held by an identifiable community of interdependent users. Users exclude outsiders while regulating use by members of the local community."[9] Controlling access to the commons can be difficult and costly (think of regulating fishing or groundwater). Increasingly, legal and private property systems characterize the commons as subtractable or zero-sum, meaning that what is gained by one user is lost by another.

The enclosures in Europe, and particularly in Great Britain, were some of the first moves toward territorial privatization, moving away from systems of public access to land. Enclosures came in the eighteenth and nineteenth centuries in the form of a movement to kick peasant populations off communal land they had used to graze their animals to supplement their livelihoods. Some began as early as the twelfth century, but by the eighteenth century, elite ruling and expanding capitalist classes in England enclosed much land for their private use, through various Enclosure Acts and often with literal fences or walls. As Karl Polanyi observed, enclosures and commodification of land created some of the first and starkest forms of social dislocation and disruption.[10]

While the notion of the *urban commons* draws upon this older idea of the commons, more contemporary writers have used the idea to describe shared collective, non-commodified spaces within cities. The urban commons is aspirational—a concept employed to help create new ways of living in cities specifically. When philosopher Henri Lefebvre wrote that "the city is dead," he meant that urban spaces no longer seemed like communal places where residents could fulfill their social needs (for community, entertainment, knowledge, play, and the like).[11] Runaway urbanization, he argued—in Paris, New York, Chicago, and London at the time—prioritized economic exchanges over relationships and privileged rationality, efficiency, and profit maximization over vibrancy of human life within cities. In recent decades, these processes combined with neoliberal reforms to shrink safety nets, decrease public access and public space, and decrease support for grassroots movements.[12] Lefebvre's thinking birthed a generation of research on what is called the "right to the city," exploring urban residents' ability to mobilize and thrive in cities.[13]

The *commons*, though, does not refer only to physical spaces. The concept of the public sphere also refers to interactive spaces of public interest—spaces where people develop our identities and cultures and become who we are; spaces where we undertake collective action; spaces that allow societal representation, collective expressions, and political freedoms; spaces advancing the condition of equality; and spaces reflecting democratic formation of opinion and public will.[14] Further, in line with environmental justice's inclusion of the built environment (spaces where we live, work, play, and pray), public spaces cross urban and rural boundaries—and include not only public and wild lands conceived of as wilderness areas and constructed as a result of violent removal of Native populations[15] but also commons and public spaces within built environments.

In 1968, Garrett Hardin popularized the idea of the "tragedy of the commons,"[16] predicting the overexploitation and degradation of resources held communally (also discussed in chapter 3). Hardin asked readers to imagine what would happen to a metaphorical village commons if all of the herders were to add a few animals to their herd, imagery that highlighted the divergence between individual and collective rationality. If each herder found it more profitable to graze more animals than the pasture could support (because each took all the profit from an extra animal but bore only a fraction of the cost of overgrazing), the result would be degradation and loss of the resource for the entire community. Hardin concluded that "freedom in the commons brings ruin to all."[17] His observations were almost immediately adopted as *the* definitive insight on collective resources, and this conclusion has been accorded the status of scientific law, becoming part of the conventional wisdom in environmental studies, resource management and science, economics, ecology, and political science, among other fields.[18]

However, Hardin's claims are premised on ethnocentric, patriarchal cultural ideas that privilege rationality and individualism. He makes a number of faulty assumptions about human nature and behavior, including: that all people work within wage-based or market-based economic systems (as opposed to communal or subsistence systems); that people (whom he refers to as "peasants") will not communicate with one another about individual or collective needs; that people always and only look out for themselves; and that the commons are open to everyone equally and not subject to complex systems of social control and protection.

Further and more importantly, Hardin's observations are not supported by empirical research, which has repeatedly shown different outcomes of communal management or stewardship. Elinor Ostrom and her protégés[19] found abundant cross-cultural empirical evidence of the following: that social protections can actually *preserve* the commons for generations of people; that many cultures and peoples still do not operate solely within market-based economic norms; and reiterated that collectives have successfully managed common resources for centuries. As communal management of systems like fisheries and water resources has been lost, the real tragedy has resulted from commodification and concomitant loss of the commons. This includes loss of connection to community and loss of the cultures, worldviews, and even languages that are parts of those spaces.[20]

For us, the true tragedy of the commons seems to actually be *brought on* by privatizing these spaces. Ironic, then, that Hardin's thought experiment has so encouraged privatization—and that this pillar of neoliberalism is now so taken for granted. As Polanyi[21] observed, the commodification of land is inherently destabilizing and disruptive. Perhaps it is not surprising, then, that significant pressures are mounting against privatization, particularly of water, which we will turn to shortly.

Privatizing Vital Commons: Water and Extractive Energy Production

Perhaps no action is more audacious than privatizing water. Water is the consummate communal resource—or relation. And privatizing it is, perhaps, the ultimate act of dispossession by accumulation.[22] All people (indeed, most beings) need water to live. And we need water to facilitate all forms of civilization. In fact, water—access to it, its quality, its quantity—is becoming the defining issue of the twenty-first century, driving global conflict and resource wars alongside global climate change.[23]

Water privatization is the practice of commodifying and marketizing water so that access to it and use of it is limited to those people and groups who can purchase it in a private, market-based system—at market prices and/or at a price set by the so-called owner. Yet, erecting these barriers to accessing water is ethically dubious; it blocks people from accessing a foundational building block of life.[24] When water is privatized, a vital necessity gets a price tag on it—one that billions of people cannot afford.[25] Further, privatizing water commodifies rivers and watersheds, which are relations for many Native nations and which are increasingly recognized as having legal rights.[26]

More concretely, when social scientists study the consequences of privatizing water systems, they typically find that the colorful promises of "water for all" are not fulfilled.[27] Water rates tend to increase drastically, people who worked for the public utilities are laid off in significant numbers, access can diminish, and the quality of water often suffers as the bottom line replaces concerns about water's safety and accessibility.[28] In the United States, we need not look further than notorious cases such as in Flint, Michigan, or the entire U.S. Southwest, to appreciate the part that privatization—even partial privatization—has played in corrupting water quality and access.

Globally, water privatization has become a loan conditionality for powerful lending agencies such as the World Bank, which oversees hundreds of loan contracts, forcing countries to privatize at least portions of their water systems under the premise that water demands can be met only through mega-infrastructure projects funded by private institutions.[29] These loan conditions create spaces for multinational companies to stake claims and privatize ownership—often invisibly, as corporate conglomerates in sectors like food and energy production benefit from major water grabs.[30] Indeed, water has become characterized as the next big business opportunity for venture capitalists and international developers.[31]

To make these ideas more concrete and to contextualize water protection case studies later in this chapter, we will dig into Stephanie's data on oil and gas production *to show how privatizing resources—especially where food, energy, and water systems intersect—tends to redistribute wealth toward private companies while socializing costs and risks to the public.* When oversight of food, energy, and water becomes privatized, it means that, ultimately, private owners control access to those systems—and our lives will literally depend on those companies.

Using representative information from five years of fieldwork and over 100 interviews conducted in northern Colorado, we show how leasing of water and land by private oil and gas corporations diminishes public power and water access while enhancing power, profit, and access for private companies. This representative example helps illustrate the ways private fossil fuel companies benefit from and use—to exhaustion—some of the world's most valuable and increasingly scarce resources (like water) even as they pollute other communal resources (like air). This case helps show how, in direct contrast to Hardin's tragedy thesis, private control of vital resources like water can encourage the *degradation* of those resources and the loss of public access to them—given that private profit is the key motivation rather than stewardship.

Unconventional oil and gas production, best known for hydraulic fracturing ("fracking"), uses a combination of vertical and horizontal drilling to access small deposits of oil and natural gas in shale rock layers. To frack just one well once takes between two and five million gallons of water, tons of sand, and over five hundred chemicals.[32] Drillers push this concoction down into the well after the vertical well has been drilled and sealed with concrete, after directional drills have been bored for up to four miles horizontally through the shale layer, and after small explosions have been set off along the horizontal pipe to fracture the shale rock and release the hydrocarbons. Hydraulic fracturing relies heavily on water (hence the hydraulic)—and those millions of gallons of water are used to extinction. In other words, after water becomes radioactive, briny, and full of chemicals, it then sits in ponds or is reinjected underground and no longer reintegrated into the hydrologic cycle.

The industry impacts land in a variety of ways; it especially affects the food web because it depends on accessing and leasing agricultural spaces. Private farmlands, ranchlands, and water are used to set up well pads and other infrastructure like pipelines. Brokers called landmen visit homes door to door and attempt to negotiate individual leases—which often have environmental injustices associated with them.[33] Private oil and gas companies also rely heavily on public lands and waters and on lands and minerals leased from the federal government. Each year between 1988 and 2016, about 3.4 million acres of public lands were leased to oil and gas companies, and by the end of 2016, over twenty-seven million acres of public lands were controlled by private interests—with that number only increasing under Trump's administration.[34] (This leasing remains contested under President Joe Biden's leadership.) Finally, public/private institutions, like ditch companies described below, can also facilitate the industry's access to communal water resources.

Here, we show how oil and gas companies' private investments in public goods such as water can create wicked problems, especially where food, energy, and water systems intersect. A quick overview of relevant terms will help clarify these mechanisms related to water privatization and use.

- *Water rights* are complex systems of water diversion, allocation, and allotment. Some of the oldest (most senior) water rights are allotted to farmers and ranchers, mining companies, and descendants of other settlers who established these systems in the mid- to late 1800s—as the Homestead Act of 1862 stole land and water from Indigenous populations and made it available to white settlers. Those who have more senior water rights have stronger claims to divert water for designated beneficial uses like growing crops, raising livestock, or running a city. They are first in line. Those who have more junior water rights have more precarious access to water, especially during drought years.[35]
- *Ditch companies* formed as settlers irrigated the American West. They represent groups of water users, or shareholders, allowed to divert water for agricultural, municipal, and other uses. Members pay assessments, and these help keep the ditch companies running. They have interesting capitalist/socialist modes of organization, working within market-based business models but also depending on collective participation and communal management by members.
- *Conservancy districts* manage water rights and access and often can help transfer water rights from some uses—agriculture, for instance—to municipal uses.

Privatized access to water amplifies the wealth of oil and gas corporations and operators, while transferring costs and uncertainty to the public. Certainly, corporations' private investment in water has short-term benefits for some large ditch companies and farm operations. For instance, as observed by a ditch company president we interviewed, leasing water to oil and gas companies is appealing because they offer short-term, lucrative benefits: "It's been good for them, the farmers and the ditch companies. I know several ditch companies that have capitalized big time from just using their ditches and infrastructure to deliver water from the river to a pump somewhere, take it to a frack job."

Yet, setting aside temporary pay-outs, this approach has substantial drawbacks. Another ditch company president observed that leasing water could persuade farmers to "sit out" farming. He said: "If they [farmers] have a senior right, and oil and gas will pay enough, they just won't farm. Because they can afford to sit out for a year, or farm half their ground." So, *if* farmers or ranchers have senior water rights, and *if* they have a substantial amount of land, they can benefit during years when water is plentiful and the industry pays handsomely. But these financial benefits are temporary—and may result in disruptions to growing food.

A water rights attorney we interviewed, who oversaw many of these contracts, observed that the benefits accrued only to very few farmers or ranchers and ditch companies, even as the public and smaller operators saw mostly costs and conservation programs were edged out. He explained: "I think very few farmers have benefited. . . . I mean, the ditch companies, some of them have some pretty lucrative contracts to actually carry this other water different places. . . . The guys that don't have the minerals [or water rights], they just absolutely hate it. They struggle with the surface use agreements, they feel like they get run over, roughshod." The industry's presence can run up prices in private water markets, which has significant impacts on democratic access to those markets and participation of smaller or newer farmers. One well-established and large-scale grain farmer observed: "That's why, if you ask farmers who don't own their mineral [or water] rights, they'll say they're against it [oil and gas production] because it's costing them more money on the water rental."

Importantly, when the prices run high, participation in water markets can be limited to a few wealthy private landowners and companies—and can stall other, more communal markets that have more public benefits, like programs where municipalities work with farmers to lease their water in some years but also keep farms operational and livelihoods intact. The water rights lawyer we previously quoted explained, "In terms of the development of the kind of markets we'd like to see—where farmers are farming some years and providing water to municipalities in others—it's sort of suppressed those markets, because of the hyper-inflated [water] price." Rather than public entities like municipalities collaborating with farmers, then, private companies buy or lease water to enrich their bottom line. Systemic disruptions occur, too, in public food, energy, and water systems as oil and gas companies and large agricultural firms (including confined animal feedlot operations) consolidate power and control of vital public resources.

These dynamics create longer-term environmental problems and risks to the food system, externalized by private companies. Public and intergenerational costs, in turn, rise. A water and irrigation engineer and farmer, who owned his water rights, explained:

> The thing is, once again, we're [the public] paying for it [the industry's use of water]. We're subsidizing the industry. There is no telling how many related charges go into it—that somebody else is paying for. And it puts a strain on our municipalities to produce high quality, consumable water. And they're [oil and gas operators] just using it like it's an endless supply from the Poudre [River].

Not only does this externalize costs and risks onto the public; it is ecologically unsustainable. A grain farmer with wells on his land observed: "My great grandfathers and everybody would say 'you're ruining your farm by drilling oil wells.' . . . No, they wouldn't appreciate this. They'd drive down the road, say . . . 'they ruined that farm, they ruined that farm, they ruined that farm.'" Another farmer and ditch company manager observed:

> Just clean this water up! Because the stuff that comes out of these wells . . . [trails off]. There's water trucks up and down, going to tank batteries on a daily basis, picking up dirty water. And what they're doing is injecting it down in these injection wells. . . . No! It's water! We have a finite amount of water on this planet. And any time you take it and put it down in the injection well and put it out of the system, you've taken water out of the system.

So, we can see how privatization of a vital communal resource like water can have detrimental material outcomes and, specifically, how *degradation* of communal resources can occur when the profit motive intervenes. This brings significant social and environmental justice costs for the public, too—as private investors enjoy profits generated by their use of communal resources, even as the public and future generations contend with resultant pollution and the large climate and consumption footprints and costs of fossil fuel industries.

As much as the oil and gas industry offers negative examples of privatization, movements are emerging to protect urban and rural commons and vital relations such as water. So next, we will take a look at urban commoning, as illustrated by Meghan's data on urban street bands.[36] Then, we will explore various forms of activism around water protection, which fight neoliberal privatization and instead assert and institutionalize the rights of nature.

REIMAGINING PUBLICS: COMMONING IN URBAN SPACES

While the previous section illustrated nefarious effects of privatization, the remainder of this chapter focuses on alternatives: different ways communities can rethink democratizing public and shared spaces.

The idea of the commons is expansive; community gets created in both urban and rural spaces, in so-called natural spaces and in built or urban ones. In fact, separating the two (or insisting that urban spaces are not part of nature) reinforces the idea of nature as something external to humans, when it is a constitutive part of people and our lives. Today's existential environmental threats and rampant social inequalities demand different approaches and more unified visions of various spaces as natural. Urban issues *are* environmental issues, just as much as rural issues are; the environments just look different. But both kinds of environment demand critical assessments of enclosures and practices of privatizing spaces to develop land, water, or other so-called resources for profit—which have accelerated under neoliberalism. Indeed, as some commentators note,[37] a mere revival of the social democratic agenda of the 1940s and 1950s would be insufficient; people are clamoring for more local and collective control of the land on which they live in the face of starker forms of austerity and privatization. And today's challenges, unlike those of the postwar period, include climate crises.

In response, a new kind of urban commons showcases how the public manages shared resources in cities, rather than, for instance, only in the explicitly agricultural, rural examples in Hardin's work. The commons framework is not only about physical space, as we pointed out earlier. Rather, commons are made by their uses. For instance, a park becomes a public good and its meaning changes depending on its use: it becomes a ball field as people toss around a baseball; it acts as a library when people read on a park bench; it becomes a home and a site of protest if people participate in actions like Occupy demonstrations.[38] Physically, urban common spaces are spaces within a city that are for public use and collective possession and belong to the public authority or to society as a whole. They include, for example, spaces for circulation (such as a street), spaces for recreation (such as a park), and spaces designated for conservation (such as an ecological preserve).

Economic and environmental injustices play out regularly in cities. In the United States, for example, 1980s-era policies of deindustrialization encouraged a "race to the bottom" for corporations looking to move their manufacturing centers to the cheapest labor markets, gutting inner cities and their employment opportunities.[39] So-called barbell economies have formed in many global cities wherein an elite upper class of professionals (such as bankers, lawyers, and those serving ever-growing financial sectors) became the 1 percent, even as they required a cadre of low-wage workers to meet their needs, from housekeeping to food service to retail.[40] Though massive economic inequalities first became visible in global cities such as New York, London, and Tokyo, most cities have since become hubs of stark economic disparities.

Commoning activities,[41] as well as coalition-building, nurture important resistance to economic inequality and to the public's forced exclusion from many urban spaces. Participatory art, including street bands, is one avenue that has been used to create the commons at the community level.[42] Participatory art is itself an implicit critique of many top-down urban strategies aimed at fostering a "creative class" or a "creative city"[43] as an avenue toward wealth generation. After all, despite catchy city slogans, these public relations efforts to create so-called creative spaces often do little to disrupt power differentials and market-based private development like gentrification.[44] Participation—particularly in the arts—is a rejoinder to hierarchical and undemocratic urban processes and a process by which social alternatives emerge.

Case Study 1. Urban Street Bands and the Built Environment

The relatively recent, fast-growing activist street band phenomenon is especially relevant to understanding how the urban commons are being (re)imagined. This transnational movement of street bands—particularly brass and percussion ensembles—play primarily in informal public spaces and are often loudly costumed. They quickly formed a nascent network of activist street bands—in the United States and globally. Our data here come from the HONK! festival network of street band festivals that began in Somerville, Massachusetts, in 2006, consisting of thirty interviews with participants from nine street ensembles. Such groups—which often have an explicitly political orientation—are riffing on, and redefining, brass band traditions and, as a community, have been called "probably the most vibrant incarnation of the protest music tradition in America today."[45] While they often play at protests and other political events, part of what distinguishes their social agendas are their participatory, anti-hierarchical, and inclusion-oriented practices of self-governance.[46]

Brass band traditions are, of course, old—during the nineteenth century they thrived all over the United States and Europe, often attached to towns, congregations, and even factories and serving as both a creative outlet and a symbol of community solidarity.[47] Bands also have a deep connection to the Southern United States: benevolent societies (also known as mutual aid organizations) were social organizations that emerged in the late 1700s to help free and enslaved Black Americans cope with financial hardships (including illness and funeral costs) in New Orleans and elsewhere.[48] These groups eventually metamorphosed into "social aid and pleasure clubs," which, in addition to supporting community members, were the community-based force behind the parades for which New Orleans became famous. Beyond the colorful parades, however, the clubs have been pillars among working-class Black communities for more than a century.[49] The contemporary HONK! movement both builds on this history and embraces broader urban themes and struggles, influenced particularly by the anarchism and punk scenes. The Boston HONK! festival describes itself in the following terms:

> Acoustic and mobile, these bands play at street level, usually for free, with no stages to elevate them above the crowd and no sound systems or speaker columns to separate performers from participants. These bands don't just play for the people; they play *among* the people and invite them to join the fun. They are active, activist, and deeply engaged in their communities, at times alongside unions and grassroots groups in outright political protest, or in some form of community-building activity, routinely performing and conducting workshops for educational and social service organizations of all kinds.[50]

In this context, street bands reclaim physical space in cities; in doing so, they create new public spaces that both call attention to inequities, and suggest new ways of using cities. The processes are interdependent; indeed, simply by claiming physical space, a street band offers an inherent critique of how power is organized in urban areas.[51] For one woman, the acoustic, mobile nature of her band helps her think about music and performance as something that is inherently democratic and accessible to all. She said: "[Our] band was partly founded with the idea that a mobile project, that wasn't tied to a bunch of gear, would be really cool. Because then it could be a band that would play anywhere. And that's a pretty awesome concept. So we never play with mics; there are no instruments that would require any kind of gear like that."

Most of these bands also have some commitment to playing in public and in the streets and to mixing the experience of the audience member with the experience of the performer. One woman described what appealed to her initially about joining a street band: "It's the idea that it was music, there was no electric amplification necessary. . . . It was free, so anybody could access it. It was on the streets, with the idea of democratizing public space. There was a community behind it." Another person described walking down the street and encountering for the first time what would become his band:

> I think [the fact that] the energy was conjured up out of nowhere in the most unexpected of ways pulled me. And you could watch everyone else in the crowd—it pulls you from your daily experience. That is magical! It was this tapping into something "other." Also, just the sheer—not just energy, but passion! I don't know, an almost violent passionate energy of goodness and sound and music. You don't get that in a whole lot of places in this world. . . . But it's walking down the street and seeing that magic in someplace unexpected that has such a pull.

As a part of this commitment to street music, some bands hold their rehearsals in public spaces, either in parks or alleys or as informal parades through town. HONK! festivals are particularly designed to upend the normal operation of a city, albeit for short periods of time. Another woman talked about the festivals and the values they express: "I feel like just being in a public space, having a free event that's family friendly, bringing in kids to start thinking about music, and to get to participate, I think that's political. It's just spreading the joy and meaning-making, and anybody can be a part of that." For her, the very publicness of HONK! is part of what feels unusual and transformative.

A musician from a different band talked about the ancillary shows that are performed during festivals and how these can create bridges between seemingly disparate groups looking to claim the commons in urban spaces for all members of the public:

I've been part of some of the actions that HONK! has done and they've been awesome, playing at the ICE detention facility or outside of it, playing with striking workers at Harbor [Hotel]. Those have been really high points for me. . . . I know that at its core [HONK] is a really beautiful idea, and I appreciate that there's continued work—in the way that bands are asked in their applications about what they care about and why they want to be part of the festival. . . . I can see the work happening. So that's really cool.

She pointed out that the internal logic of HONK! festivals—the commitment to playing shows for progressive causes or community benefit and the ways in which the festivals themselves are curated—is deeply meaningful for those who participate in the festivals, either as musicians or as organizers. These actions draw an audience from the general public, who may or may not perceive the broader political implications.

Regardless, these street bands claim spaces for the public—and, perhaps most important, they bridge divides that have been created among different groups who live in these (privatized) cities. By marching outside (often private) U.S. Immigration and Customs Enforcement (ICE) detention centers, for instance, street bands use public spaces to make visible the injustice of private incarceration, which can be so *invisible* even in densely populated urban centers. Another woman felt that such shows are themselves inherently political:

And then you can get to some of the really political stuff that they're doing in Boston [during HONK!], going to play at the ICE detention centers. You know, that's giving people hope. It's showing, "We see you. You're not invisible. And we're trying to include you in this thing." I do think that HONK! has a positive effect on politics, that it amplifies voices. It fosters a sense of inclusion.

In general terms, the combined commitment to public space and the power of participatory music become part of how these bands aim to activate the commons and open up enclosures—in ways that are sometimes very literal and sometimes less so. One person describes the connection she sees between playing in the streets and other types of political mobilization:

What I think that the HONK! bands provide is. . . . It turns it into a celebration of "We can do this." . . . And I think that my vision for social movements . . . and just to give you some context, I'm a union organizer, and I was a political organizer before that. So I've been involved as an activist for many years. And I've always thought that we're doing it wrong. Why would you want go to a party that nobody wants to go to? And so my thought is that to make political change, you need to be *throwing* the party that everybody wants to go to. And that involves a great band. When there's an intersection between political events and music, it will draw more people to the political issues if it looks like a fun thing to do. And so I believe that the more . . . I think that the involvement that street bands have had in the past has been helpful to engagement of the community in general. And I think more involvement will be more helpful and more engaging.

As one group put it, their band's goal is to "interrupt your regularly scheduled life with spontaneous moments of raucous musical joy." In doing so, these groups retool the built environment as a way both to invite participation and to lay claim to physical space in cities. The combination of participatory musical performance and commitment to public space marks a material change away from the neoliberalized and privatized city to one that is more accessible and inviting. These bands use a model of celebratory change that takes exclusion seriously but aims to tackle it by modeling inclusivity. They also illustrate how "democratizing the commons" is an ongoing process; it happens in fits and starts or at certain times of day. Part of HONK!'s contribution is simply to spark the public's imagination about what cities can be. It makes democratizing the commons an enjoyable—even danceable!—space meant to elicit feelings of camaraderie, celebration, and happiness.

It is particularly meaningful here that the groups' commitment is largely to playing outside and in the streets—because the streets, after all, are often the primary link with nature for people who live in cities. The street is both a built and a natural environment; street music weaves together the built environment with the outside richness of urban spaces, drawing people out of their homes to see "what all the noise is about."

Now we will turn to additional cases that highlight how organizing can dismantle privatization by creating new ways forward—now returning to the context of water. These organizations illustrate how building more accessible, public, and intergenerational communities and systems of communal management of water privilege the rights of nature, while counteracting privatization of the kind we see in oil and gas production.

Case Study 2. Urban Spaces of Hope: Indigenous-Led Action for Water Protection and Intergenerational Equity amid Oil Refineries

Our second case study also explores urban activism, focusing on a coalition of Indigenous-led organizations based in California's San Francisco Bay Area: Idle No More SF Bay, Movement Rights, signatories of the Indigenous Women of the Americas' Defenders of Mother Earth Treaty, and the Society of Fearless Grandmothers. The two women we interviewed—Pennie Opal Plant and Alison Ehara-Brown—guide these efforts. But the organizations represent entire communities and coalitions, some of them global. These groups have collectively counteracted private oil corporations, refineries, and privatization of water by asserting the rights of nature. They institutionalize those rights across a host of environmental justice (EJ), water protection, and community-building actions spanning decades—and show that, as Plant asserts, "communities can create our own regenerative economies." These organizations mirror similar work done by many Native and Indigenous nations.[52]

These groups have organized in the "Refinery Corridor" in the northeastern part of the San Francisco Bay Area around Richmond—amid concentrated contamination from multiple oil refineries, marine terminals, and petrochemical facilities. The area includes the Tesoro and Shell refineries in Martinez, the Chevron Richmond Refinery, the Valero refinery in Benicia, and the Phillips 66 San Francisco refinery in Rodeo. The Refinery Corridor has created environmental injustices where minoritized communities are inequitably exposed to higher levels of water contamination and air pollution and are treated as sacrifice zones by the city and state. Here, people have elevated risks of dying of heart disease and stroke because of their exposure.[53] These negative health impacts are clearly racialized and disproportionately affect children. More than 80 percent of Richmond residents are people of color, and Richmond children's asthma rates are nearly twice those of children living in other areas of the county.[54]

Resonant with a central theme of this chapter, these refineries are privately owned by large corporations headquartered elsewhere, and yet the negative consequences are borne by the public and surrounding ecosystems. Each Refinery Corridor facility contributes significantly to systemic regional problems of water and air pollution,[55] creating the worst sources of pollution and emissions in the region. The Tesoro and Shell refineries have the highest per-barrel emissions of hazardous air pollutants for facilities in this region, for instance. The Valero refinery emits the highest per-barrel amount of "criteria" air pollutants, which include sulfur dioxide, oxides of nitrogen and carbon monoxide, and $PM_{2.5}$ (particulate matter, or fine particles from soot, smoke, and other pollution that can seriously damage lungs when inhaled). Water pollution from refinery activity has been equally serious and impactful, with pollutants such as nitrates, methanol, methyl tert-butyl ether (MTBE, a gas additive), ammonia, zinc, nickel, and phenol regularly released into local waterways.

The Chevron Richmond facility stands out as the worst in a lineup of bad actors. The facility had serious fires in 1989, 1999, and 2012—with the 2012 blaze sending around fifteen thousand people to local hospitals with respiratory problems.[56] The refinery processes about 250,000 barrels of oil each day and has recently ramped up flaring, the burning off of so-called excess natural gas in large smokestacks and sending black plumes of noxious smoke over surrounding communities. This facility emits the most greenhouse gases in California and is the largest polluter in the region.[57] However (in a familiar scenario), it is also the primary employer in Richmond and has contributed handsomely to local political candidates to protect its three-thousand-acre campus and its right to pollute.[58]

Instead of surrendering to these corporations, Pennie Opal Plant and Alison Ehara-Brown work with others to organize community-based alternatives. They use nonviolent strategies based in cultural traditions from their own backgrounds as Mohawk (Ehara-Brown) and Yaqui, Choctaw, and Cherokee (Plant) women. Each tradition elevates respect for all people—even the workers implicated in this puzzle of pollution, dependence, and environmental injustices. This coalition of organizations strives to embody the principles of decommodification and communal management—asserting the rights of future generations, marginalized communities, children, and nature to clean air and water.

Plant explained: "We stand for clean air, clean water, and clean soil, for health and sustainability for future generations, for equity, for Indigenous rights. . . . We organize people to get into the streets." These groups operate using Erica Chenoweth's[59] theory that "it takes 3.5 percent of people, nonviolently working together, conducting nonviolent direct actions and strikes . . . for a very rapid policy change. . . . We are all like a school of fish going in the same direction." Each organization counters environmental injustice with persistent, positive direct action based in connection among people rather than professionalized models of advocacy.

Plant and Ehara-Brown's organizing began in the early 2000s as part of a small Native grandmothers' circle that came together each month to pray for the sacred system of life. This grandmothers' group later expanded to guiding Idle No More SF Bay and includes signatories of the Indigenous Women of the Americas' Defenders of Mother Earth Treaty (described later in the chapter). By 2018, seeing a need for all older women to "step up and put our bodies between younger people and the police," said Ehara-Brown, they created the Society of Fearless Grandmothers to train grandmother-age women to risk arrest, block the streets, and be liaisons with police to protect the generations below them by using nonviolent direct actions. Plant sees their model of organizing as inclusive and protective of younger generations:

> There is a different thing that happens when grandmothers step into the role of being responsible for future generations. And it's not necessarily an Indigenous thing, it is an all-women kind of thing. When women accept that role, then we provide the training for those women to become the people that stand between the law enforcement and all of the younger people behind us at nonviolent direct actions.

As water protection has spread in recent years, and as nonviolent direct action against petrochemical companies, refineries, and pipelines has become more common, members of the Society of Fearless Grandmothers (SFG) have created more mechanisms to share their multigenerational approach to getting in the streets. Their goal has remained nonviolent opposition to private industries and community organizing focused on intergenerational injustices. Ehara-Brown explained: "SFG has trained many women since 2018. Locally at this time, some of the women we trained—who are willing to risk arrest—in our ally group, 1000 Grandmothers Bay Area, are active in blocking the streets for actions. And women in other parts of the country have either attended live trainings with us, or online training and are using this approach where they live." SFG also (re) claims space in urban settings, then, though its methods differ meaningfully from the street bands we discussed earlier.

Plant and Ehara-Brown carefully distinguish most *people* working for these facilities—police forces hired by the refineries or workers employed by them—from the corporate cultures and elite classes controlling and profiting from them. They implicitly encourage organizers to look differently at the connection between individual and systemic factors—and to build collective communities rather than create further division. Ehara-Brown observed:

> We're not naive about police and military—but we have tried to honor the human essence in everyone. . . . Often [when] we would do some nonviolent direct action at a refinery . . . we would have a prayer circle and put out prayers for the people in charge—for their hearts to be open, [and] for security guards and the people working there. . . . That is a big part of our vision, and I think it's also a really big part of Indigenous values. When people are coming from a place of anger and depression, our [Native] cultures have been generally places where we are welcoming strangers, seeing the human in people.

Plant echoed her collaborator, seeing people's actions as direct results of the privatized, colonial, divide-and-conquer capitalist systems in which many people are embedded: "It's not their fault. Everybody needs to have a job. It is the corporate directors that are so addicted to creating more wealth for themselves, that they are literally destroying the world for their own progeny. It is a type of insanity . . . maybe the Romans had it. It might be one of the outputs of empire building." By seeing these problems like this, rather than as a collection of evil security guards protecting a morally bankrupt institution, these women explicitly draw attention to the *systemic* nature of the problem, leaving additional space for the formation of ally relationships, learning, and growth.

In 2012, as members of the Native grandmothers' prayer group saw their "sisters in Canada" rising up, they were inspired to formalize solidarity with the First Nations Idle No More movement in Canada. Plant and Ehara-Brown and the other grandmothers then launched Idle No More SF Bay. Water protection remains their central concern, in the face of what they call "corporate extreme energy." Idle No More SF Bay hosts teach-ins, builds coalitions, coordinates direct actions against fossil fuel operators, and organizes Healing Walks and opportunities to get into the streets in peaceful protest. In the context of water protection, this group actively participates in reshaping spaces that have been sacrificed for private profit.

The group's mission centers on Native-led, women-led, multigenerational, and inclusive activism in pursuit of a world free of fossil fuels, emphasizing a just transition and sustainable jobs in refinery communities. Members envision current oil workers leading remediation efforts, seeking to link an old industry—and its workers—with the new. Rooted in multiple Indigenous practices, Idle No More SF Bay focuses on nurturing what they term the "sacred system of life" for younger and future generations. Group members orient themselves toward fighting the ideologies of colonialism, capitalism, and ecological destruction rather than people. Non-Indigenous allies are included as part of the movement, enhancing organizations' capacities for collective coalition-building.

Between 2014 and 2017, Idle No More SF Bay hosted Healing Walks—visionary fusions of teach-ins, intergenerational healing ceremonies, and creative arts. Each walk included a fourteen- to sixteen-mile journey amid refineries, inspired by First Nations actions to protect Canada's tar sands. Guests were included, mostly Indigenous women from other communities similarly impacted by fossil fuel economies. The walks created awareness and time for quiet, ceremonial, mobile contemplation of all the refineries surrounding San Francisco Bay Area communities. Plant vividly described one of the walks: "Here we are with these horrendous fossil fuel facilities that have destroyed the land that they're on. . . . We walked through refinery structures. We walked through pipes overhead that were rusting and pools of water behind the fences that were toxic. . . . Sometimes we would get sick from what was being emitted that day walking through it all."

These walks invited people to *just be* with the present infrastructure and all of its baggage; to consider and contemplate and, especially, envision. Community-building, artistic projects, and positive visioning prefaced each Healing Walk—focused on how to replace the destruction by building something better, as envisioned by community members. Ehara-Brown noted:

> We would do an art party in the refinery community [before walks]. . . . We would find community space and silkscreen T-shirts, paint signs, talk to people about what it was that we were walking for. . . . We tried to keep a really clear focus on what we were *for* more than what we were *against*. So we would focus on clean air, clean water, healthy soil, and healthy future for the generations to come. . . . We did a lot of community-building. . . . A lot of kids got involved that way, and we were really trying to have there be a lot of positivity.

The Healing Walks began early in the day. They included water ceremonies and visits to refinery sacrifice zones and ended with prayers, collective visioning, and quilting. The walks created community amid destruction and aimed to

connect people in decommodifying these urban spaces. They inspired participants to create collective solutions for claiming and healing sacrificed spaces and
their communities—healing metabolic rifts by envisioning how to move beyond
the blight left by private companies extracting wealth and emitting pollutants.
Ehara-Brown observed: "We would always begin with the water ceremony. We
would stop at a Superfund site, or sometimes it would be a community garden.
Different places where we were really taking a look at the destruction and the
sacrifice zones that we live in—but also the places where there was hope and
something different going on." The quilting helped refocus people's attention on
what *could* be, on what they would like to see in place of the industrial, contaminated landscapes. Ehara-Brown continued:

> We had a couple quilters in our group, and we would bring one-foot by one-foot
> squares of muslin. About a mile before the end of the walk, we would have people
> spend some time in prayer, really trying to put their attention on their visions for
> the future. What would society free of fossil fuels look like? What would it be like
> for humans to be back in alignment with our original instructions? How did people
> envision what schools would be like—and communities? Where would we get our
> food? . . . People put their visions down on squares . . . made into a Refinery Walk
> Envisioning Quilt. . . . And that's been another important value for us, to . . .
> empower people to imagine a different future and collaborate with the people in
> those communities that were already creating that future in different ways.

This part of the Healing Walks led to the River of Time Project, creating permanence out of transient events and bridging Idle No More SF Bay and Movement Rights (described in the text that follows). The project is positive and
prefigurative: it is designed to help communities envision what they want, and
the idea is that a goal more clearly illuminates the path. Envisioning the collective path forward empowers people to see that different systems are possible—
and achievable. Plant said:

> We started training our younger members of Idle No More. . . . It's so important
> that we imagine what we want. Otherwise we're not going to get there. It's called
> the River of Time. It's those rolls of paper that you can put up on a wall, . . .
> divided up by decades. Initially, we had 2100 at one end, and 2019 at the other
> end . . . though we've now flipped it. And on the bottom would be a little line
> drawing of the industrial world, where we are now, that's killing off the sacred
> system of life. And then how that could change visually by 2100. And the exercise
> is to have people break up into groups and imagine: "So that's where we want to
> go. How do we get there?" . . . To get there, in the 2090 decade, we need to almost
> be done with all of the polluting, harmful industry, and ways of colonization.

The culmination of these local actions—and Plant's participation in the 2010 People's World Conference on Climate Change and the Rights of Mother Earth in Cochabamba, Bolivia—was the formation of another organization, Movement Rights, in 2014. Movement Rights aims to "align human laws with Natural Law" by focusing on three pillars of action: "a) empowering communities to write their own rules; b) movement building for the rights of nature; and c) advancing Indigenous rights and traditional knowledge." This involves hands-on community organizing and education offered by Movement Rights, through which, as Plant put it (with her characteristic wit): "We do trainings for people on 'how the hell did we get here?'"

Movement Rights uses the Rights of Nature framework at local, state, and international scales to reprioritize the "rights of communities, Indigenous peoples, and ecosystems." It rejects the legal treatment of private corporations as persons and asserts that Indigenous peoples should define collective paths forward, *shaping* those actions. Movement Right's mission statement attests: "As the defenders of the most diverse places on Earth, Indigenous peoples have a leadership role to play in the transformation of our culture and law toward ecological balance." Plant explained: "The Rights of Nature/Mother Earth movement . . . came out of the People's Climate Summit. . . . The majority of the 30,000 people that were there were Indigenous people. Some people walked for days to get to this summit. And that is where the Declaration of the Rights of Mother Earth was written. . . . It is an amazing paradigm shifting document." Much like the Declaration on the Rights of Indigenous Peoples, it is now under consideration by the United Nations.

Subsequently, Plant and six other Indigenous women leaders from the Arctic to the Amazon drafted the Indigenous Women of the Americas' Defenders of Mother Earth Treaty in 2015. Idle No More SF Bay and Movement Rights members signed on, as did hundreds of others. The treaty identifies central responsibilities of human communities, including protecting "the safety, health, and wellbeing of our children and those yet to come, as well as the children of all of our non-human relatives, the seeds of the plants, and those unseen."

The treaty directly challenges the tenets of neoliberalism; it identifies market-based capitalism and privatization as major drivers of climate crises and ecological devastation:

> The economic system of the world has exploited and abused nature, pushing Mother Earth to her limits. . . . Mother Earth is the source of life which needs to be protected, not a resource to be exploited and commodified as a "natural capital." We are seeing the world expanding the commodification, financialization and privatization of the functions of Mother Earth that places a price on forests, air, soils, biodiversity and nature, causing more inequality and destruction of nature and the environment.

The treaty calls for "no more commodifying and privatizing of the earth, air, water, soil and natural systems. Mother Earth and her natural resources cannot sustain the consumption and production patterns of this modern industrialized society." Women, especially women of color, have been diminished and terrorized through colonial and capitalist systems—and the treaty recognizes a leading role for Indigenous women in creating new systems. Indigenous women and their allies are called upon to participate in direct, nonviolent action until "'business as usual' is halted and life on Mother Earth is safe for generations to come."

These four organizations form a powerful coalition fighting privatization, pollution, and environmental injustice—focused on solutions. They counter neoliberal norms with creative, community-generated visions for how to build something better, collectively. They illustrate the power of nested scales of action and public coalition-building. What began as a small group of Native grandmothers who met each month to pray expanded to the Healing Walks and the community-building action of Idle No More SF Bay. Momentum then propelled Movement Rights and the treaty signing, accomplished on a global scale and with the involvement of many Indigenous communities. These organizations, then, exemplify collectives *within* each organization and collectives *among* organizations, as they weave coalitions from threads of action. This rich, multi-scalar tapestry of organizing illustrates how to counter privatization, build capacity for reciprocity, and reclaim and sustain common spaces. These organizations utilize actions that build reciprocity and relational systems over time, including positive visioning and bridge building across divisive segments of society; rejection of commodification and privatization of animate beings like water; clear identification of the *systems*, not people, creating environmental injustices; and spiritual connections among people, more-than-humans, and ecological systems.

These four organizations have shaped their environments in lasting ways. Especially through the Society of Fearless Grandmothers and Idle No More SF Bay, these organizations create spaces for training, community connection, and nonviolent direct action in polluted places, diffusing both knowledge and organizing skills. Their actions, and especially the Healing Walks, promote taking to the streets to build community that is unified by connecting to water, land, and one another. Through their Healing Walks and Movement Rights, Plant, Ehara-Brown, and those they work with have helped generate community-led public visions for how to build better systems—and then helped build them. They have also worked to reassert the rights of Indigenous and Tribal nations and nature and the importance of protecting the commons, through these organizations and through their participation in the treaty signing. All of these material changes accomplish cultures of peace and spiritual progress as well; they promote non-anger and compassion toward all beings and the hope that people can still build a better world.

We will now move from these urban organizations, street bands, and coalitions fighting industrial pollution to a more rural, but no less impactful, effort to protect water amid uranium exploration.

Case Study 3. Rural Spaces of Hope: Havasupai Tribal Nation's Water Protectors and the Threat of Uranium Mining near the Grand Canyon

Many readers will have seen photographs of the iconic waterfalls at the bottom of the Grand Canyon: blue-green water cascading down brilliant orange canyons and cliffs, looking like a surreal paradise. Each year, people enter permit lotteries to access these sacred spaces, to photograph them and spend a few days. But for the Havasupai, this beautiful space is still their home—despite centuries of displacement. For centuries before the arrival of European settlers, the Havasupai Tribal nation spent spring and summer seasons gardening and farming in this rich, abundant oasis, migrating back out each fall and winter to live, hunt, and gather, mostly around the South Rim of what is now called Grand Canyon National Park.

The Havasupai Tribe[60] has called this spot home since "time immemorial." They shared this spot with other Native nations who trace their lineages back to these stunning spaces, but the Havasupai are the only community that still lives within the Grand Canyon. We learned this history from Ophelia Watahomigie-Corliss—a Havasupai Tribal Councilwoman, community organizer, and Water Protector fighting to prevent nearby uranium mining. In the past century or so, the Havasupai Tribe has been deeply disrupted—first as the Fred Harvey Railroad arrived, industrialization ensued, and waves of visitors and settlers invaded, and then as Grand Canyon National Park steadily eroded the Tribe's rightful access to their ancestral lands and waters. Their territory used to be roughly the size of Delaware, in and around the canyon. As Watahomigie-Corliss explained, this land is part of the Havasupai, and the Havasupai, then and now, are part of this land. The land is part of their identity as the *Havasu Baaja*, or "People of the Blue Green Waters."

As is true for most Native nations in the United States, the history of the Havasupai Tribe has been tumultuous and traumatic since Europeans arrived. They saw their lands, their access to water, and their sacred spaces gobbled up by settlers and privatization schemes. This created ongoing struggles over the Havasupai Tribe's sovereignty and rights to their ancestral lands. Between the arrival of the railroad at the Grand Canyon's South Rim in 1901 and the official designation of Grand Canyon National Park in 1919, all Havasupai people were kicked off their land. They were removed from a particularly contentious space popularly called "Indian Garden" and forcibly relocated to railroad work camps. What followed, as Watahomigie-Corliss related, was cultural and ecological devastation: "These were heartbreaking times for us, as our home became a tourist attraction. We had to endure constant racism; people . . . were given the last name 'Burro,' for example, as if we were no more than pack animals."[61]

As Fred Harvey and other settlers continued to industrialize and privatize the South Rim, the Havasupai endured more decades of violence. The Supai reservation was established in the 1880s, but once the new national park started to bring in serious tourism, the U.S. government again violently displaced the Supai people. By the early 1930s, "the Park Service burned Supai Camp to the ground, and our people, including elders and children, were loaded into covered wagons in the snow, taken to the canyon's rim and forced to walk down a grueling 17-mile trail to Supai Village," recalled Watahomigie-Corliss. Their home was gone, and the assaults kept coming as the park's 1970s-era superintendent further abused the Havasupai by shutting off their septic system and water supply.

In a staggering expression of grace, the Havasupai Tribe is finding ways to, as Watahomigie-Corliss explained, "collaborate and work with the National Park Service" despite this traumatic history. The relationship is less adversarial now, and about 426 Tribal members currently live at the bottom of the canyon. But this has been a paradoxical case (as with many spaces holding ancestral and sacred significance for Tribal nations) of so-called public lands areas still excluding Native people from their ancestral lands. Watahomigie-Corliss observed:

> Where I'm walking right now was reservation lands that was one mile by three miles that we can live on. Anything south of those waterfalls—those famous waterfalls—was owned by the Park Service. . . . And then the damn eight mile trail that you walk into Supai—that belonged to Kaibab National Forest. So, we were just so trapped. And these tourists don't know that. We couldn't even walk that trail that they're walking. We couldn't even go look at the waterfalls that everybody comes to look at. So it's a little infuriating.

While collaboration is a goal, then, Watahomigie-Corliss possesses extensive cultural memory of the intergenerational trauma from settlers' de facto privatization and co-optation of Tribal lands and waters. The area around the Grand Canyon became "public lands" only through the Havasupai's violent removal. Reminding tourists and state agencies of this history is a crucial part of justice-seeking, and of Watahomigie-Corliss's work. As she told us, the National Park Service needs to "have Native histories and visions as central to the Park," so part of her outreach work focuses on "educating people about who the Supai are, that we even exist, what the [Indian] Garden history is, and what the Tribal issues are."

The Havasupai Tribal Council and Tribal members want the millions of Grand Canyon visitors each year to learn this history and appreciate that their community still lives there. Watahomigie-Corliss says that the National Park Service should recognize the Havasupai Tribe's own history and reidentify spaces throughout the park with the appropriate Havasupai and Native names, making room for more complex histories and present experiences. "It offends me that people don't know [the history of this area]. . . . It started to perplex me that millions and millions of people would come to the Grand Canyon and have no idea who the Havasupai are. And they're so in love with Indian Garden, yet they have no idea that Havasupai grew [food] there."

These historical traumas were aggravated again recently by another threat—private uranium production. For decades, uranium extraction has affected—and been fought by—many Tribal nations in the Four Corners area.[62] Uranium mining and milling—spearheaded by Energy Fuels Inc.—threatens to return to the Grand Canyon and affect the waters that the Havasupai depend upon for daily life in their remote community. Uranium mining and milling arrived in the area during the era of the Manhattan Project and the Cold War—and created troubling histories of environmental injustice in the Four Corners region. This is especially true for Native communities like the Havasupai, the Hopi, the Diné, and other Tribal and Pueblo nations, who still deal with legacies like cancer clusters, abandoned mines, and contaminated water, land, and homes.[63] Despite protections enacted in 2012, environmental deregulation under the Trump administration opened the lands to private uranium mining.

Energy Fuels—a Canadian uranium corporation with a near monopoly on U.S. uranium production—has been attempting to mine uranium here since the mid-1980s, when the USDA Forest Service first allowed a permit. But the site has been a seesaw; after Energy Fuels built the mine in the 1980s, it put the mine on standby in the 1990s because of low uranium prices. In 2012, the Presidential administration of Barack Obama protected about one million acres of public lands around the Grand Canyon, effectively blocking any uranium mining from taking place—and immediately sparking lawsuits from the company. But because Energy Fuels has mineral rights and has had a mining permit for decades, it has been exempted and allowed to drill the shaft to access uranium deposits, now reaching a depth of 1,470 feet. The Pinyon Plain Mine (renamed from the Canyon Mine in 2020) is the only mining operation allowed within the area protected in 2012, and it is also within the Red Butte Traditional Cultural Property. Still, a federal judge ruled in favor of Energy Fuels and its mineral rights access in the spring of 2020, allowing it to reopen the mine.

Now Energy Fuels wants to reopen its private mining enterprise there, using and potentially contaminating the Havasupai's main water source and occupying their Tribal lands. The Pinyon Plain Mine shaft starts atop the Grand Canyon and is near the sacred Red Butte Mountain, not only revered by the Havasupai but also considered sacred in the traditions of the Hopi, Hualapai, and Diné Tribal nations. The Havasupai see Red Butte as their lifeline to the spiritual realm. Uranium contamination from ore dust and increased truck traffic from the transport of ore across the plateau could risk environmental injustices all over again—in sacred spaces. Further, the mine shaft has repeatedly flooded with millions of gallons of water each year since it was sunk. In 2019 alone, about 10.7 million gallons of potentially radioactive water had to be removed from the mine shaft after it flooded—and some of it is sprayed on surrounding land or leaked during transport, despite assurances by Energy Fuels that flooding would not occur.[64]

These allowances for a private company challenge the Havasupai's Tribal sovereignty and their rights to clean water and land. This concerns the Tribal Council and community members. Watahomigie-Corliss explains collective concerns about corporate takeover of Havasupai land, yet again, since it counters their sovereignty: "Uranium mining is a long-standing issue for Tribal Council.... The reservation has had land taken or ... [has been] restricted on how to use it. [We've] not been able to keep all the mining rights that come with actually being sovereign and owning your land. Those are problems Tribal Council has to be able to speak about.... But it's like a grassroots movement, not just for the Council."

Havasupai people feel particularly concerned about threats to water. For millennia before their resettlement, and now again, the Havasupai Tribe has relied on the water that would be most affected if any sort of mining spill or accident were to occur. Not only would the Colorado River potentially be impacted by accidents, but the Redwall-Muav Aquifer would also be contaminated by any spills or leaks from the mine shaft or Pinyon Plain Mine.

This risk inspired Watahomigie-Corliss and other Havasupai Tribal members to organize as Water Protectors, protesting the private Pinyon Plain Mine and renewed uranium mining. They mobilize frequent protests, peaking with their annual four-day Red Butte Gathering, where celebration and protest blend. The Tribe's sacred existential ties to the water drive their collective activism. Explained Watahomigie-Corliss: "The Havasupai *are* water, and that's why we're Water Protectors. For our everlasting survival. The company's inability to promise that it [the water and aquifer] won't be contaminated is a gamble on all of our lives." Here, we see fundamental distinctions between commodifying uranium and using water for private gain, and the Havasupai's resistance due to their cultural, spiritual, and reciprocal ties to the lands and waters. Watahomigie-Corliss explained the community-wide concern, particularly among the Tribe's eldest members: "The Tribe is good. They come out as a group to protest and protect.... It isn't just the annual gathering, it's whenever we feel like it. For a long time, we had it [the Red Butte Gathering] for five years straight. But that is a protest, usually a four-day protest. And we don't let the public show up until the third and fourth day."

The Tribe's concerns are well-founded. Energy Fuels promises to avoid spills, accidents, and water contamination. But, as the Grand Canyon Trust, Uranium

Watch, the Ute Mountain Ute Tribe, and Stephanie have established—and as Watahomigie-Corliss consistently pointed out—Energy Fuels has a troubling environmental record.[65] For example, it owns the White Mesa Mill in Blanding, Utah, which has historical and current violations, including a contaminated plume in the water aquifer adjacent to the mill. The corporation's record also includes several fines and accidents at its mines and other facilities.[66] Given this, the company cannot promise that there will be no accidents—which could pose an existential threat to the Havasupai's home and water.

The Havasupai Tribe has commissioned scientific studies on possible impacts to the aquifer to counter Energy Fuels's claims that it will be completely safe. The company's activity has already depleted the springs on which the Havasupai depend—and gives warning signs that if future water consumption were to ramp up alongside uranium production, water availability would be compromised along with water quality. Watahomigie-Corliss can now use her position on the Tribal Council to fight for water protection, along with some of her fellow council members. She and another council member traveled to Washington, DC, in support of the Grand Canyon Centennial Protection Act, which would solidify protections for one million acres around the national park from uranium mining—including the Supai Village land, where Tribal members live. Watahomigie-Corliss has returned several times to lobby congressional representatives for this and other legislation related to water and land protection (and the Tribal digital divide), sometimes as "the sole representative of a Tribal government."

The Tribe's efforts as Water Protectors have been sustained since the Pinyon Plain Mine was permitted and will continue as long as their sovereign right to protect water is challenged. At the core of the community's actions lies a fundamental disagreement about private use of and possible contamination of water that, for them, means life for their community now and for future generations. They reject the prioritizing of private corporate profit over environmental well-being—and over the Havasupai's health, perhaps even their lives. Watahomigie-Corliss captured this when she observed:

> If there was any breach, any possibility of contamination, 95% of that [aquifer] is the water I've been swimming in the last days. It is the water from the spring I drank last Thursday. That's the Havasu Creek ... that's how we survive ... the Havasupai, who have been here since time immemorial. ... That is the reason we're able to live and survive out here, as Havasupai of the blue-green water. As the vice-chairman says, the Havasupai *are* water. And that's why we are Water Protectors.

She continued: "I'll repeat: their [Energy Fuels's] inability to promise the water will never be contaminated is a risk on all of our lives—*our lives*. And they have the gall to argue about monetary gain versus the life of hundreds and hundreds of people down here. It's ridiculous."

For Watahomigie-Corliss and other Havasupai activists, the stakes are existential, collective, and intergenerational. And, now, the stakes also mean life or death for the Havasupai community. Watahomigie-Corliss's orientation is long-term and connected to place, and it informs everything she does:

> It's easy to stand up and fight for the right to live . . . on land that we've been living on from the beginning of time. Versus these fools who have showed up from a foreign country, who think they're allowed to dig and contaminate the land. And when they're done doing that, they're just going to leave. . . . They're not going stay and clean it up. And their need for monetary gain is supposed to be more powerful than the lives of people? The ethics there are wrong, and the politics protecting that argument are wrong. . . . We have to fight against this. . . . People have been wondering why such a little tiny tribe is bothering to fight against such a large corporation.

"We are fighting for our lives," Watahomigie-Corliss concluded. "It doesn't matter if people want to tell us they have all the money, that they're gonna win because they have big lawyers. It doesn't scare us."

In this case, we see similar strains of community-led action for collective and communal rights of waters, of lands, and of Native nations. Much as with the coalition of organizations in San Francisco, fundamental distinctions are drawn between privatized and commodified land and water and the cultural worldviews of Indigenous, Native, and other nations living in affected spaces. And the work is ongoing: a fight for cultural and Tribal sovereignty in the face of multinational corporate power and resources is not something that should be underestimated. It is an exemplar, however, of community-based persistence and vision.

CONCLUSION

One strong link among these different sites of organizing is the conviction that space should belong to communities rather than to corporations and that the way to create that outcome is by building relationships *among people and places and with the land and water.*

Of course, these relationships remain fraught—because the influence of neoliberal systems is never absent. Community orientations conflict with the larger systemic norms, particularly regarding concepts like rights and ownership of resources/relations. There are ongoing questions, for instance, about what it means for the Havasupai to effectively own their water within a capitalist system—even if the Tribe would never put it into play as something to be bought and sold. In other words, in order to protect the water, the Havasupai Tribe must own it, in a manner of speaking. Various Native nations have formed corporations to benefit their members in similar ways. Neoliberal capitalism forces some acquiescence to its own systems even as groups work to do things differently. Importantly, though, these actions are undertaken with fundamentally different intentions; the goal is not to privatize profit and socialize risk to the public but to empower Tribal nations to protect their communities and homelands for the *benefit* of the collective, which includes those places and all beings within them. And they do illustrate—just as the divestment case study in chapter 4 does—that moving into new institutions typically requires a degree of engagement with existing ones. This is part of the process.

Still, these tensions require both scholars and organizers to grapple with the consequences of materialist society even as transformations occur within it. "Owning" land and water become a means of survival within a brutal system. And these conventions are deeply ingrained and stubborn in settler societies; for instance, we have shown how the profit motive can manifest in powerful ways in the context of oil and gas production, naturalizing and normalizing efforts of private companies to control water. The project of dismantling big, painful systems takes time and involves a lot of metaphorical gray area—and in the meantime, people still suffer from the immediate consequences.

As is the case with much community organizing, tidy metrics do not do these cases justice or reflect their significance. Organizing is about building collective power; it is about fighting for narratives that feel authentic to the issues at hand, about setting out a vision for action at multiple levels, and about moving communities and institutions into something better. How do we, for instance, measure the impact of a street band? How do we assess the contributions of a community of people fighting long-term violence and dislocation? Is it at all meaningful to attempt such measurements in the context of the cases we have explored?

We think not—at least, not in those terms. We are more interested here in how these projects and communities offer different ways of thinking about existing challenges. Just by their presence, these and other organizations and coalitions chip away at the hegemonic control and power of private interests. Street bands show how to celebrate and claim urban spaces, from which many people have been excluded, despite their roles in building them. Groups like Movement Rights highlight how to heal, how to build community on its own terms, how to build coalitions across scales, and how to assert the Rights of Nature at multiple scales. And the Havasupai Tribe displays how to fight for self-determination in the face of private industrial development and in spite of centuries of forced displacement.

In these spaces, *organizing* has immense power. Belief in and hope for something better motivates action. And that, so far, has not been privatized.

6 · MORE THAN THE MARKET
Practicing Social and Ecological Regeneration

In this chapter we offer a final recommendation, one that is to us the most fundamental: we must build economic systems that serve our communities and our planet. These systems must be embedded in everyone's daily lives and at multiple levels; they must value well-being and be built on equitable social norms and ecological realities. In this chapter, we will talk about why this should be the goal and explore some communities already doing this work.

Dis-embedded political-economic systems hinge on an absence of social protections, limits, or environmental regulations. Indeed, this is the central meaning of "dis-embedded"—a market system floating around in (and governed by) its own internal logic, without being grounded in the needs or norms of the ecological systems, people, and communities or societies on which it depends. But purely dis-embedded markets are not truly possible—after all, markets are inherently social and depend on finite resources, for instance—and even if they were, they should not be the norm. The first step in creating different systems is envisioning alternatives and trying them out: when communities reject basic tenets of neoliberalism in favor of different (more embedded, distributive, and regenerative) approaches, other options suddenly become possible.

Here, we explore how communities are dismantling a third pillar of neoliberal norms: deregulation and reregulation of market systems or corporate activity (defined in detail in chapter 3).[1] De- and reregulation protect and accelerate dis-embedded economic and extractive activities because they release corporations and/or industries from providing or adhering to ecological, social, and economic safety nets and protections. They facilitate the privatization we examined in chapter 5, too.

Yet, to build better societies and socially and ecologically sustainable systems, this has to change. The focus must be on building systems that work for all of us—the economy is just one of those systems. Here, alongside our discussion of neoliberal norms of de- and reregulation, then, we look at groups and communities building social and ecological protections, where economic norms are *embedded within* those needs, rather than the other way around. We examine how communities fortify social protections, building community-based safety nets and focusing on regenerative ecological models. Through case studies in this chapter, we explore the many ways that groups are doing this: by starting and nurturing cooperatives, by building regenerative agricultural systems, and by crafting community-based and community-benefiting enterprises that prioritize social protections and environmental regulations over markets.

First, though, we want to spend a little more time on context. As we have discussed, one of economic historian Karl Polanyi's keenest observations was that capitalism inherently dis-embeds markets from the social, political, and ecological contexts in which they operate.[2] Dis-embeddedness means quicker extraction of profit, fewer messy rules interfering with business, and faster growth. Dis-embedded markets have also produced the expectation that industrial sectors or corporations should (and can!) self-regulate, monitoring their own performance related to social, ecological, and economic outcomes. But enormous social, economic, and ecological upheaval results because, simply put: there is no incentive for companies to self-monitor well, when profit is the goal.

Dis-embedded economies create severe cases of what Polanyi called *social dislocation*: vulnerability, instability, and feelings of uncertainty and powerlessness as people try to navigate daily life in volatile or unstable ecologies or market-based systems.[3] Émile Durkheim offered an early illustration of social dislocation's potentially stark outcomes. In *Suicide*, published in 1897, Durkheim found that increases in suicide in France were based on social imbalances in urban and industrial settings; suicide reflected an individual's moral confusion and lack of social direction and was linked to social and economic upheaval.[4] Durkheim argued that social upheavals were symptomatic of a failure of economic development and division of labor—and an economy that produces no solidarity or sense of connection among people themselves. Some of these patterns seem to persist across time and space; even today suicides increase in times of economic strife and uncertainty.[5]

In less tragic scenarios, Polanyi observed that people may contend with disruptive experiences of social dislocation by attempting to *embed* markets into their social and ecological contexts. In other words, they mobilize. They organize. They try to make markets accountable to community and environmental needs through social movements. This may mean fighting for stronger state regulations that limit pollution or making corporations more accountable to the people and ecosystems on which they depend. It may mean demanding living wages or labor protections. Examples emerge in the reformist U.S. environmental movement beginning in the 1960s: a suite of environmental regulations were passed after people got fed up with rampant air and chemical pollution, and a river (the Cuyahoga) that was literally on fire. During the height of the COVID-19 outbreak, social movements demanded paid sick time and hazard pay for people classified as essential workers (and in some cases, they got it). Simply put, in many situations, people who experience social dislocation counter it by trying to embed markets, industries, and corporations—making them more accountable for their social and ecological effects.

A note here on our terminology in this chapter: Researchers often call this social activism "re-embedding the market." But here, we use the term "embedding the market." We do this because we want to be critical about what, exactly, *re*-embedding means. Patriarchy and colonialism often preceded, and also undergird, neoliberal capitalism. So, is the goal to *re-embed* economies into *those* systems, which are so oppressive to women, BIPOC communities, and religious minorities, among others? It is not—at least not for us. And while re-embedding is not about how to "make America great again," of course, it can certainly sound that way. People have to make something new, rather than going back to patriarchal, white, male, midcentury perspectives. Therefore, using the idea of *embedding* the market enables us to imagine a future that starts to redress some of history's wrongs.

So for us, the goal in fighting social dislocation is to embed markets into their social, ecological, and intergenerational contexts. People most often do this by countering de- and reregulation and the corporate self-monitoring these measures encourage. In a bigger sense, though, the goal becomes building better systems: fundamentally rejecting the systems in which benefits accrue to private companies and a handful of billionaires while risks and social, ecological, and health costs accrue to the rest of us, more-than-humans, and future generations. Instead, the goal of embedding markets becomes building more distributive and regenerative systems, as our cases illustrate later in this chapter. First, we reexamine Doughnut Economics, which helps visualize *how* to build them.

GETTING INTO THE DOUGHNUT

In chapter 2 we introduced the work of Kate Raworth,[6] whose metaphor of a "doughnut economy" offers a way of thinking about embedding markets. Within that doughnut hole are the twelve social foundations below which no person should fall in an equitable society. Outside the doughnut lie the ecological measures that society must not overshoot—the upper limits of systemic disruptions that life on Earth can sustainably survive. In the middle lies "the safe and just space for humanity."

Using this metaphor, *embedding markets* means *creating* that doughnut, where societies enact rules to prevent markets and corporations from tearing apart social fabrics and ignoring ecological boundaries. This "ecological ceiling"[7] includes air pollution, ozone layer depletion, climate change, ocean acidification, chemical pollution, nitrogen and phosphorus loading, freshwater withdrawals, land conversion, and biodiversity loss. While standards do not yet exist for each category (for instance, chemical pollution), there are measures to tell us we have already overshot in four categories—climate crisis, nitrogen and phosphorus loading, land conversion, and biodiversity loss. Raworth expands on observations made by systems thinkers like Donella Meadows—and she elaborates on observations made decades ago by environmental sociologists like William Catton—whose work anticipated the threats posed by climate crises and other ecological pressures.[8] Raworth's unique imagery offers valuable conceptual building blocks for envisioning better systems.

Embedding markets in their social and ecological contexts, then, demands creating and institutionalizing political-economic systems and structures that are fundamentally different from those of neoliberal capitalism. Raworth offers recommendations for this project:

- looking beyond gross domestic product as a solitary measure of society's success and ending cultural addictions to unending economic growth;
- seeing the big picture, where the market is simply one part of an embedded economy—which also includes the commons, households, and states;
- treating human beings as social, adaptable beings rather than rational economic actors;
- engaging in systems thinking; and
- working to build distributive and regenerative systems.

Central to re-visioning and embedding markets are *distributive* and *regenerative* systems, reviewed here. The scholarly literature is starting to catch up with this phenomenon, and more studies are emerging on long-standing practices in Indigenous and Tribal nations.[9]

Raworth argues that *distributive systems and economies* (as opposed to divisive ones that encourage competition and scarcity mindsets) can reduce the massive economic inequality people face under neoliberal capitalism. What is more, distributive economies can transform capitalist notions of ownership and property. Redistributing ownership—of land, information, technology, or time—is a central pillar of a distributive economy. For instance, Raworth suggests a global design repository, where people could access free, downloadable designs for hundreds of items important to different enterprises, ranging from agriculture to tech. At local levels, examples of distributive economies include collective rights to land; enterprise ownership and worker-owned cooperatives; scaling down of large organizations to smaller, community-controlled enterprises; and universal basic income. Raworth posits that if a "global wealth tax" of just 1.5 percent of net worth were placed on all billionaires (there are roughly two thousand worldwide), that alone could generate about $74 billion per year in revenue—enough for, she says, every child in developing nations to attend school and access basic health care.

Attempts to distribute justly have met with mixed results, as we will see, and that is in part because it is tough to do in some places while still operating in the larger context of a neoliberalized global economy. At times, scale is hard; for instance, the collective responsibility of community self-monitoring of the commons may not necessarily reproduce at any social size. Working through these processes at different scales is an ongoing social experiment—and indeed, many thinkers suggest that some of these processes are better rooted in communities than in nations. Or successes may lie in scaling up to those bigger systems: Naomi Klein characterizes movements toward global commons largely in a language of leaderless networks.[10] And David Bollier[11] imagines commons at a national scale, in terms of parks and public lands. Scholars highlight various Indigenous notions of commons that were nearly obliterated under the racial capitalism of settler colonialism and will need to be centered and amplified; for instance, observing the commons must include more-than-humans, be scaled to place, and reincorporate (or perhaps give the reins to) land-based cultures and practices.[12]

Building *regenerative socioeconomic systems* compliments distributive economies while also beginning to address some of the legacies of racial capitalism.[13] Regenerative systems move beyond industrial, military, and corporate pollution of environments for profit, and they even aim to move beyond "doing no harm." Rather, regenerative systems can *enhance and enrich* environments and ecosystems. For instance, some regenerative agricultural enterprises aim to restore soil and sequester carbon through soil storage and other techniques; the Native-owned company American Indian Foods provides an excellent example of this, and we will see more later in the chapter. In particular, the Hemp and Heritage Farm focuses on rematriating seeds and cultivating hemp, which can bioremediate soil while providing an array of materials. Soul Fire Farm uses regenerative practices to restore soil while supporting farmers of color and practicing rematriation of land. Biomimicry—the design of materials, structures, and systems that are modeled on biological processes—is a key design philosophy of regenerative systems. Minimizing waste also matters; rather than losing energy and materials at each phase, regenerative systems take biological nutrients and technical capacities and harness the value created at each stage of production by limiting waste and focusing on restoring, repairing, reusing, refurbishing, or recycling materials.[14] Regenerative approaches include closed-loop systems, where the waste from one industry is used as fuel for another. We already see these approaches in states like Vermont, for instance, where the Cabot Creamery Co-operative uses animal and food waste and production by-products to create renewable energy. Cities such as Amsterdam, London, and Glasgow have also begun to adopt closed-loop practices.

This orientation can be used at multiple scales and across multiple issues. For instance, Amsterdam responded to the COVID-19 pandemic's economic effects by creating a "City Portrait,"[15] aiming to build more affordable housing while avoiding further use of raw materials and creation of carbon emissions. New buildings will get a "materials passport" (showing the composition of reusable materials) so that demolition companies have a better idea of which materials to keep. Amsterdam also plans to regulate construction materials to be recyclable, which gives them less of an environmental impact; through this approach, the city plans to address the lack of affordable housing and sustainable building issues at once.

Other examples include community-owned approaches to solar and renewable energy,[16] which we explore through our Indigenized Energy case study in this chapter. Earthships—homes that are built from natural and recycled materials, collect and filter their own water, internally process waste, naturally regulate their own heating and cooling, generate wind and solar power, and allow for some food processing—also provide excellent examples of smaller-scale regenerative design systems, covered masterfully by sociologist Chelsea Schelly.[17]

Capitalism erects significant barriers to transformation, of course, and there are real political challenges to regenerative systems-building—not the least of which are capitalist institutions and a global elite with tremendous power, wealth, and incentives to retain the status quo. And as nice as these projects sound—and as worthwhile as we think they are—these are not straightforward processes. For instance, closed farming systems are rarely initially as profitable as open ones. Developing wheat as a perennial (rather than an annual) crop sequesters carbon. As a consequence, bread would get both scarcer and more expensive, and some number of children would be hungrier than they would have otherwise been. Yet future generations of farmers would not be faced with dead soil. These tensions are real and consequential, and pretending them away does not help.

To us, this is where state support comes in and where public investment becomes crucial. The doughnut perspective, after all, reminds us that the economy is not just composed of markets and of farmers growing wheat—but also the state, commons, and households. Transitioning away from dead-end systems requires social support for the most vulnerable: in the example just given, such support might come in the form of food subsidies and subsidies for farms that switch to growing wheat as a perennial. This kind of subsidy would reduce the immediate risk for farmers who make the transition and would help families feed their children in the meantime. The doughnut model offers some specifics for how we might go about this, and our case studies in the second half of the chapter look at how groups around the country are transforming current systems.

EMBEDDING ENERGY MARKETS AMID
NEOLIBERAL HEGEMONY

These efforts take vision, time, and investment—as well as buy-in from a critical mass of people. Given the hegemonic power of neoliberalism, not everyone connects social dislocation to dis-embedded markets or capitalism—or even sees it as a problem. Instead, some see social dislocation as a sign of individual people's lack of merit, work ethic, or adaptability. As some of Stephanie's work shows, neoliberal norms can encourage people to accept the risks of industrial systems based on nuclear or fossil fuels, for instance, rather than changing to more regenerative models.[18] In these "sites of acceptance," regulations, for instance, are met with disdain and skepticism. This is especially true regarding issues of environmental protections and social safety nets, which are seen as government handouts.

For instance, communities with histories of uranium mining and milling still live with risks such as abandoned mines, contaminated land and water, and cancer clusters, and yet some people within such communities continue to support renewed uranium mining. People attribute the social dislocation that they experience (like persistent poverty) to *government regulation* of industry rather than to the industry itself; people perceive uranium markets as part of their community's social fabric, and they trust corporations more than the state.[19] Sociologist Arlie Hochschild has explored this process, too, documenting how governments also tend to punish "the little guy" more harshly for small peccadilloes (like a leaky motorboat engine) while letting large corporate actors off the hook for tremendous environmental sins (like dumping thousands of tons of industrial waste into a bay).[20] This frequently results in anti-government sentiment.

Before we present some examples of fundamentally different distributive and regenerative actions, then, we will explore the experience of communities fighting unconventional oil and gas (UOG) production in places where corporate self-regulation and drilling are defended as parts of the social fabric. We return once more to our oil and gas case, showing how people mobilize to embed energy markets and fight deregulation even in deeply divided spaces. We present this here because it serves as a reminder of just how important, yet difficult, change is—and just how powerfully familiar neoliberalism can be. Even in places fighting UOG production, as we show here, neoliberal structures both shape and muffle the goals of activism.

These data also demonstrate the impacts of federal de- and reregulation, or dis-embedded markets. The Halliburton loophole in the Energy Policy Act of 2005 created a scattered matrix of state and local regulations for UOG production; it also exempted the industry from almost half of all federal environmental regulations (including the Safe Drinking Water Act and Clean Water Act).[21] Communities in states like Texas, Colorado, and Pennsylvania, then, find *themselves* enforcing corporate accountability, because neither the oil and gas industry nor the federal government is required to do so. Individual community members reported monitoring drilling operations just to *feel safe in their own homes*, since no other entity was doing it. Small state budgets for enforcing regulations also feed into this problem: for instance, in heavily drilled Colorado (where these data were collected), only 24 field officers enforce regulations for the state's 60,000 oil wells (meaning that one officer oversees approximately 2,500 wells, a nearly impossible workload).

Strong patterns emerged from our interviews with people about how federal de- and reregulation devolve regulatory responsibility. Their observations provide examples of how difficult it can be to embed markets and how stubborn capitalism can be. After all, the data here show that sometimes people's tactics emerge from the rule book of the very firms they fight. But they also mobilize, which speaks to the power of organizing—even if it is primarily in self-defense.

Interviewees were savvy, aware they were limited by the structures of de- and reregulation. They knew the Halliburton loophole created a regulatory void, forcing individual states to scramble to figure out how to regulate (and how to afford it). They also knew the industry ignored its self-regulation responsibilities—and that it was up to the public to demand protections. For instance, Thom, a study participant with drilling rigs visible from his deck, described instability created by federal deregulation. His social dislocation motivated him to the fight:

> The [loss of] federal oversight, as far as clean air and water provisions—the Halliburton loophole, specifically—really bothers me. It's a built-in for the industry, which is what it was designed to be. I mean, look who it came from [then vice president Dick Cheney, former CEO of Halliburton]. . . . Because of that, it has forced state governments . . . to come up with this spur-of-the-moment decision on what's going to be allowed, what's not going to be allowed. And that's putting an unfair burden on the state governments, for something that should be overseen at the federal level. . . . In Colorado, we've come so far that now it's [pauses] falling to the county governments to come up with the oversight that's necessary for oil and gas.

The vast majority of interviewees in this study observed lopsided power dynamics, with state agencies supporting oil and gas operators. In states like Colorado, agencies get much of their funding through permitting fees, and so even though people spend immense amounts of time fighting for better protections, they often feel defeated and ignored even as public health risks accumulate. After *ten years* of extensive oil and gas expansion, community activism continues as the industry has grown, reminding us that organizing can be lengthy and ugly and often can feel pointless when the goals are incremental changes that allow UOG production to continue more or less without interruption. While some degree of community control remains the goal, activists encounter immense barriers. They often fail. For instance, Tammy, a teacher in her forties who organized her community as oil well pads surrounded a neighborhood school, observed how people keep fighting for more social and environmental protections, daunting as it may be:

I don't think we are satisfied that the state can regulate and protect us, because some of these bottom feeders, like [a specific local operator], are buying up [drilling rights] that are unacceptable for the more reputable companies. So they're likely to drill right in the middle of neighborhoods. . . . There was a meeting yesterday, and they're going to put 22 wells in—and sandwich them between all these homes and these neighborhoods. . . . So even on a local basis, it's very hard to be heard. . . . And that's why people get very disheartened and disillusioned.

Another interview participant, Paul, had twenty well pads going into the open space behind his home. He said, "I would still like to see a federal law in place that would cover our whole country. State-to-state regulations, you know, they're gonna be so varied. . . . I do think that there should be some state laws that would positively pre-empt local work. [So] we are working on a state initiative as well. . . . I think that should be created and mandated by the vote of the people." Paul and others want uniform oversight of the industry, however elusive the goal feels.

As people observed, self-regulation in practice meant underregulation. And people related this to the market being privileged above people's health. For instance, Maria, a woman in her thirties who joined a community group over concerns about her children's health, observed: "There is just so much money in it. There's no way people are going to regulate it, unless there's a punishment to not regulating it." Cultures of corporate self-regulation and underenforcement created enormous barriers to implementing broader accountability. Instead, community activists had to fight for much smaller goals. Maria continued:

They [the well pads] are in somebody's backyard. And just that, right there, is an injustice for humankind—to have a freaking oil well in your backyard! It's not good. And they [industry operators] continually get away with these things because . . . there's just not enough people on the line. And part of that comes from not having the right regulations and not having the right people to enforce the regulations.

In this extractive context, we can see how de- and reregulation force people to monitor operators. We also see how Maria's community is treated as a sacrifice zone—where people's suffering is justified under the auspices of progress and protection of the economic development UOG production claims to create, despite boom-and-bust cycles and externalized social, health, and environmental costs.

But operators set the rules of the game within the context of capitalist fossil fuel production,[22] and community organizations have so far met with only partial success. Public gatherings, sustained activism, and dedicated sites of resistance are gathering steam; significant numbers of people are already choosing (or trying to choose) environmental health, air quality, intergenerational equity, and ecological sustainability over dis-embedded markets. Yet, working within the logics and norms of neoliberal capitalism truncates their organizing power and limits the reach of what they can do. They are forced to take baby steps toward change when they want to sprint toward different systems.

STUDIES IN TRANSFORMATION—BUILDING REGENERATIVE AND DISTRIBUTIVE SYSTEMS

Now we will turn to examples of these different systems in progress—to places where people construct nonextractive distributive and regenerative systems. Our earlier case studies, especially Thunder Valley Community Development Corporation and those in chapter 5, also modeled some of these visionary efforts. The boldest actions in this direction occur powerfully at the food-energy-water nexus. They aim to completely transform extractive systems and instead build regenerative systems where social, ecological, and economic well-being intertwine. The idea is not only that markets are embedded in these organizations and communities but also that they are *transformed* to serve societies and ecological systems. Importantly, these cases act as representative examples of similar organizations and communities in the United States and globally.[23]

Case Study 1. Indigenized Energy, Standing Rock, and Community Solar Cooperatives

Cody Two Bears is the executive director of Indigenized Energy, a nonprofit solar cooperative based in Cannon Ball, North Dakota, on the Standing Rock Sioux treaty lands. He also served as a Standing Rock Tribal Councilman from 2013 to 2017. Indigenized Energy works to build more self-sufficient, sustainable, and regenerative systems on the Standing Rock Sioux Reservation, focusing on solar energy production and community development. Indigenized Energy's work is distributive in its commitment to low-cost energy for all, using a cooperative model, focusing on both renewable energy and intergenerational healing from centuries of collective trauma.

Two Bears was a part of the well-known No Dakota Access Pipeline (NoDAPL) movement that began in 2016 and which is still a suite of continued actions against fossil fuel–based extractive development.[24] The nonviolent Standing Rock camps (the Oceti Sakowin, Red Warrior, and Sacred Stone Camps) were attacked by militarized police and private police forces later that year and forced to close. The Dakota Access Pipeline (DAPL) was eventually pushed through by an executive order from Donald Trump (who had economic interests in the project)—though at the writing of this book, DAPL had been successfully challenged in court and that battle of appeals continued. The NoDAPL movement became a transnational, cross-cultural solidarity movement and coalition-building effort around global anti-extractivism, Tribal nations' sovereignty, and pipeline protests.

A brief history lesson helps contextualize why this matters so much—and why this case of *Indigenous* environmental injustice creates such strong foundations on which to build distributive and regenerative systems. [25] When DAPL was approved by Trump's executive order—even after the permits were defeated under Barack Obama's administration—the power given to the U.S. Army Corps of Engineers represented only the latest in a series of historical thefts for the Standing Rock Sioux and other Native nations across the Missouri River Basin. This conflict is part of one of the largest and most protracted land thefts in U.S. history (which also deeply impacts the Thunder Valley Community Development Corporation highlighted in chapter 4).[26] In 1803, the fledgling U.S. government claimed 827 million acres from the French Crown during the Louisiana Purchase, which instigated the Lewis and Clark expedition. These "French lands" were Native nations' homelands—and no Native nation approved the sale. More fundamentally, no Native nation thought in terms of owning and selling land as private property. Over the next one hundred years, Native people—specifically the Oceti Sakowin, or the People of Seven Council Fires (also called the Great Sioux Nation)—were systematically evicted from their homelands, even after entering into the Treaties of Fort Laramie with the U.S. government in 1851 and 1868. These treaties defined a 25 million–acre territory that became the Great Sioux Reservation. White settlers continued to claim these lands, however, leading to incredibly violent, genocidal state-led campaigns against Native nations. These campaigns included the killing of more than 10 million buffalo in order to starve Native people, and settler invasions of the Black Hills territory to claim gold.[27] Over time, these treaties were unilaterally voided by U.S. policies such as the Indian Appropriations Act of 1876 (repealing treaty-making with Native nations) and the Black Hills Act of 1877. As North and South Dakota became states, they contributed to further land theft and genocidal violence against Native nations, including the Ghost Dance War in 1890–1891, when over three hundred unarmed Lakota Sioux—many of them women and children—were violently attacked and killed by U.S. forces at Wounded Knee.

The Dawes Act of 1887 broke up the Great Sioux Nation, facilitated theft of millions of acres of land, and eventually created a battle over Native nations' water rights when settler populations wanted to initiate large-scale irrigation systems on the Great Plains. The U.S. Supreme Court ruled that taking Native nations' water was unlawful, but subsequent policies (such as the Flood Control Act of 1944) gave the Army Corps of Engineers unprecedented control over water and further disenfranchised the Oceti Sakowin Confederacy of Nations (a confederacy of several Tribal nations that speak Lakota, Dakota, or Nakota language dialects). Thousands of acres of Native lands were flooded because of the Pick-Sloan dams,[28] while the 1953 House Concurrent Resolution 108, the Indian Relocation Act of 1956, and Public Law 280 essentially wiped out Tribal sovereignty. The U.S. government did not recognize some Tribes and even moved large parts of these communities to distant urban centers.

In response to the ongoing assaults, the American Indian Movement (AIM) mobilized, and there was a standoff at the Pine Ridge Reservation in 1973. Then, in 1974, thousands gathered at Standing Rock to form the International Indian Treaty Council—which helped craft the 2007 United Nations Declaration on the Rights of Indigenous Peoples. So, when the Army Corps of Engineers claimed the right to permit DAPL on Standing Rock Sioux lands—after moving its path from predominantly white Bismarck, North Dakota—it hit a nerve.

The Standing Rock Sioux Nation—with efforts organized in part by Two Bears—has continued to build community-based distributive and regenerative systems and to fight for climate justice, joining the substantial work by others in this region and in other Native nations.[29] During the NoDAPL protests at Standing Rock, Two Bears visited the camps regularly and witnessed intense state-led violence against protestors. Yet, he also saw self-sufficient production of what he referred to as "indigenized energy," which inspired him to work toward founding a solar cooperative in his community—despite all the barriers to renewable enterprises in oil-dependent North Dakota. He told us, "I told myself I don't just want to protest about it, I want us to *be* about it now." He leveraged public interest and media attention to build something led and owned by the community, reaching out to potential investors such as GivePower, Empowered by Light, and JinkoSolar. These partners helped him form the Cannon Ball Community Solar Farm.

Two Bears founded Indigenized Energy in 2017 as a nonprofit, community-based enterprise. Its biggest accomplishment to date has been the construction and operation of the Cannon Ball Community Solar Farm—North Dakota's first solar farm. The solar array—built in part by community members—has 1,100 solar panels and a capacity of 300 kilowatts. This will be enough to power Standing Rock homes in Cannon Ball—once they can get access to the transmission lines, which are currently off-limits due to local and state regulations that favor fossil fuel–based utilities. Even though they can produce their own energy, they are not allowed to use it—yet. In an excellent example of reregulation's effects in the United States, local ordinances that favor fossil fuels have also kept Indigenized Energy from installing solar panels on people's homes. Installation is the plan for Phase 2, once those ordinances are revoked.

For now, Indigenized Energy uses a power purchase agreement to sell the energy through its cooperative to the North Dakota state grid system. The state grid buys the energy for only 2.25 cents per kilowatt-hour—one of the lowest rates in the nation, and far less than the 14 cents per kilowatt-hour that people pay for their electricity in the Standing Rock Nation (the highest rate in the state). Indigenized Energy agreed to this because it allows the cooperative to get its foot in the door of state energy markets, bringing in renewables to the second-largest oil-producing state in the United States. The agreement also makes more transparent the enormous disparities that lead to energy poverty in this community—not only the exorbitant rates but also the poor insulation and construction in government-built homes, which makes heating and cooling costs especially prohibitive.

Eventually, the goal is to have the array and solar panels on households providing most, if not all, of the power in Cannon Ball. The group has plans for additional panels on schools and community buildings—plans slowed by COVID-19. For now, even with that low rate of return on what they generate, the energy created continues to save the community an estimated $7,000–$10,000 annually in electricity bills. This money is used to offset the costs of electricity for the community's Veterans Memorial Center (which serves eighty meals per day to elderly community members) and the community-based Cannon Ball Youth Activity Center. The income also supports Indigenized Youth, a related nonprofit, especially its youth athletic programs and educational programs for reintroducing and retaining Lakota (and Dakota) languages. For instance, there is a language immersion school on the reservation for children from infancy through age seven, and the program is supported in part by this income.

Indigenized Energy has also begun to train community members and young people in solar installation, and Two Bears himself has learned how to install panels. Indigenized Energy formally partnered with United Tribes Technical College in Bismarck to initiate a training program in renewable energy and solar installation and other technologies related to the cooperative. They want to be as self-sustainable as possible and have all the skills needed to take care of the community and solar technologies within the community itself. Two Bears observed: "I live in a state where it is all coal, all oil. . . . So [I] reach out to people and tell them the benefits of how great this technology is and how wonderful it would be if we can all work together. . . . When people start joining on, this movement will get bigger and bigger."

He explained what self-sustainability and the concept of indigenized energy means for the community. The nonprofit's regenerative vision and its embeddedness in the community's social and ecological needs defines Indigenized Energy's mission, as Two Bears explained:

Having to rely on outside resources is a big problem. Moving forward, people and communities can work in this way of not having to outsource any more and to have everything in-house. And that even includes energy. Indigenized Energy was born because . . . at the [NoDAPL] encampments, people created their own energy through solar panels, little wind turbines, things like that. And I [thought], "That's Indigenized Energy." And "indigenized" basically means doing it your own way, what you feel like within your own communities. With Indigenized Energy, we are creating energy within our own reservation boundaries—and using that energy in a way that benefits our people in the way that it should.

The solar cooperative has been important for the energy it provides, but it has also been symbolically important—an emblem of progress and self-sustainability, led by and embedded in the Standing Rock Sioux Nation. Its existence is an accomplishment, as Two Bears explained: "We produced the largest solar farm in one of the toughest states in the country to produce solar or renewable energy—North Dakota . . . [and] about 3 miles away from the [Dakota Access] pipeline. So, pretty cool [laughs]. . . . The goal is not necessarily to build the biggest solar farm in the world—but to build enough solar [to meet] our needs. . . . [Growing to] 5 megawatts would generate about half a million dollars a year. With that . . . we could continue to educate, continue to set this platform up, continue more [home] installs on our reservation for free."

The community hopes that Indigenized Energy will remain generative for the Standing Rock Sioux Nation for many generations. The organization's central goal in creating embedded, self-sustainable energy markets is to build regenerative enterprises that will help Standing Rock reclaim its sovereignty and achieve ecological and intergenerational equity, even in the midst of oil country. Two Bears observed:

> [Our] ultimate goal is to control and maintain our own Tribal utility. . . . To build solar through the whole reservation. Once we get our own Tribal utility twenty years down the road, then we will be in control of our own destiny as far as energy. We will have all of the knowledge of food sovereignty, in medicine, traditional cultural ways of praying. What more do you need to not have to outsource anymore? So this is kind of just the start to get people educated, to get the youth involved . . . to have those next generations . . . know everything that [we] taught them, to carry it on. Otherwise, it is for nothing. So that is why the youth programming is so important.

For Indigenized Energy, renewable, cooperative solar energy production embeds an energy market in the social fabric of the Standing Rock Sioux community while moving them away from settler colonial histories and extractive industries. Renewable energy capacity combines with forms of knowledge that have carried forward, such as Lakota language dialects and land-based approaches to health and well-being. Moving away from fossil fuels connects the nonprofit with its NoDAPL movement origins—and grounds the community in renewable energy systems that enhance their long-term sovereignty and self-sustainability. Indigenized Energy's focus on training and empowering young people, veterans, and future generations builds community and stitches together multiple generations of social fabric.

By building a Tribally owned and operated utility, the community aims to move off the grid and away from the structural violence and persistent poverty induced by settler colonial policies. As Two Bears explained, part of the work is to disentangle the community from exploitative corporate utility rates. Solar power offers economic independence:

> On Standing Rock, in particular, we pay the highest utilities rates within the whole state. We pay 13.77 cents per kilowatt-hour, and . . . some places pay 14 cents on the reservation. And you go right off the reservation, 6–7 miles down the road to the next community, they are paying half of that, at 7 or 8 cents. . . . The next highest that we saw was in Fargo, at 10 cents. So we pay almost double compared to every-one else, [and] people never really knew or understood what we were paying. . . . So that is . . . another wrongdoing of the energy companies, keeping high-poverty communities down in the dirt so that they can't really flourish.

The Standing Rock Sioux Nation is located in one of the poorest counties in the United States, with close to 70 percent unemployment rates and poverty rates at 60 percent.[30] With the history of ignored treaties, land grabs, and other con-temporary aspects of settler colonialism on full display, these inequities are pal-pable. But still—when we talked with Two Bears, we got excited about how the world can be. As the community works to build this system, Two Bears hopes that Indigenized Energy can become "a model for other high poverty places, even those that are non-Native."

Indigenized Energy has a specific set of goals that guide its work. These are not new goals. Importantly, they carry traditions and systems of knowledge that have remained durable, lasting through land grabs, attempted genocide, and immense pressure to become additional nodes in the neoliberal political econ-omy. The visions of connection to land and place through regenerative prac-tices have persisted and been sustained even in the midst of settler colonial cultures that normalize metabolic rift, or separation from nature. Two Bears explained:

> For some reason Indigenous communities around the world, after all of the atrocities, all of the genocides, and the governmental systems trying to change the way they live, Westernize them, Christianize them, whatever it may be. . . . For some reason, they held on to those cultures. They held onto those ways of life. . . . There is a reason for that. The Creator has given us a spirit about these Indigenous communities that will never ever ever give in and still hold true to who they are. . . . So Indigenous people, we still carry that knowledge today. We

still hold it. For some reason, we are holding it for everyone who has lost that way of life. I call it, "The Disconnected Ones." ... I've been in New York City, D.C., ...

He paused as he considered, and then he continued:

They don't really know what is around them. They are just so disconnected from the Earth. They know that there is something bigger we need to learn, something bigger we need to be a part of. COVID-19 is just one example, a tiny taste, of what it looks like. We call it mass hysteria, where people are going crazy thinking "I need this, I need that." ... And I think this is key for all Indigenous communities. ... We know how to grow foods right now. We know how to find where these traditional medicines are if we get sick. We know our traditional ceremonies and how we pray and how we have guidance from the Creator. We have all of these things already. But you look at one aspect that we don't have ... but it could boost us ... for the next 150 years. And that is energy. If we can learn how to use energy, self-sufficiently, and teach our people the way of this new technology ...

Two Bears connects Indigenized Energy's mission with the long-term survival of his community and their culture. Ultimately, these Tribal nations have a lot to teach others about how to embed markets, and why:

[We] use energy, especially renewable energy, wind and solar, especially solar, as a way to use this last branch to be fully sustainable. ... You always know that you have to get sick to feel better. The Earth has to regenerate herself to feel better. ... People have to change the way they do things—and this is just the beginning. ... People now are starting to reach out to Indigenous cultures, Indigenous communities, all over the world and try to get this knowledge, to get back to their traditional roots. ... Because these big old shiny expensive things aren't glamourous like they used to be. People don't want those things anymore. They want to go back to a simple way of life, learning how to be regenerative. ... But if we don't have a platform ready for that, if we're not ready to be able to transition for that, then you are going to see a lot more people suffer.

The efforts of Two Bears and Indigenized Energy are materially visible in a way that not all the cases profiled in this book are: they have built the first solar farm in North Dakota and established a foothold for renewable energy in a heavily oil-dependent region. They have carried on some of the momentum of the NoDAPL coalition-building and action by making themselves a renewable part of the state's energy economy. In doing this, then, Indigenized Energy helps fortify the Standing Rock Sioux Nation's social fabric, and it has done so despite a marked lack of action at state and federal levels. It is worth reemphasizing that

Indigenized Energy's work emerges, in part, from a wealth of knowledge accumulated over centuries of human and ecological relationships and traditions.

This work is complex. And it makes goals fraught and slow: building renewable and regenerative systems in the midst of one of the biggest oil patches in North Dakota and the United States is a large task. Political context does not help these efforts, and it also remains deeply neoliberalized and extractive. This is why, for instance, it will take about twenty years to build Indigenized Energy's capacity to be self-sustaining.

These systems can be built at smaller scales, but the scaling up requires at least some extra fortitude—and an appetite for engaging in institutional and regulatory systems. But the coalition-building around the NoDAPL action reminds us that institutions like Indigenized Energy can inspire coalitions, too. They can help inspire similar efforts[31] that can create momentum, connection, and critical capacity across scales and places to accomplish these complex, challenging material changes.

Case Study 2. Winona's Hemp and Heritage Farm: Community Enrichment and Building Regenerative Systems

We could easily focus on Winona LaDuke herself for this entire case study. She is a force of nature: at once funny and wise, energetic and humble—ready to dismantle capitalist patriarchy and build the "post-petroleum economy," as she calls it. An Ojibwe activist and organizer, LaDuke is the only Green Party candidate to have earned an Electoral College vote. And in conversation, she is motivated by fortifying community, building collective and regenerative systems *now*, and even risking "spectacular failures," as she puts it. As LaDuke said in our interview and has said in many other talks, she is here to help humanity realize the prophecy of the Anishinaabe.[32] Societies have a choice between the two different paths at the center of this prophecy, as LaDuke tells it: "the choice between the familiar, worn path that is scorched" and the less-trodden path that is greener, more alive. Her job, her calling, involves showing people how to take that second, green path and abandon the scorched path of, as she puts it, "dumb ideas from silly white men" that have reached the status of gospel for five hundred years.

While it is tempting to tell LaDuke's story, we instead tell the story of her community organizing and the organizations that have been the fruit of that thirty-nine-year effort—shaped and fortified by the energies of so many others.[33] In particular, we focus on Honor the Earth and the regenerative, community-led Hemp and Heritage Farm. As part of the Anishinaabe Agriculture Institute, the farm aims to become a living model of an organic, Indigenous-led, women-led, community-based, and post-petroleum economy where food, energy, and water are not simply so-called natural resources but are understood as members of the community. The farm works to build a "hemp renaissance," creating vertically integrated nodes of the hemp industry centered on producing textiles that are stronger, more sustainable, and homegrown.

Rural economic development is not just LaDuke's academic expertise; it is also the core of her organizations and farm, which is near the White Earth Nation in northern Minnesota. But she wants to rewrite stereotypes of "rural economic development," moving away from inequitable, unsustainable industrial growth. As she said in a recent talk at the Flow Cannabis Institute, collective change toward building regenerative systems is the goal:

> Let's be awesome. Let's be the kind of ancestors that our descendants will be proud of. Let's do some epic stuff. . . . I come from the land where the wild things are. We call it "Omaa Akiing," or the land to which the people belong. It's not the concept of private property. *The land to which the people belong*—think about that. This is a worldview we really need to work on having. . . . What is our covenant? Where do we belong?

This flip—from *owning* to *belonging to*—is the crux of her work. LaDuke, along with Amy Ray and Emily Saliers (both of Indigo Girls fame), founded Honor the Earth in 1993 to address environmental injustices and climate crises and to support Indigenous environmental efforts through the arts and media. They have raised over $2 million, which has been given back directly to over two hundred Native nations.[34] Honor the Earth supports societal transformation and relationships based on just transitions away from settler colonialism. It aims to heal metabolic rift through regenerative practices—"to restor[e] a paradigm that recognizes our collective humanity and our joint dependence on the Earth." To aid humanity in choosing "the green path," Honor the Earth supports Native efforts to build "land-based economies," reject extractivism, advance intergenerational and interspecies equity, and carve out spaces for Native nations to lead regenerative projects.

The organization has become vital to mobilizations against pipelines, fossil fuel infrastructure, and the Rights of Nature movement discussed in chapter 5. Honor the Earth trains the next generation of community organizers and fights current fossil fuel–based systems, aiming for renewable and sustainable post-petroleum futures. The organization's recent work has focused on fighting Enbridge's Sandpiper pipeline and Line 3 pipeline, has provided some of the most significant support behind the water protection movement, and has been central in supporting the protests against the Dakota Access Pipeline.[35] Through its nonprofit community development corporation, Akiing, Honor the Earth and other supporters including the Rural Renewable Energy Alliance, founded 8th Fire Solar, the first Native-owned solar thermal manufacturing company.

The White Earth Nation and other Anishinaabe people and communities figure centrally in these collaborative efforts and are supported by a coalition of
organizations and funders. LaDuke asserted in our interview: "My work is for
my community. I have, you know, we have some businesses, we have some
nonprofit organizations. We have some Tribal schools that are all part of this
collaborative." Collaboration and cooperation guide these efforts, using logic
fundamentally different from the competition that shapes neoliberal market
economies. LaDuke recalled:

> I was at the UN Climate forum a couple years ago, and I ran into Philip White-
> man, from Northern Cheyenne. . . . And so we were hanging out and he says,
> "Winona, I gotta tell you this. I gotta tell you this." He says, "The next economy is
> about cooperation, not competition." That's what he said. And so that's kind of
> the thesis upon which I am formulating what we're working on. If we wanna sur-
> vive, we've got to work together. . . . I've got some new ladies coming to my com-
> munity. And I said, "You know, we've been working on this for 25, 30 years. . . .
> This is what it looks like." Then there's a set of organizations and what I'm doing is
> working with a lot of other people to weave us together to transition our commu-
> nity into a more safe and secure place.

Resonant with the Doughnut Economy's formulation of "safe and just space,"
LaDuke helps forge this path by also building physical, material parts of a post-
petroleum economy. The Anishinaabe Agriculture Institute and the Hemp and
Heritage Farm model the "Indigenous Green New Deal," as LaDuke calls it, and
the new economy. Together, she said, they work to "light the 8th fire, the regeneration of the good life," represented by that less-trodden path of Anishinaabe
prophecies. These organizations help LaDuke contribute to building a system
that rejects capitalism and embraces more regenerative Indigenous lifeways and
knowledge systems. As she reflected in our interview, "Indigenous economics,
or earth-based economics, is really the only kind that is gonna work. . . . This
capitalist patriarchy needs to be sent to the ditch. . . . We have a really well proven
case of the failure [of it]. . . . From COVID to nuclear power and beyond."
The Anishinaabe Agriculture Institute represents the nonprofit arm of these
efforts and focuses on research, development, and various educational endeav-
ors related to growing hemp and localizing the food economy. In 2008, LaDuke
completed a study on the White Earth Nation and found that reservation
households spent about $8 million per year on food, with almost all of it leaving
the community. The money spent on the reservation went to chain convenience
stores and to buy processed foods.[36] This information provided an impetus for
change. As a research nonprofit, the institute focuses on learning and then teaching others how to "restore food ways, rematriate seeds, and make a new economy

based on local food, energy, and fiber."[37] The institute sits at the food-energy-water nexus; this is the focus for building a new regenerative economy because, as LaDuke has said, "we have to change the materials economy to make change in the system . . . to move to the post-petroleum era." From this perspective, the distributive potential of the farm's work is not only about economic revenue but also about building equitable distribution of nutrients, access, and food security.

The Hemp and Heritage Farm, purchased in 2017, sits on forty acres (and growing!) outside the White Earth Nation's land. The farm activates the institute's food sovereignty and security missions by acquiring land and by farming heritage crops and hemp. It works to heal the land and build up the soil, create space for ancestral crops to thrive, train the next generation of Anishinaabe farmers, and help launch the hemp economy. Together, these efforts work to build the "new economy, which is [again] about cooperation, not competition," and to revitalize the visions of the long-running White Earth Land Recovery Project.

The Hemp and Heritage Farm grows heritage crops and varietals—especially corn, beans, and squash (raised together as the Three Sisters staple crops[38]), heritage potatoes, Jerusalem artichokes, traditional tobacco varieties, and fiber hemp. Maple syruping has long been a key part of this land, and LaDuke greeted us with "So, the new year just started in our country. Maple syruping is the new year . . . so happy new year!" Horses figure centrally as well, since the farm relies on horsepower to plow the fields. The farm also runs a Youth Horse Cultural Trainings program in which Native youth spend therapeutic time with the horses to heal from various intergenerational traumas and the stresses of poverty, while learning about farming.

Hemp epitomizes the farm's regenerative goals. The farm grows primarily fiber hemp—to be used for clothing and products like rope—and also hemp for CBD strains and products. The farm produces hemp oils, hemp milk, and even hemp pastas, which the farmers have collaboratively created using North Dakota's prized semolina wheat varieties. The farmers see hemp as "magical" and as "part of forming a covenant with the Earth." Hemp cultivation has become part of the farm's collective efforts to be "doulas of the next economy," premised on building "an Indigenous, women-led, regenerative economy that is kind to the Earth." Growing hemp helps regenerative measures such as building up of the soil and bioremediation by filtering out toxic chemicals, which is especially important because the farm is surrounded by an immense potato farm that used fossil fuel and chemical-heavy approaches to agriculture. Hemp requires little water to grow; it resists mold and ultraviolet light's impacts; and all parts of the plant make useful products.[39] As the community works to eventually construct a hemp mill, find a decorticator, and expand its rope-making machinery, people on the farm see some of the strongest roots of the new regenerative economy taking hold. A main pillar of LaDuke's vision for the new economy is "to build an ecologically based textiles industry that isn't based on chemicals and slave labor. How are we going to do this?! I want to build a hemp mill with vertical integration, use all our land to build a model that others can replicate."

The overarching vision has always been to fight extractive, fossil fuel–based injustices—and to build more regenerative economies with potential to distribute benefits throughout the community. Mistakes will happen, of course, as LaDuke recounted, but the stakes are less ecologically disastrous in a regenerative enterprise:

> I make mistakes. You know, I got wind projects, wind turbines that flew off the top of their shells. I mean, that was a spectacular one, out in South Dakota. I have had some spectacular failures. [Laughs.] The only way you learn, you do your best and sometimes you're gonna make a mistake. Try not to make it a big one that fucks shit up. . . . Build it and they will come.

Leading by example and holding bold visions have helped these groups establish regenerative, community-led systems. LaDuke recounted how her organizations and community scale up. The key, she said, is not being overwhelmed by alienating market systems, and building something better to which people can happily transition, leaving behind the fear—and the old systems. She said:

> Start small and scale up. That's my other thing. . . . So I don't wait till all the foundation money is in to do something. My experience is as a community organizer since basically 1981. So that's 39 years of community organizing work. . . . You know, you figure out what's going on [in the current economy], people know what's going on. And then you have to give people a way out. And so you work to create something better. If you want to be a Water Protector, you have to make a future that protects the water. We organize against. . . . [Pauses.] We've fought off a lot of dumb shit coming to our reservation. And we're about to defeat the Enbridge company. Because they don't have any oil, as you've noticed. They're laying people off right now. . . . All together, we're gonna defeat these guys. But, you know, don't spend a lot of time thinking about what you're doing. Pray hard and do it . . . because someone's got to show the example. If people are afraid, they don't know. So you got to show them. You've got to reassure them it's okay, kind of take their hand a little bit. And then off you go.

And, indeed, off they have gone—joyfully modeling regenerative community development for the rest of us. Through Honor the Earth and her long-term humanitarian organizing, LaDuke's organizations have supported and activated integral parts of the Water Protector movement. They have also funded and built Native-owned and -operated businesses like 8th Fire Solar. The Anishinaabe

Agriculture Institute and the Hemp and Heritage Farm, meanwhile, model how to build nodes of the post-petroleum economy and "change the materials economy." They have started to rebuild collaborative, cooperative, and regenerative parts of this economy, such as hemp cultivation, all while enriching soil health and spaces of intergenerational healing. And, even after her thirty-nine years of organizing, one gets the feeling that LaDuke has not shown the world all that she is capable of building.

Case Study 3. Soul Fire Farm: Regenerative Farming to Dismantle Layered Oppression

Soul Fire Farm embodies intersectional regenerative practices (see chapter 2 for a review of intersectionality[40]). It is one of many farms doing similar work,[41] including the Black Dirt Farm Collective in Maryland, the California Farmer Justice Collaborative, Urban Tilth in the San Francisco Bay Area, and the global La Vía Campesina. Soul Fire Farm focuses on agriculture, of course, but it operates with a keen awareness of historical and institutionalized systems of oppression, and it engages in current policy debates. It is an "Afro-Indigenous centered community farm"—one that exists to serve and create safer spaces for farmers (aspiring or experienced) who are Black, Indigenous, and/or members of communities of color.[42] It aims to localize the food system, at once breaking free of industrial farming and addressing the historical exclusion of marginalized peoples from these spaces. The farm itself provides a strong rejoinder to a history of exclusionary landownership; between 1910 and 1970, "Black Americans were uprooted from 90% of the land that they and their ancestors had stewarded in the United States."[43] As Soul Fire leaders note, this history mirrors the centuries of forced displacement of Native and Indigenous peoples from their ancestral lands as settlers spread across the Americas and violently took the land through removal and various (violated) treaties. (As we edited this book, in May 2021, the Joe Biden administration announced a loan payoff program for minority farmers, responding to systemic discrimination perpetrated against farmers and ranchers of color by the U.S. Department of Agriculture. Agriculture Secretary Tom Vilsack called it one of the biggest civil rights bills in decades, but it has faced significant legal challenges since being announced—signaling the structural persistence of institutionalized racism in these spaces.)[44]

Leah Penniman founded Soul Fire Farm in 2010, on eighty acres in the Hudson Valley of upstate New York.[45] Soul Fire focuses on its community-supported agriculture (CSA) program and on cultivating fruits, plants for medicine, pasture-raised livestock, honey, mushrooms, vegetables, and preserves. The Soul Fire team brings its regenerative, environmentally just vision to life—and has become a beacon for others looking to deconstruct racism and environmental injustice while getting their hands dirty growing food. The farm focuses on regenerative practices while slowly healing historical racialized traumas and creating space for people to reconnect with the land and with one another. And it has a wide reach: in 2019 alone, over eleven thousand people attended its various talks; it fed over 350 people in its sliding scale CSA; participated in over ninety media spots; and trained 286 participants in farming and construction.

We interviewed Larisa Jacobson, who then served as one of the farm's co-directors and its partnerships director. Jacobson has twenty years of educational and experiential background in public and community health, social injustice, policy, herbalism, learning programs, and environmental justice work—and we hear from her throughout this case study. Part of what drew her in was Soul Fire's multi-scalar approach. She explained: "I loved this pairing of structural-level change with a very hyper-local approach, doing direct action work, direct service work, getting very concrete things to people and communities like food, gardens, experiences, healing, learning. But also working at the level of policy change and advocacy and shifting public understanding of land and the history of this country related to the food system."

Soul Fire's strategic goals center on regenerative ideologies of justice, ecology, and healing. Justice happens, Jacobson says, when historically marginalized communities are at the center of the food system and are empowered to revolutionize it and to claim their roles as stewards of the land. Soul Fire is motivated to realize this change because of the structural, racialized inequities baked into American food systems, as its institutional reports attest: "Black farmers currently operate around 1% of the nation's farms, having lost over 12 million acres to USDA discrimination, racist violence, and legal trickery. 85% of the people working the land in the US are Latinx migrant workers, yet only 2.5% of farms are owned and operated by Latinxs."[46] That is, the notion of family farms in the United States largely corresponds to *white* family farms, landowning enterprises that follow patterns of dispossession in settler colonies. These imbalances create "food apartheid" across the United States.

Soul Fire centers on ecological balance and moving away from industrial agriculture toward more sustainable, regenerative approaches of agroecology. They see their farm as a space of healing—and also aimed at linking with Black and Indigenous people living in *urban* spaces, where many people have ended up after being repeatedly displaced from land. By cultivating immersive farming programs, community gardens, and urban spaces and training young farmers from minoritized groups, they model how to address systemic racism in the food system. Soul Fire equips participants to farm and mobilizes food communities fighting for access to land and equitable farming policies and institutions. This not only includes working on the farm but also centers on nurturing links to "mycelial support," as Jacobson puts it, on and off the farm. "Mycelial support" likens Soul Fire's efforts to complex, multilayered, and living mycelial, or fungal, networks that thrive in healthy soils and keep spaces like forests interwoven and strong. They often operate at the microscopic level, but mycelial networks are vast, vital, and unify interstitial spaces—in much the same way that Soul Fire works to build foundational and enduring links across multiple spaces and efforts.

Soul Fire demonstrates what intersectional, cross-cultural approaches to regenerative farming can look like, bringing together a mix of "Afro-Indigenous agroforestry, silvopasture, wildcrafting, polyculture, and spiritual farming practices ... [and using] ancestral farming practices [to] increase topsoil depth, sequester soil carbon, and increase biodiversity."[47] As Jacobson explained, these practices are aimed at regenerating the eighty acres of mountainside at Soul Fire, refortifying the soil while decolonizing this space. In their practice, the land is understood as alive and deserving of stewardship rather than domination or industrialization. Jacobson explained:

> We are focused on the land. . . . And we talk about the land at Soul Fire in many different ways, either as a respected elder, [or] as a community member. For me, it's a collective of beings. And we have an obligation as a member of that collective, both to the whole community of beings [and] to our ancestors, in this moment of climate crisis, as carbon is being released into the atmosphere at very large scale because of human actions. . . . And so at Soul Fire, one of the things that we hope to accomplish is regenerating land that has been depleted by the very practices that descend from colonialism and other forms of extraction and domination that have taken place on the land.

As with some of the case studies in previous chapters, Soul Fire Farm has a spiritual component tied to decommodifying land. Instead of using metrics of efficiency, farming strategies are rooted in a connection between land and community, relationship with land as its own being, and reciprocity—all meant to demonstrate these approaches to teach others:

> We [regenerate] through agroforestry, through our spiritual farming practices, through cover cropping, and soil-friendly practices. And it's also a demonstration. So we're showing how you can live and work in cooperation with the land, and then take the abundance from the land and offer it to your local community in order to build very local communities—food sovereignty for people who are living under food apartheid—which is again a human created system. . . . And then we're hoping to accomplish regenerat[ing] the land and shift[ing] relationships to land in this country, from what it has become, through many years of history—which is land as a commodity, land as something to be bought and sold. Moving from "land is a material resource that can be extracted from" to "land as elder or community member."

Soul Fire's vision ties deeply to *rematriating* the land: recognizing the land's original inhabitants by returning Indigenous land to Indigenous people and communities. The farmers use a connotation of "mother" rather than "father" when talking about this. Jacobson explained that Soul Fire works on a

> vision of advancing land and food sovereignty in the northeast by securing permanent and non-predatory, non-exploitative land tenure for Black, Indigenous and other people of color farmers who plan to use the land in a regenerative way, in a sacred way that honors our ancestors. So for sustainable farming, for habitat, for ceremony, for ecosystem restoration, for cultural preservation. And so, we're establishing a nonprofit land trust that will accept land, offer cultural respect easements to the original stewards of the land, and in some cases, rematriate land to the original stewards and create this ability for our Black and Brown farmers and land stewards to access land.

This practice includes honoring the original inhabitants and stewards of the land—who are the Muheconneok, known more commonly as the Mohican people. In 2019, Soul Fire Farm completed a complicated process of converting its private ownership of eighty acres to a collective land trust, or "land stewardship collective," that allows it to honor the original Native inhabitants. In concrete practice, this means that Mohicans can acquire shares of this collective space, which then gives them access to voting on future missions and goals of Soul Fire Farm—a key piece of its distributive potential. As with other examples in this book, here a community engaged the existing legal system—in a complex process—to better act on its own values. Importantly, as part of Soul Fire's regenerative vision and practice, the *land itself* also has a vote in these processes. The land is represented in various ways by different farmers and practitioners at Soul Fire, but as Jacobson described it, they hold regular divination ceremonies, many of them based in West African Ifa practices, whereby the land's voice is heard.

Equipping and mobilizing Black, Indigenous, Latinx, and other minoritized farmers and aspiring farmers are two other pillars of action for Soul Fire Farm. This work happens on several levels, one of which is through distribution of the food itself. Soul Fire provides no-cost doorstep delivery of vegetables, fruits, medicine, eggs, and value-added products to people living under what they term "food apartheid" in the Albany-Troy area, as well as free and low-cost bulk products to community groups.

Soul Fire's work also links to urban spaces, where programs focus on training young people—through grants, through immersion training programs on the farm, and through off-farm support via its Soul Fire in the City program. Farmers are active in policy making and in speaking at an array of venues about their vision for regenerative farming by Black, Indigenous, Latinx, and other minoritized people. Jacobson explained:

> We hope to equip hundreds or thousands of adults and youth with skills—so that they can become leaders in farming and food justice. Particularly Black and Brown youth and adults, to heal that relationship with Earth that has been disrupted by slavery, colonialism, and genocide. And to use that relationship with land as one way of healing from the trauma that's arisen from all those historical things. . . . And in that process, what we're hoping to accomplish is to reverse this trend of so few farms or . . . conservation projects being led and owned by people of color. So to really create leadership and . . . pathways to support that. Finally, I hope to mobilize people, to raise awareness about what has happened in the history of the food system—about stolen land and stolen labor. We also look at policies that are currently unjust in terms of farm worker rights, in terms of Black farmer land access. And discrimination that might be faced in all the supports for being on land—like capital, loans, technical assistance, crop insurance. So the way that we seek to mobilize is by getting the word out, speaking, writing, and then facilitating workshops for activists, including white activists, to share ways that they can take action in the food system. *And shift the ways that resources have been taken and distributed throughout the history of what's called the United States.*

Undoing the entwined effects of settler colonialism and neoliberalism informs all of these goals, including Soul Fire's relationships with international farm sites and communities. Jacobson's explanation of this approach requires no further elaboration:

> We don't have any faith that neoliberal capitalism will work or lead to justice in any way, because it's built out of these systems that are inherently unjust and extractive. In this moment, we see the disproportionate impact of COVID-19 on Black and Brown communities. We see the disproportionate impact of climate change and chronic diseases and environmental issues and food apartheid, lack of access to healthy, affordable, culturally relevant food, lack of access to land—all of that. Part of our task is to call attention to the fact that the systems have *always* been broken. *But* that they did not break. *They were built to function exactly as they are.* They were built to function on stolen land and stolen labor. . . . We can't operate in a free market or deregulated way because those systems are built on exploitation and oppression.

As we see from both the Hemp and Heritage Farm and Soul Fire Farm, groups aimed at regeneration possess keen awareness of the ways that their localized efforts are embedded within larger systems. By enriching and connecting to the different nodes within larger structures, these organizations exemplify pursuing alternatives within big systems—of "getting into the doughnut" and scaling up. They are doing the daily work on the ground, restoring soil and rematriating land and seeds, for instance—but they are also linking to broader coalitions and networks, both living within and working against larger political and economic systems. At multiple scales, then, they explore their own versions of safe and just spaces for humanity, where social equity and ecological well-being are prioritized and protected. But they also show how larger structures can act as barriers *or* as allies, accomplices, and conduits for change.

CONCLUSION

As these cases show, regenerative systems fight the third pillar of neoliberalism—practices of de- and reregulation that dis-embed markets from social and ecological protections. Regenerative systems embed markets into what is real—land, ecosystems, and relationships. Regeneration offers alternatives to existing systems. But it is a process rather than an outcome. It is always incomplete—that is the point.

Even in the middle of the oil patch in a deeply politically conservative county, people have growing awareness that building something better is humanity's only option for survival. Indigenized Energy models community-based progress away from centralized, colonial, fossil fuel–based control over energy production and toward systems that are owned cooperatively by and for Native communities, with intergenerational environmental justice as central goals. The Hemp and Heritage Farm and Honor the Earth build visionary components of just transitions. Through their Indigenous- and women-led efforts, they move past neoliberal systems and into a post-petroleum economy based in communities with hope, while using hemp cultivation to heal the soil and craft multiple plant-based goods. Soul Fire Farm illuminates how change and engagement can happen at multiple levels, attending at once to practical realities and to historical and contemporary structural and racial inequities. By rematriating land, healing soil, and creating spaces within the food system for Black, Indigenous, Latinx, and other minoritized farmers to heal from historical and current traumas, they tread paths toward regenerative growth.

These organizations certainly model local and regional experiments in new systems—bold experiments at that. But institutional change is complex, and it rarely emerges through small-scale organizations alone. To borrow Jacobson's analogy once again, these small groups can form "mycelial support networks" to inspire and mobilize shifts elsewhere, creating networks and coalitions of organizers with similar goals. As LaDuke said, starting small makes sense. But mycelial networks formed by these smaller-scale organizations have to be able to link to broader structures—eventually, ideally, into polity and formal systems.

They can form a solid doughnut for everyone to get into; but it is easier if there is something bigger to align with, including a bigger version of justice. Neoliberal norms and structures, as Jacobson and LaDuke both observed, antagonize equity, justice, and safety, and battling them constantly is tiring, expensive, and time-consuming.

So we leave you with this: multi-scalar approaches help local changes take hold. The strong mycelial networks of smaller organizations root better when they have firm soil supporting their growth and regeneration, though. Part of the work, then, is envisioning how these smaller groups can connect with system-wide changes.[48] Black Lives Matter protests, for instance, have birthed a campaign to defund the police and focus on community-based public safety; but those ideas did not emerge overnight. Rather, they came from many years of community work and organizing, bursting forth in moments of political urgency. Similar work has been happening in these spaces—and is also ready to burst forth, at a time when it is desperately needed. As LaDuke said, "[They] didn't end the stone age because they ran out of rocks. We gotta be moving on, and it's all about who controls the change."

7 · CONCLUSION
Building Something Better

In october 2020—several weeks before the presidential election and as we were finishing the first draft of this book—police in Providence, Rhode Island, hit a young Black man on his moped with a cruiser. The man's name was Jhamal Gonsalves. Three days later, hundreds of masked protesters filled the street on an eerily warm late fall day; nineteen were arrested, and tensions ran high. As we finished our writing, the officer involved was put on desk duty, but no charges against him had been filed, and the interlocking crises of racism, climate change, and a global pandemic continued to unfurl in this small city.

Around that same time in Colorado, wildfires took over hundreds of thousands of acres. Each successive fire set new records, becoming the largest in Colorado's history. One fire burned about one hundred thousand acres in a matter of hours. Fire engulfed forests made vulnerable by beetle-killed pine, warmer temperatures, and severe drought conditions—all related to the climate crisis. Mountain towns were evacuated, ash fell from the sky, and the new reality of climate change set in as midafternoon looked like a strange orange-gray twilight. Rocky Mountain National Park was closed, along with all national forests in several counties. The most vulnerable evacuees, forced into crowded shelters, were exposed to COVID-19—which was simultaneously escalating again. As we finished our writing, many were not able to return home, return to their jobs, or rebuild. And even with the fires over for the moment, it was uncertain whether the forests would grow back, what the water quality impacts would be, and what was ahead as drought conditions continued. Here, too, climate crises, environmental injustice, and global pandemic intertwined in devastating ways.

As we completed the second draft of the book in 2021, things looked somewhat different: the Joe Biden–Kamala Harris administration had forcefully articulated a commitment to tackling climate crises; Derek Chauvin was convicted in George Floyd's murder; various components of the American Rescue Plan infused states with infrastructure and public health dollars; and other safety net supports were under serious consideration. A COVID-19 vaccine was available.

We finished writing in early June, putting the finishing touches on a book filled with alternatives—explorations of how things might change and examples of how they already are changing—and even still, the world's grimness remained on full display. The year to date had broken heat records; the Northeast was already in a drought, and so was much of the West. Just eighteen weeks into 2021, the United States had already experienced 194 mass shootings—averaging about 10 per week.[1]

This entwining—of progress and crises, of crises and progress—remains something that we live, to different degrees and in different ways, on a daily basis. The paradoxical discomfort is part of many people's realities. And from this bizarre, critical inflection point, it is clear that no decision—indeed, no work—is straightforward, clear-cut, or without contradictions.

The case studies we have presented in this book offer insights into how different communities step out of existing systems, living into a world of different possibilities. Deeply related to rejecting and dismantling capitalism comes the complementary project of decolonization—of acknowledging the ways that historical and continuing colonialism facilitated white supremacy, deep inequalities, and abundant environmental injustices.[2] At the same time, the data here show that extractivism and limitless growth cannot provide sustainable, equitable paths forward for current or future generations or for more-than-humans. Instead, these cases illustrate collective interdependence of humanity—on one another, on past and future generations, on more-than-humans, and on the ecological systems that undergird life.

Each of the communities profiled in this book has shown how to look at histories: to understand them, learn from them, and then recenter just action to tread paths out of this quagmire. The Havasupai Tribal nation, the Hemp and Heritage Farm, and the coalition of San Francisco Bay Area organizations, for instance, orient their work around Indigenous and women-led knowledge, elevation of more-than-humans, water as a relation, and prioritization of intergenerational equity. They also remind us of the vital role that people can play, and have played, as Water Protectors. Street bands show us how to democratize and take back privatized urban spaces with celebratory and musical activism. Youth movements illustrate the power of young people's active pursuit of climate justice, their systemic thinking, and their political savvy. Indigenized Energy, the Hemp and Heritage Farm, and Soul Fire Farm are examples of building community-centered, community-powered distributive and regenerative systems. They show how to decolonize systems of energy and food, even as they illustrate how to move away from extractivism.

And while these groups reckon with historical and contemporary inequities in their own ways and on different scales, they also deal with the difficulties of being embedded in larger systems that are still deeply capitalist and market-centered.[3] They all face uncertainties about whether and how to scale up and how to exist within big neoliberal systems that can feel all-consuming. The organizers who we interviewed are clear that, while their interventions are typically at the community level, they require some connection to institutional and, indeed, political structures at larger scales.

So, here we offer one final case study to illustrate how one community has approached restoration and the challenges of institutional transformation. And this case study makes an especially important point: it engages deeply in processes of *restoration* and *amends*. The lesson is this: nothing can be fixed without each person and community acknowledging how we got here and changing those patterns. Only by understanding the past and taking responsibility for it can these sorts of efforts succeed in the present—at multiple scales and in many different communities.

Restorative justice practices offer one model for how to build more *socially distributive and regenerative systems*. The term "restorative justice" refers to a wide array of concepts, but at its center is the idea that crimes and wrongs can be addressed in more mediation-based, people-centered, and thickly democratic ways—that communities can, to some degree, restore what has been lost or taken. Restorative justice is a practice aimed at repairing harm done. Restoration can happen in meetings, it can happen in other facilitated settings, and it can also happen by restructuring larger systems and ideas of punishment and reconciliation. In the United States, the concept is most frequently used in relation to issues of crime—bringing together victims, offenders, and community members. But the concept is bigger than that; it emphasizes accountability, amends, and fairer systems. And it can apply to many kinds of social and relational spaces. The approach—based on trusting, respectful, and nonviolent human relationships—can be used at multiple social scales and in many spaces, from families and households to neighborhood conflicts, schools, government agencies, and even entire cities. Smaller groups and lower-level conflicts can be dealt with in discussion circles and with informal processes meant to build trust and empower people to communicate relationally and peacefully. Higher-level, more complex or historical conflicts can require more formal, structured processes and facilitation.

This translation across scales, spaces, and peoples is tricky—but doable. Scale matters in a deep sense. Looking at smaller scales of interaction and community can help people envision systems that might better address the needs for consensus and restorative approaches to justice at the level of the state (or even internationally!). Restorative justice has also become central to environmental justice efforts.[4] Here, we offer a short case study of Whanganui, New Zealand—a place working to build what it calls a restorative city. This case shows how one city is continually reckoning with a colonial past and working to scale up transformative community-building.

We note, of course, that the restorative city model is not the only way to do restorative work. Around the world, conversations are unfolding about how to acknowledge the past while building better futures. Those conversations range from restorative justice, to reliance on Traditional Ecological Knowledge (or Native science), to reparations for racial violence done over time, to gender quotas in public representation, to universal basic income and other progressive policies and practices that seek to equitably integrate the past with the present.[5] Universal basic income may end up being one of the most promising solutions for realizing environmental justice, since it de-commodifies people and opens up more democratic access to safety nets. But it is just one approach in a sea of options. There is no silver bullet that will simultaneously right the wrongs of colonialism, sexism, racism, and environmental breakdown—nor the compounded crises that emerge as a result of their intersections. Justice and knowledge are contextual—and the context often has complex, fraught layers.

RESTORATIVE CITY MODELS AND THE WHANGANUI RESTORATIVE JUSTICE TRUST

The Whanganui Restorative Justice Trust shows just how intricate and delicate the process of building restorative systems can be—and also what possibilities may exist when people unleash their collective imagination. Like the United States, New Zealand is a settler colony, and it has a violent and fraught history with the Indigenous Māori people who inhabited Aotearoa long before it was called New Zealand. This illustration—the final one we offer in our book—is about restorative practices that support justice amid intersecting injustices.

The Whanganui Restorative Justice Trust (also called the Whanganui Restorative Practices Trust) was formed in 1999 and then established as a nongovernmental organization (NGO) in 2012 with the goal of scaling up—expanding restorative approaches to other institutions and social systems in the city. The trust helps guide an entire city through complex, time-intensive processes of putting restorative justice principles into action. Whanganui is one of the few cities in the world working to become a restorative city—by building restorative institutions; restorative justice approaches to criminal justice, school systems, workplaces, and governance interactions; and sustainable, Indigenous-led, and multigenerational environmental policies. The trust works to "creat[e] the environment for all Whanganui people to thrive and succeed together through respectful relationships."[6]

Relationships, or relational dynamics, lie at the heart of restorative justice principles that the trust teaches about and uses.[7] Its restorative practices, derived from those principles, are designed to heal relationships in which parties have been harmed in some way—and these harms range from small interpersonal misunderstandings to serious harm, like crimes and historical oppressions. The goals are peaceful relationships embedded in more sustainable, equitable systems. These efforts are best scaled up beyond small groups when operating within safe and calm contexts where people are treated with respect and dignity, different cultural identities are recognized and equally valued, and all people can take responsibility for their actions. Metrics for success in a restorative city, meanwhile, are also assessed by markers of social justice, including decreased child abuse and other forms of domestic abuse and violence; decreased absenteeism in workplaces and schools; higher academic achievement; increased satisfaction with and trust in government organizations and NGOs; a greater sense of community cohesion and belonging; and a stronger sense of being safe at home and in the community.[8] The Whanganui Restorative Justice Trust belongs to a coalition that includes other places aspiring to become restorative sites as well, including Vermont in the United States; Wellington, New Zealand; Canberra, Australia; Halifax, Nova Scotia, Canada; and Leeds and Hull in the United Kingdom.

We interviewed two leaders of the Whanganui Restorative Justice Trust: Jenny Saywood, a founding member of the trust in the 1990s and current chair of the trustees, and Debra Smith, the coordinator for Whanganui restorative practices. They both recognized that institutionalizing restorative justice requires immense patience and time, working through many different levels in society, and that it is ultimately something to be strived for yet never perfectly realized. Their work began in Whanganui as part of criminal justice reform in youth courts, eventually expanding to adult criminal justice approaches. These initiatives were so successful that local judges, Saywood, and others saw its potential beyond criminal justice.

The trust has worked since 1999 to bring these models into the wider community. The project has always been about more than solving conflicts, more than reforming only the criminal justice system; the entire community and its varied institutions had to get involved in creating positive transformation. As Saywood observed, the interconnections that could be achieved could transform other spaces, too, as these approaches rely on "this idea that we're all interconnected, and we need each other. I had applied it to what we were trying to do [in earlier criminal justice work]. So that was a useful sort of connection, really, that communities can only be healthy when people are all working together and have a voice and a value."

When she joined in the 2000s after transitioning from her work as a clinical pharmacist, Smith saw immense potential for this approach to heal communities and practitioners. She explained: "One of the reasons why I want to stick with this work ... is that it has the potential to be really responsive. ... We are able to enact something for our community that is quite free, and it's an empowering way to work as opposed to working in a large organization or a large institution. ... That's one of the other reasons why this work is so captivating—not only can you see potential for positive change, I see the teacher being really affected in that positive change." She went on to explain the role that intergenerational justice played in restorative work: "I saw the need for all of our community leaders to know how to use restorative practices as an everyday tool. . . . I want to help build this future for our children and the community around our families."

These realizations helped the trust shift to broader restorative practices by 2012 as the members realized how to move beyond a conflict-based approach. Saywood explained:

> There were a lot of really good things about the approach. So we thought, "Well . . . we can take it out into the community." And we got stuck. . . . We thought: "How do we do it? And what are we actually doing this for?" We got hooked on thinking about conflict all the time, and about how we would use this process to address conflict. That's negative, and we thought people weren't really grasping it. And most people thought, "Well, we haven't got victims and offenders . . . so it won't apply to us."

Saywood continued, assessing their breakthrough about process as they envisioned what they wanted to *build*, as opposed to focusing solely on conflict they wanted to *avoid*:

> So we had to rethink that—and think about what it was that we were really wanting to do—which was creating a healthy community where people would address each other respectfully and understand each other. And so, there was more to it than just this idea that we would use the process for addressing conflict. It was more about building healthy societies to create a cohesive society where when things went wrong, people were more resilient.

This approach aligned with, and drew from, the ways Indigenous Māori communities interacted socially and with more-than-human relations. Smith observed that the trust had "done a lot of work around decolonization as an organization and recognizing the importance of partnership." Saywood also explained: "Indigenous practices aligned with restorative approaches. So our Mother Earth and the connection with the people and everything that is part of that has its ecological nodes. It's acknowledging the synergies of our ecology and people living in it." These synergies—understood as relationships—form the crux of the work.

So, restorative approaches, in this perspective, also must consider the ways that rivers, mountains, and other relations are treated and perceived. And Māori communities led these efforts. The Whanganui River, for instance, has recently been recognized as having human rights—the same rights as people of the Māori Indigenous community and specifically the Whanganui iwi (tribe), who call the river the Te Awa Tupua. Though these efforts have been about so much more than achieving legal personhood for the Whanganui, this legal strategy provided the closest approximation to conveying the intrinsic value and centrality of the river to Māori life. The Māori have been working for over 140 years to negotiate this recognition, given that the river is seen as an ancestor from whom they originate. While this legal designation has been made for other bodies of water since then, it marked the first time in the world that a river was granted this sort of status—the right to thrive and exist with the same rights and standing as a legally recognized person.[9] The Whanganui River thus has to be defended and protected legally as a living being. And the Whanganui Tribe of the Māori now has significant resources to institutionalize this revolutionary legal agreement.

This case illustrates how communities can begin to take responsibility for the harms of the past and work at multiple scales to restore and transform those relationships. It is also an important illustration of how community-based work can reshape citywide and even regional institutions in settler colonies, transforming them away from the colonial, patriarchal, and capitalist systems that have created layered injustices. Their mechanisms for building procedural equity, trust, and intergenerational and interspecies recognition can happen within neighborhoods and also within nation-states. The work is not easy. It will not—and it should not—look the same everywhere. But it does offer some options for thinking through more inclusive futures, and it enlivens hope in a fraught and chaotic time.

RELATIONSHIPS, ACTIVE HOPE, AND JUSTICE

As detailed in the introductory chapter, each case presented in this book gives examples of communities building something better—transforming their own relationships among people, with the Earth, and with more-than-humans. Similar themes run through many of them, as we have discussed: each addresses capitalism and the inequality it has generated. Each shows how identity matters most when fused with collective and historical contexts—and that intergenerational equity and reciprocity must be fundamental goals for social transformation. Each prioritizes noneconomic concerns; each rejects racism and sexism; each considers structure and systems while also focusing on a clear set of community-level goals. In each case study, we see engagement with context and place, we see attentiveness to intersecting experiences, and we see how these deeply grassroots organizations build coalitions and eschew professionalization. The work done is emotive and affective; groups work with their relationships and connections to one another, seeing in them significant power to transform.

One of the most important questions we face, though, is how neoliberal societies like the United States—and a neoliberal international order like the one shaping many people's lives—can quickly and holistically retool enough to sustain life amid climate crises. But that question reveals another, deeper question: *Are people capable of reimagining the world to prioritize our relationships with one another and with the planet, instead of our relationships to wealth?* Each case study within this book answers this question affirmatively—but they all model paths forward that require substantive and significant transformation beyond neoliberal ideologies, policies, and cultural norms to do so. Each group has started doing this work—toward systems, structures, relationships, and lives that are fundamentally more balanced, reciprocal, and whole.

This is where the insights from scholarship can help with community organizing. Research from within sociology has shown that strong, loving, reciprocal relationships can move mountains—and that *community organizations* are the driving logistic and organizing forces behind social change.[10] One clear example is the U.S. civil rights movement, which was built on the organizational and community structure of Black churches. All of our case studies show the same thing: that relationships (with other humans and with more-than-humans) constitute the core of this work. Indeed, community groups are usually the *only* forces moving mountains. Politics tends to lag behind community organizing, not lead it. And right now, we have some serious mountains that need moving— political, economic, social, ontological, and ecological.

The central idea from much sociological research, then, is that people are much more likely to take risks for the other people, communities, and natural spaces that we love: we will sit in for them, march for them, risk arrest, or run for office to ensure a better world for them. And the structures we build around the communities that we love—our congregations, our parenting groups, our neighborhood groups—can be the backbone of the political work that needs doing. Those groups give us strength, fuse our identities to something bigger, hold us accountable, and make logistics easier—in large part because we already care about and trust people within them. In these spaces, the restorative work we highlighted earlier can happen more organically. Nonpolitical groups help build relationships that can be transferred to organizing work[11]—and the power of the people is much more easily evoked when we are fighting for, and alongside, those we love. Indeed, this may just be the secret ingredient in learning to think intergenerationally, expansively, and transformatively.

But what do those connections actually look like for most of us? A 2018 study showed that the average American had not made a new friend in five years, and more than one-fifth of people in the United States always or often feel lonely[12]—a problem that has recently reached the status of a public health crisis. There are many reasons for this, but it suggests that *one of the first and most obvious steps anyone can take is to connect with other people—by making new relationships and strengthening existing ones.* Have a drink with a colleague after work. Write letters for a local political campaign; check on an elderly neighbor; walk your dog with a friend. Global pandemics complicate these efforts, of course; but people's creative innovations for connecting with one another even amid COVID-19 have shown us just how determined human beings are to remain social and connected to others. So seek others out; no problem is solved alone, especially not problems as big as these.

Organizing collectives and collective action are at the heart of this. Organizing is a process, it looks different from one context to the next, and it has to be done with other people.[13] It is messy, tedious, frequently vexing, and daunting for cultures conditioned to crave instant gratification. But *organizing—working with others to change systems*—is what defines each case we have presented in this book. At the core of all these organizations, as different as they may be, is people getting together, hammering out a vision for change, and doing the tough work of transforming the world around them—for the sake of other people and more-than-humans.

One challenge within sociological, political, and economic environments so focused on humans alone is expanding and evolving that love for others to include not only more people but also more-than-human relations. The trick is learning and relearning humanity's connection with the world outside the built environment and expanding people's thinking to make this part of how teaching, learning, and action happen in all institutions. The task becomes evolving beyond worldviews that emphasize separation from and domination of nature, of perceiving nature as something "out there." It also means fighting the urge to surrender to business as usual, fighting the urge to give up as climate crises and other existential dilemmas encroach from all directions. As Potawatomi scientist and writer Robin Wall Kimmerer reminds us, love and action matter here, too, perhaps the most; when extended to more-than-human communities, the power of love and reciprocity can enliven and enlighten even the darkest contexts. She says:

> Despair is paralysis. It robs us of agency. It blinds us to our own power and the power of the Earth. . . . But how can we submit to despair when the land is saying "Help"? Restoration is a powerful antidote to despair. Restoration offers concrete means by which humans can once again enter into positive, creative relationships with the more-than-human world, meeting responsibilities that are simultaneously material and spiritual. It's not enough to grieve. It's not enough to just stop doing bad things. . . . Here is where our most challenging and rewarding work lies, in restoring a relationship of respect, responsibility, and reciprocity. And love.[14]

As people have withdrawn socially, many have also withdrawn indoors. Those in industrialized nations have become an "indoor species," spending about 90 percent of their time inside—with some dire consequences for psychological, sociological, and spiritual well-being, including "species loneliness," where people feel "estrangement from the rest of Creation."[15] *This suggests that the second step people can take involves connecting with the more-than-human world,* whatever that means in different contexts. Get out for a walk or a hike; eat a meal on the grass or on a patio; sit or camp with the trees and be still; plant a garden in pots on your porch; or hang out on the fire escape and take in the cityscape. Look at the stars from a mountaintop or a rooftop.

Some cultures have never forgotten how to do this. Some younger generations, too, have put words around this shift, and they try to explicitly reject loneliness and materialism. This premise—that humans are far less exceptional than we often think, and far more dependent on more-than-humans than society likes to recognize—is only recently accepted in sociology and still less in mainstream politics. It is readily accepted, though, in the organizations and organizing we have showcased here.

But even with a more expansive understanding of interconnectedness, big transitions are rocky—especially in mainstream political, economic, and cultural life. Weaning ourselves from dead-end systems necessarily requires support for the most vulnerable—what is often called a *just transition*. That is: crises can offer opportunities to rethink systems, but only when people have one another's backs and when people create institutions that put supports in place to help everyone weather hard times.

For instance, food is plentiful and cheap in wealthy parts of the world because prices are kept down by massive subsidies for large operators, massive quantities of fertilizer, and industrial farming practices.[16] Those same practices are heavily dependent on fossil fuels, both directly and indirectly—in energy use for fertilizers, pesticides, and machinery production.[17] To transition away from that—to more sustainable kinds of farming, for instance, that do not leave the soil dead for future generations—requires that states and communities support those who are likely to struggle when food prices rise as productivity declines. This is fully *possible*: research has found that a decline in world energy production could be accommodated by state support for agriculture and sustainable practices.[18] But to be *doable*, such transformations require structural support for investment in public safety nets, and a lot of it—both in the agricultural systems themselves and in people's well-being as systems transform. COVID-19 has given rise to some similar experiments; for instance, Chelsea, Massachusetts, piloted a universal basic income program for its lowest-income residents in 2020, addressing the havoc of the pandemic, and Stockton, California, initiated a similar program in 2019.[19] Amsterdam has initiated an economic transformation based on Doughnut Economics. The idea here is that transitions need to be supported by collective and embedded systems. These transitions persist and thrive at multiple scales only when there is a larger mycelial network with which to connect.

The third point we want to make here is that Politics—with a capital "P"—matter, and they require community participation. In the United States, for instance, the health of democracy matters, and it matters especially at regional, state, and local levels, where political action is often more sensitive to the needs of constituents and less gridlocked than federal politics. This is an important insight related to our discussions of scaling up, but one we have spent relatively little time on in this book, as focused as we have been on community-based action. (It is also odd, since Meghan spends so much of her time in explicitly political arenas.)

But our point is this: community-based knowledge and organizing exist within larger structures and contexts—and there still is considerable promise within U.S. democracy for shaping larger contexts. The many small systems we have explored here are both bound to that larger system and powerful within that larger system. Although we have focused on community-level work, we wish to underscore what most of our interviewees have said: *all* of the work matters, at each scale. Political and policy organizing can be less satisfying than community-based work because it takes longer and requires a lot more compromise (as our interviews with the divestment activists illustrated). But it is still crucially important. There are still opportunities within democracy to shape large-scale political contexts and to strengthen them through engagement, collective vision, and love. With record numbers of women and Black, Indigenous, and other people of color running for office at all levels, this democracy is poised to become a more inclusive and representative system. The wave of new recruits to office has also inspired hope among many. And currently, this democracy— with all its flaws and room for improvement remains a very important tool that the United States has to enforce some of the regulations and incentives required to pull us back from the climate crisis cliff.[20]

Fourth, hope matters. Specifically, we assert—following thinkers like Joanna Macy, Chris Johnstone, and Rebecca Solnit[21]—that hope is an *active* process. It is feeling that is linked with doing. Passive hope is about waiting for external forces to bring about what we desire. Active hope is about *becoming* participants in bringing about the things we want; active hope is about agency, participation, organizing, and empathy. It is about *doing* that restoration work we discussed. Hope is a practice; it is something we do rather than something we have. As a practice, hope can be applied to any situation by taking a clear and empathic view of reality, identifying what we hope for, and taking steps in that direction. Since hope, by this definition, does not require optimism, we can practice it even when we feel hopeless—it is about intention, as well as about outcome.[22]

Democracy and community organizing are sticky issues for many reasons, and one of them is that the process and the outcome are blended. Certainly for some classic writers like Alexis de Tocqueville, democracy *transforms* people even as it creates political outcomes.[23] The same thing is true of efforts to re-envision social systems in this time of crisis: some of our case studies focus on the distributive *outcomes* of (in)justice; some focus on regenerative *processes* of justice. These two dynamics link, but they are not identical.

This is the beauty of the cases profiled in this book—they demonstrate how communities engage multiple strands of environmental justice in various stages and at different scales, from distributive to procedural and from practicing recognition to working on restoration. They illustrate different ways, then, in which communities are getting into that safe and just space, that doughnut. These cases highlight instances of communities collectively engaged in *processes* of dismantling neoliberalism's most harmful tenets—of doing the work focused on equity, of honoring human and ecological systems and participants. They show emergent *outcomes* as well—what equitable, distributive, regenerative systems can look like, where (all kinds of) wealth, comfort, safety, and control belong to everyone.

The relationship between process and outcome brings to light *a fifth insight: the question of time*. Social change takes place over both long and short terms. In our graduate classes especially, both of us teach our students to identify systems and systemic effects—indeed, we have just written a whole book about systems. Systemic analysis is the crux of sociology. What we *do not* want to encourage, however, is a focus on systems that ignores the current realities of people within those systems and within shorter time frames. In other words, it is all well and good to push for systemic change—as so many social movements do (rightfully, in our opinion) and as we, as scholars and organizers (and for one of us, as a politician), also clearly do. However, it is also crucially important to recognize and honor that systemic change is a long-term goal, and there are lots of ways people can suffer before it is realized. For instance, building more affordable housing is critical and can be accomplished over the span of a few years. Yet, it is also critical to recognize that *right now*, thousands of families in the United States live in cars and need safe places to park at night and access to bathrooms. Short-term realities matter even as we seek long-term change. And, to return to one of our early and essential points: the perfect cannot be the enemy of the good as people work toward changes at multiple levels.

The work of building better systems is slow, and it is decidedly less glamorous than pointing out systemic problems. Ignoring or discounting immediate needs in exclusive pursuit of systemic change is a failing strategy. Both must happen simultaneously.

This leads us to our final observation: there is no silver bullet. Social change is a complex process that needs work on all fronts—it is unpredictable, and only part of it is under human control in the best of times. Find where you feel best and plug in—and remember that everything is interconnected. We cannot have a conversation about schools without also talking about race; we cannot talk about politics without talking about women's representation; we cannot talk about climate without talking about labor. We must both build up good things and break down bad things. We must make amends while also re-envisioning alternatives. As we said in the introduction to this book, these processes are linked. We need everybody's good ideas to get through what humanity faces. And every little transformative, hopeful effort and action helps build something better.

"Hope," Rebecca Solnit wrote in *Hope in the Dark*, "is not a lottery ticket you can sit on the sofa and clutch, feeling lucky. It is an axe you break down doors with in an emergency."[24]

Hope is an active process—let's get to it.

ACKNOWLEDGMENTS

FROM BOTH AUTHORS

We owe a tremendous debt of gratitude to the people who lent us their time and expertise as we developed this book. The members of communities and organizations we interviewed were exceptionally generous with their perspectives—and this book would lack richness and depth without their contributions and insights. Thank you to Alissa Cordner, Dave Ciplet, and Jill Harrison for your time, your heartfelt and thoughtful feedback, and your brilliant analytical minds. You have helped shape this book. India Luxton, Thalia Viveros-Uehara, and Micaela Truslove, thank you for your support, spectacular attention to detail, keen intelligence, and overall support of the manuscript. To our editor, Peter Mickulas, and the series editor, Scott Frickel—thank you for your support of and belief in this project and your principled leadership of this series.

FROM STEPHANIE

I feel immense gratitude to many people and organizations for supporting me as we wrote this book. We talk a good deal about "mycelial networks" here—and I would not be able to survive without my own network of professional and personal connections that keep me going. First, thank you to Meghan for being a spectacular collaborator, friend, sociologist, and political force! Though the pandemic stopped us from getting all the in-person writing retreats we wanted, the ones we enjoyed were lovely. And co-creating with you is a joy. I hope this is the beginning of many projects.

Thank you to the institutions that inspire and support me as a scholar, including my home, the Department of Sociology at Colorado State University; the Center for Environmental Justice at CSU, which I cofounded as we wrote; the Colorado School of Public Health; and the Colorado Water Center and School of Global Environmental Sustainability at CSU. Thank you as well to Brown University, Utah State University's sociology folks, the Western Rural Development Center, and the mentors who helped me get my footing during my graduate training and postdoc—especially Phil Brown, Peggy Petrzelka, Christy Glass, and John Allen. My colleagues and friends in these circles have made my work life fun, productively challenging, and collegial—which makes me happy to continue in a profession that at times can be all-consuming. These institutions and relationships have empowered me to focus on examining the relationships among people, the planet, and more-than-humans, and I am grateful because I am lucky to do what I do.

The oil and gas data shared in this book were supported in part by the Rural Sociological Society's Early Career Research Award and the Colorado Water Center and as part of a multi-year, multi-community study funded by the National Institute of Environmental Health Sciences (NIEHS) (grant R21-ES025140-01). And while any opinions, findings, conclusions, or recommendations expressed in this material are mine and not theirs, their research support has been vital to the early part of my career.

On a personal note, I want to thank my little family—Matt, Logan, and our herding dog, Jasper—for their patience and support. Completing a book manuscript during a pandemic, while pregnant and then with a new baby, and without consistent child care, has been a feat that would not have been possible without my husband's unwavering partnership. Thank you also, Matt, for spending so much time with me outside—camping, hiking, and going on family walks. That is where I get some of my best ideas, and the fresh mountain air does not hurt, either. Even Jasper chipped in, spending countless hours and many late nights right next to me as I worked; I am pretty sure he thinks *he* has written a book or at least made sure the UPS delivery person did not steal my laptop. Thank you to my parents and Matt's, too, for their love and willingness to quarantine and then spend many weeks in Fort Collins, helping with Logan so I could work on this book (and everything else). I am also deeply grateful for a loving, funny, grounded circle of family and friends who give life color and laughter and remind me to relax here and there.

Thank you, everyone!

FROM MEGHAN

My community offered up its best self to me during this project, the writing of which entwined with so many other issues—ranging from global public health crises to elections. If it is true that we count time by heartthrobs and live in deeds rather than years, then the groups of people who surround me have given a decade's worth of support to this project!

Being able to collaborate with friends is one of the great joys and privileges of being in the academy, and I am deeply, deeply fortunate to have been able to write this book with Stephanie. May it be the first of many such projects!

My colleagues at the School for Global Inclusion and Social Development at the University of Massachusetts Boston have been everything that I could have asked for—and more—during this project-within-a-pandemic. Their feedback is always generative and generous, and I count myself as forever fortunate to be teaching in a program so deeply committed to applied and justice-focused knowledge.

I am very grateful to the institutions and people that have supported my development and scholarship over the course of my career—including UMass Boston,

Brown University, and the National Science Foundation, among others. Some of the research presented in this book—the data on street bands—was supported by the inaugural Wilczenski Faculty Research Award at UMass Boston's College of Education and Human Development.

I am grateful to my network of academic colleagues, especially Ora Szekely, Scott Frickel, Sindiso Mnisi Weeks, Valerie Karr, and Carrie Oelberger, for collectively helping create collaborative, feminist, justice-based approaches to scholarship and academic life. I am grateful to my network of political colleagues, especially Dawn Euer and Sandra Cano, for helping model the kind of (environmental) policy work that will get us where we need to go. I am grateful to my network of friends, especially Kassie Stovall, Zoe Gardner, Mike Gore, Jess Brown, Jay O'Hara, Josephine Ferorelli, and Nathan Ackroyd, for making the journey loving, joyful, and musical.

NOTES

1. INTRODUCTION

1. Gurminder K. Bhambra and John Holmwood, *Colonialism and Modern Social Theory* (Cambridge, UK: Polity, 2021); Crystal Marie Fleming, "No Fucks to Give: Dismantling the Respectability Politics of White Supremacist Sociology," in *The New Black Sociologists: Historical and Contemporary Perspectives*, ed. Marcus Anthony Hunter (New York: Routledge, 2018), 131–145.

2. Stephen Steinberg, "Decolonizing Sociology," *Stanford University Press Blog* (blog), 2020, https://stanfordpress.typepad.com/blog/2016/08/decolonizing-sociology.html.

3. Simbarashe Gukurume and Godfrey Maringira, "Decolonising Sociology: Perspectives from Two Zimbabwean Universities," *Third World Thematics: A TWQ Journal* 5, no. 1–2 (March 3, 2020): 60–78.

4. Raewyn Connell, "Decolonizing Sociology," *Contemporary Sociology* 47, no. 4 (July 1, 2018): 399–407.

5. Aldon D. Morris, *The Scholar Denied: W.E.B. Du Bois and the Birth of Modern Sociology* (Oakland: University of California Press, 2015).

6. Steinberg, "Decolonizing Sociology."

7. Charles W. Mills, *The Racial Contract* (Ithaca, NY: Cornell University Press, 2014), 18–19.

8. Patricia Hill Collins, "Intersectionality's Definitional Dilemmas," *Annual Review of Sociology* 41 (2015): 1–20; Nikol G. Alexander-Floyd, "Disappearing Acts: Reclaiming Intersectionality in the Social Sciences in a Post–Black Feminist Era," *Feminist Formations* (2012): 1–25.

9. Kimberlé Crenshaw, "Mapping the Margins: Intersectionality, Identity Politics, and Violence against Women of Color," *Stanford Law Review* 43, no. 6 (July 1991): 1241–1299; Kevin Duong, "What Does Queer Theory Teach Us about Intersectionality?," *Politics & Gender* 8, no. 3 (September 2012): 370–386; bell hooks, *Ain't I a Woman: Black Women and Feminism* (Boston: South End Press, 1981); Meghan Elizabeth Kallman, "The 'Male' Privilege of White Women, the 'White' Privilege of Black Women, and Vulnerability to Violence: An Intersectional Analysis of Peace Corps Workers in Host Countries," *International Feminist Journal of Politics* 21, no. 4 (August 8, 2019): 566–594; Anne McClintock, *Imperial Leather: Race, Gender, and Sexuality in the Colonial Contest* (New York: Routledge, 1995).

10. Patricia Hill Collins, "Black Feminist Thought in the Matrix of Domination," *Black Feminist Thought: Knowledge, Consciousness, and the Politics of Empowerment* 138, no. 1990 (1990): 221–238.

11. Celene Krauss, "Women and Toxic Waste Protests: Race, Class and Gender as Resources of Resistance," *Qualitative Sociology* 16, no. 3 (1993): 247–262; Kishi Animashaun Ducre, "The Black Feminist Spatial Imagination and an Intersectional Environmental Justice," *Environmental Sociology* 4, no. 1 (January 2, 2018): 22–35; Stephanie A. Malin and Stacia S. Ryder, "Developing Deeply Intersectional Environmental Justice Scholarship," *Environmental Sociology* 4, no. 1 (January 2, 2018): 1–7; Camila H. Alvarez and Clare Rosenfeld Evans, "Intersectional Environmental Justice and Population Health Inequalities: A Novel Approach," *Social Science & Medicine* 269 (2021): 1–12; Helma Lutz and Anna Amelina, "Intersectionality and Transnationality as Key Tools for Gender-Sensitive Migration Research," in *The Palgrave Handbook of Gender and Migration*, ed. Claudia Mora and Nicola Piper (Cham, Switzerland: Palgrave Macmillan, 2021): 55–72; Pierrette Hondagneu-Sotelo, "New Directions in Gender

and Immigration Research," in *The Routledge International Handbook of Migration Studies*, ed. Steven J. Gold and Stephanie J. Nawyn (London: Routledge, 2013), 180–188; Rhacel Salazar Parreñas, *Children of Global Migration: Transnational Families and Gendered Woes* (Stanford, CA: Stanford University Press, 2005); Rhacel Salazar Parreñas, "Migrant Filipina Domestic Workers and the International Division of Reproductive Labor," *Gender & Society* 14, no. 4 (August 2000): 560–580; Patricia Hill Collins and Sirma Bilge, *Intersectionality* (John Wiley & Sons, 2020); Hae Yeon Choo and Myra Marx Ferree, "Practicing Intersectionality in Sociological Research: A Critical Analysis of Inclusions, Interactions, and Institutions in the Study of Inequalities," *Sociological Theory* 28, no. 2 (2010): 129–149; Sumi Cho, Kimberlé Williams Crenshaw, and Leslie McCall, "Toward a Field of Intersectionality Studies: Theory, Applications, and Praxis," *Signs: Journal of Women in Culture and Society* 38, no. 4 (2013): 785–810.

12. Steinberg, "Decolonizing Sociology."

13. Gil Eyal, *The Crisis of Expertise* (Cambridge, UK: Polity, 2019).

14. Dorceta E. Taylor, "The Rise of the Environmental Justice Paradigm: Injustice Framing and the Social Construction of Environmental Discourses," *American Behavioral Scientist* 43, no. 4 (January 1, 2000): 508–580, 509.

15. Christen A. Smith et al., "Cite Black Women: A Critical Praxis (A Statement)," *Feminist Anthropology* (2021): 10–17.

16. Ali Meghji, *Decolonizing Sociology: An Introduction* (John Wiley & Sons, 2021); Alicia Izharuddin, "Does Sociology Need Decolonizing?," *International Sociology* 34, no. 2 (2019): 130–137; Connell, "Decolonizing Sociology"; Syed Farid Alatas and Vineeta Sinha, *Sociological Theory beyond the Canon* (Springer, 2017); Julian Go and George Lawson, eds., *Global Historical Sociology* (Cambridge University Press, 2017).

17. William R. Catton Jr. and Riley E. Dunlap, "Environmental Sociology: A New Paradigm," *American Sociologist* 13, no. 1 (February 1, 1978): 41–49.

18. Taylor, "Rise of the Environmental Justice Paradigm"; David N. Pellow, "Environmental Inequality Formation: Toward a Theory of Environmental Injustice," *American Behavioral Scientist* 43, no. 4 (2000): 581–601; Sharon L. Harlan et al., "Climate Justice and Inequality," *Climate Change and Society: Sociological Perspectives* (2015): 127–163; Theo LeQuesne, "Petro-hegemony and the Matrix of Resistance: What Can Standing Rock's Water Protectors Teach Us about Organizing for Climate Justice in the United States?," *Environmental Sociology* 5, no. 2 (2019): 188–206; Giovanna Di Chiro, "Acting Globally: Cultivating a Thousand Community Solutions for Climate Justice," *Development* 54, no. 2 (2011): 232–236; Elizabeth Hoover et al., "Indigenous Peoples of North America: Environmental Exposures and Reproductive Justice," *Environmental Health Perspectives* 120, no. 12 (2012): 1645–1649; Peggy M. Shepard, "Advancing Environmental Justice through Community-Based Participatory Research," *Environmental Health Perspectives* 110, suppl. 2 (2002): 139; Alice Fothergill and Lori Peek, *Children of Katrina* (University of Texas Press, 2015); David N. Pellow and Hollie Nyseth Brehm, "An Environmental Sociology for the Twenty-First Century," *Annual Review of Sociology* 39 (2013): 229–250; Alice Fothergill and Lori A. Peek, "Poverty and Disasters in the United States: A Review of Recent Sociological Findings," *Natural Hazards* 32, no. 1 (2004): 89–110.

19. Audre Lorde, "Learning from the 60s," in *Sister Outsider: Essays and Speeches* (Trumansburg, NY: Crossing Press, 1984), 134–144, 138.

20. C. Wright Mills, *The Sociological Imagination* (Oxford University Press, 2000), 5.

21. Crenshaw, "Mapping the Margins"; Nancy Fraser, "Roepke Lecture in Economic Geography—from Exploitation to Expropriation: Historic Geographies of Racialized Capitalism," *Economic Geography* 94, no. 1 (January 1, 2018): 1–17; McClintock, *Imperial Leather*; Satnam Virdee, "Racialized Capitalism: An Account of Its Contested Origins and Consolidation," *Sociological Review* 67, no. 1 (January 1, 2019): 3–27.

22. Rita Kaur Dhamoon, "A Feminist Approach to Decolonizing Anti-Racism: Rethinking Transnationalism, Intersectionality, and Settler Colonialism," *Feral Feminisms*, no. 4 (2015).

23. Kimberlé Crenshaw, "Demarginalizing the Intersection of Race and Sex: A Black Feminist Critique of Antidiscrimination Doctrine, Feminist Theory and Antiracist Politics," *University of Chicago Legal Forum* 1989 (1989): 139; Leslie McCall, "The Complexity of Intersectionality," *Signs* 30, no. 3 (2005): 1771–1800; Patricia Hill Collins, "It's All in the Family: Intersections of Gender, Race, and Nation," *Hypatia* 13, no. 3 (August 1, 1998): 62–82.

24. Combahee River Collective, "The Combahee River Collective Statement,"1977, unpaginated, https://combaheerivercollective.weebly.com/the-combahee-river-collective-statement .html.

25. Jennifer Daryl Slack, "The Theory and Method of Articulation in Cultural Studies," in *Stuart Hall: Critical Dialogues in Cultural Studies*, ed. David Morley and Kuan-Hsing Chen (New York: Routledge, 1996), 113–131; Collins and Bilge, *Intersectionality*; Ducre, "Black Feminist Spatial Imagination"; David Naguib Pellow, *What Is Critical Environmental Justice?* (John Wiley & Sons, 2017); Laura Pulido, "Rethinking Environmental Racism: White Privilege and Urban Development in Southern California," *Annals of the Association of American Geographers* 90, no. 1 (2000): 12–40.

26. Dorceta E. Taylor, *The Rise of the American Conservation Movement: Power, Privilege, and Environmental Protection* (Durham, NC: Duke University Press, 2016); Dorceta E. Taylor, "American Environmentalism: The Role of Race, Class and Gender in Shaping Activism, 1820–1995," *Race, Gender & Class* 5, no. 1 (1997): 16–62.

27. Cody Ferguson, *This Is Our Land: Grassroots Environmentalism in the Late Twentieth Century* (New Brunswick, NJ: Rutgers University Press, 2015).

28. Dorceta E. Taylor, "Introduction: The Evolution of Environmental Justice Activism, Research, and Scholarship," *Environmental Practice* 13, no. 4 (December 2011): 280–301, 286.

29. David Treuer, "Return the National Parks to the Tribes: The Jewels of America's Landscape Should Belong to America's Original Peoples," *Atlantic*, May 2021, https://www.theatlantic .com/magazine/archive/2021/05/return-the-national-parks-to-the-tribes/618395/; Kyle Powys Whyte, "Indigenous Experience, Environmental Justice and Settler Colonialism," SSRN Scholarly Paper (Rochester, NY: Social Science Research Network, April 25, 2016); Kyle Powys Whyte, "The Recognition Dimensions of Environmental Justice in Indian Country," *Environmental Justice* 4, no. 4 (2011): 199–205.

30. Dina Gilio-Whitaker, *As Long As Grass Grows: The Indigenous Fight for Environmental Justice, From Colonization to Standing Rock* (Boston: Beacon Press, 2019).

31. Norah Anita Schwartz et al., "'Where They (Live, Work, and) Spray': Pesticide Exposure, Childhood Asthma and Environmental Justice among Mexican-American Farmworkers," *Health & Place* 32 (2015): 83–92; Laura Pulido and Devon G. Peña, "Environmentalism and Positionality: The Early Pesticide Campaign of the United Farm Workers' Organizing Committee, 1965–71," *Race, Gender & Class* 6, no. 1 (1998): 33–50.

32. Giovanna Di Chiro, "Living Environmentalisms: Coalition Politics, Social Reproduction, and Environmental Justice," *Environmental Politics* 17, no. 2 (2008): 276–298; Krauss, "Women and Toxic Waste Protests."

33. Alnoor Ebrahim, "Accountability Myopia: Losing Sight of Organizational Learning," *Nonprofit and Voluntary Sector Quarterly* 34, no. 1 (March 1, 2005): 56–87; Angela M. Eikenberry and Jodie Drapal Kluver, "The Marketization of the Nonprofit Sector: Civil Society at Risk?," *Public Administration Review* 64, no. 2 (2004): 132–140; Hokyu Hwang and Walter W. Powell, "The Rationalization of Charity: The Influences of Professionalism in the Nonprofit Sector," *Administrative Science Quarterly* 54, no. 2 (June 1, 2009): 268–298; Meghan Elizabeth Kallman, "Encapsulation, Professionalization and Managerialism in the Peace Corps,"

International Public Management Journal (June 17, 2019): 1–30; Meghan Elizabeth Kallman, *The Death of Idealism: Development and Anti-Politics in the Peace Corps* (Columbia University Press, 2020).

34. Joan Acker, "Hierarchies, Jobs, Bodies: A Theory of Gendered Organizations," *Gender & Society* 4, no. 2 (June 1, 1990): 139–158; Eduardo Bonilla-Silva, *Racism without Racists: Color-Blind Racism and the Persistence of Racial Inequality in America*, 5th ed. (Lanham, MD: Rowman & Littlefield, 2018).

35. Mark E. Kann, *A Republic of Men: The American Founders, Gendered Language, and Patriarchal Politics* (NYU Press, 1998); Acker, "Hierarchies, Jobs, Bodies."

36. Michael A. Messner, Margaret Carlisle Duncan, and Kerry Jensen, "Separating the Men from the Girls: The Gendered Language of Televised Sports," *Gender & Society* 7, no. 1 (March 1, 1993): 121–137.

37. Verner D. Mitchell and Cynthia Davis, eds., *Encyclopedia of the Black Arts Movement* (Lanham, MD: Rowman & Littlefield, 2019).

38. Michelle Alexander, *The New Jim Crow: Mass Incarceration in the Age of Colorblindness* (New Press, 2012); Connie Hassett-Walker, "The Racist Roots of American Policing: From Slave Patrols to Traffic Stops," *Chicago Reporter*, June 7, 2019, Criminal Justice, https://www.chicagoreporter .com/the-racist-roots-of-american-policing-from-slave-patrols-to-traffic-stops/.

39. Gary Potter, "The History of Policing in the United States" (Eastern Kentucky University School of Justice Studies, 2020), https://ekuonline.eku.edu/blog/police-studies/the-history -of-policing-in-the-united-states-part-1/.

40. Reflective Democracy Campaign, "System Failure: What the 2020 Primary Elections Reveal about Our Democracy," 2021, https://wholeads.us/research/system-failure-2020-primary -elections/.

41. Lorde, "Learning from the 60s," 138.

2. A PEOPLE'S SOCIOLOGY

1. David L. Brunsma and Jennifer Padilla Wyse, "The Possessive Investment in White Sociology," *Sociology of Race and Ethnicity* 5, no. 1 (2019): 1–10; Daniel Hirschman and Laura Garbes, "Toward an Economic Sociology of Race," *Socio-Economic Review* 19, no. 3 (December 19, 2019): 1171–1199; Crystal Marie Fleming. "No Fucks to Give: Dismantling the Respectability Politics of White Supremacist Sociology," in *The New Black Sociologists: Historical and Contemporary Perspectives*, ed. Marcus Anthony Hunter (New York: Routledge, 2018), 131–145; Lynn McDonald, "Sociological Theory: The Last Bastion of Sexism in Sociology," *American Sociologist* 50, no. 3 (September 1, 2019): 402–413; Janet Saltzman Chafetz, "Feminist Theory and Sociology: Underutilized Contributions for Mainstream Theory," *Annual Review of Sociology* 23, no. 1 (1997): 97–120; Judith Stacey and Barrie Thorne, "The Missing Feminist Revolution in Sociology," *Social Problems* 32, no. 4 (1985): 301–316; Gurminder K. Bhambra and John Holmwood, *Colonialism and Modern Social Theory* (Cambridge, UK: Polity, 2021).

2. Intergovernmental Panel on Climate Change, "Global Warming of 1.5°C: An IPCC Special Report on the Impacts of Global Warming of 1.5°C above Pre-industrial Levels and Related Global Greenhouse Gas Emission Pathways, in the Context of Strengthening the Global Response to the Threat of Climate Change, Sustainable Development, and Efforts to Eradicate Poverty," 2018. https://www.ipcc.ch/site/assets/uploads/sites/2/2019/06/SR15_Full _Report_Low_Res.pdf.

3. Jason W. Moore, "Anthropocene or Capitalocene? Nature, History, and the Crisis of Capitalism," in *Anthropocene or Capitalocene? Nature, History, and the Crisis of Capitalism,*

ed. Jason W. Moore (PM Press/Kairos, 2016); Paul Griffin, "CDP Carbon Majors Report, 2017" (Carbon Majors Database and Climate Accountability Institute, 2017), 16; Rob Nixon, "The Great Acceleration and the Great Divergence: Vulnerability in the Anthropocene," *Profession*, Modern Language Association, March 2014, https://profession.mla.org/the-great -acceleration-and-the-great-divergence-vulnerability-in-the-anthropocene/.

4. Kyle Powys Whyte, "Our Ancestors' Dystopia Now: Indigenous Conservation and the Anthropocene," in *Routledge Companion to the Environmental Humanities*, ed. Ursula K. Heise, John Christensen, and Michelle Niemann (New York: Routledge, 2017), 206–215.

5. Eve Tuck and K. Wayne Yang, "Decolonization Is Not a Metaphor," *Decolonization: Indigeneity, Education & Society* 1, no. 1 (2012): 1–40.

6. Linda Tuhiwai Smith, *Decolonizing Methodologies: Research and Indigenous Peoples*, 2nd ed. (London: Zed Books, 2012); Raewyn Connell, "Decolonizing Sociology," *Contemporary Sociology* 47, no. 4 (July 1, 2018): 399–407; Joel Wainwright, *Decolonizing Development: Colonial Power and the Maya* (John Wiley & Sons, 2011); Ali Meghji, *Decolonizing Sociology: An Introduction* (Cambridge, UK: Polity Press, 2021).

7. Meghji, *Decolonizing Sociology*, chapter 1.

8. Phil Brown, Rachel Morello-Frosch, and Stephen Zavestoski, eds., *Contested Illnesses: Citizens, Science, and Health Social Movements* (University of California Press, 2011).

9. Connell, "Decolonizing Sociology," 400.

10. Paulin Hountondji, ed., *Endogenous Knowledge: Research Trails* (Dakar, Senegal: CODESRIA, African Books Collective, 1997).

11. Connell, "Decolonizing Sociology," 400.

12. Connell, "Decolonizing Sociology," 403.

13. Connell, "Decolonizing Sociology"; Julian Go, "For a Postcolonial Sociology," *Theory and Society* 42, no. 1 (January 1, 2013): 25–55; Stephanie A. Malin and Stacia S. Ryder, "Developing Deeply Intersectional Environmental Justice Scholarship," *Environmental Sociology* 4, no. 1 (January 2, 2018): 1–7.

14. Raoul S. Liévanos et al., "Challenging the White Spaces of Environmental Sociology," *Environmental Sociology* 7, no. 2 (2021): 103–109; Michael Warren Murphy, "Notes toward an Anticolonial Environmental Sociology of Race," *Environmental Sociology* 7, no. 2 (2021): 122–133; Michelle M. Jacob et al., "Indigenous Cultural Values Counter the Damages of White Settler Colonialism," *Environmental Sociology* 7, no. 2 (2021): 134–146; Tracy Perkins, "The Multiple People of Color Origins of the US Environmental Justice Movement: Social Movement Spillover and Regional Racial Projects in California," *Environmental Sociology* 7, no. 2 (2021): 147–159; Louise Seamster and Danielle Purifoy, "What Is Environmental Racism For? Place-Based Harm and Relational Development," *Environmental Sociology* 7, no. 2 (2021): 110–121; Laura Pulido, "Geographies of Race and Ethnicity II: Environmental Racism, Racial Capitalism and State-Sanctioned Violence," *Progress in Human Geography* 41, no. 4 (2017): 524–533; Kishi Animashaun Ducre, "The Black Feminist Spatial Imagination and an Intersectional Environmental Justice," *Environmental Sociology* 4, no. 1 (January 2, 2018): 22–35; Sirma Bilge, "Whitening Intersectionality," *Racism and Sociology* 5 (2014): 175; April Karen Baptiste and Hubert Devonish, "Freedom and/or Development? Scale and Intersectionality in an Industrial Public Debate," *Environmental Sociology* 4, no. 1 (January 2, 2018): 93–106; Brett Clark, Daniel Auerbach, and Karen Xuan Zhang, "The Du Bois Nexus: Intersectionality, Political Economy, and Environmental Injustice in the Peruvian Guano Trade in the 1800s," *Environmental Sociology* 4, no. 1 (January 2, 2018): 54–66; Ducre, "Black Feminist Spatial Imagination"; Elizabeth Hoover, "Environmental Reproductive Justice: Intersections in an American Indian Community Impacted by Environmental Contamination," *Environmental Sociology* 4, no. 1 (January 2, 2018): 8–21; Catherine Jampel, "Intersections of Disability Justice, Racial Justice, and

Environmental Justice," *Environmental Sociology* 4, no. 1 (January 2, 2018): 122–135; Michelle L. Larkins, "Complicating Communities: An Intersectional Approach to Women's Environmental Justice Narratives in the Rocky Mountain West," *Environmental Sociology* 4, no. 1 (January 2, 2018): 67–78; Theo LeQuesne, "Petro-hegemony and the Matrix of Resistance: What Can Standing Rock's Water Protectors Teach Us about Organizing for Climate Justice in the United States?," *Environmental Sociology* 5, no. 2 (2019): 188–206; Rachel G. McKane et al., "Race, Class, and Space: An Intersectional Approach to Environmental Justice in New York City," *Environmental Sociology* 4, no. 1 (January 2, 2018): 79–92; Anja Nygren and Gutu Wayessa, "At the Intersections of Multiple Marginalisations: Displacements and Environmental Justice in Mexico and Ethiopia," *Environmental Sociology* 4, no. 1 (January 2, 2018): 148–161; Lauren Richter, "Constructing Insignificance: Critical Race Perspectives on Institutional Failure in Environmental Justice Communities," *Environmental Sociology* 4, no. 1 (January 2, 2018): 107–121; Jamie Vickery, "Using an Intersectional Approach to Advance Understanding of Homeless Persons' Vulnerability to Disaster," *Environmental Sociology* 4, no. 1 (January 2, 2018): 136–147; Ingrid Waldron, "Re-thinking Waste: Mapping Racial Geographies of Violence on the Colonial Landscape," *Environmental Sociology* 4, no. 1 (January 2, 2018): 36–53; Kyle Powys Whyte, "Settler Colonialism, Ecology, and Environmental Injustice," *Environment and Society* 9, no. 1 (2018): 125–144; Patricia Widener and Carmen Rowe, "Climate Discourse: Eluding Literacy, Justice and Inclusion, by Evading Causation, Privilege and Diversity," *Environmental Sociology* 4, no. 1 (January 2, 2018): 162–174; Kyle Powys Whyte, "The Dakota Access Pipeline, Environmental Injustice, and US Colonialism," *Red Ink: An International Journal of Indigenous Literature, Arts, & Humanities* 19, no. 1 (February 28, 2017).

15. Emile Durkheim, "What Is a Social Fact?," in *The Rules of Sociological Method: And Selected Texts on Sociology and Its Method*, ed. Steven Lukes, Contemporary Social Theory (London: Macmillan, 1982), 50–59; Max Weber, *The Theory of Social and Economic Organization*, 1st American ed. (Oxford University Press, 1947); Max Weber, *Ancient Judaism*, ed. and trans. Hans H. Gerth and Don Martindale (New York: Free Press, 1967).

16. William R. Catton Jr. and Riley E. Dunlap, "Environmental Sociology: A New Paradigm," *American Sociologist* 13, no. 1 (February 1, 1978): 41–49.

17. Dorceta E. Taylor, "Women of Color, Environmental Justice, and Ecofeminism," *Ecofeminism: Women, Culture, Nature* (1997): 38–81; Dorceta E. Taylor, *The Rise of the American Conservation Movement: Power, Privilege, and Environmental Protection* (Durham, NC: Duke University Press, 2016).

18. William R. Freudenburg, Scott Frickel, and Robert Gramling, "Beyond the Nature/Society Divide: Learning to Think about a Mountain," *Sociological Forum* 10, no. 3 (September 1, 1995): 361–392.

19. Garrett Hardin, "The Tragedy of the Commons," *Science* 162, no. 3859 (1968): 1243–1248.

20. Elinor Ostrom, *Governing the Commons: The Evolution of Institutions for Collective Action* (Cambridge University Press, 1990); Elinor Ostrom, "Coping with Tragedies of the Commons," *Annual Review of Political Science* 2, no. 1 (June 1, 1999): 493–535.

21. Kevin N. Laland and Gillian R. Brown, "The Social Construction of Human Nature," in *Why We Disagree about Human Nature*, ed. Elizabeth Hannon and Tim Lewens (Oxford University Press, 2018), 127.

22. R. A. Sydie, "Nature/Nurture: The Sociological Fathers and Their Sociobiological Descendants," in *Nature: From Nature to Natures; Contestation and Reconstruction*, ed. David Inglis, John Bone, and Rhoda Wilkie (Taylor & Francis, 2005).

23. Karl Marx, *Capital: A Critique of Political Economy* (Penguin Books, 1976); Karl Marx, *Capital*, vol. 3 (Penguin UK, 1992); see also John Bellamy Foster, "Marx and the Rift in the Universal Metabolism of Nature," *Monthly Review* 65, no. 7 (December 1, 2013): 1–19.

24. John Bellamy Foster, "Marx's Theory of Metabolic Rift: Classical Foundations for Environmental Sociology," *American Journal of Sociology* 105, no. 2 (September 1999): 366–405; Foster, "Marx and the Rift"; John Bellamy Foster and Brett Clark, "The Robbery of Nature: Capitalism and the Metabolic Rift," *Monthly Review* 70, no. 3 (August 7, 2018): 1–20; Stefano B. Longo, Rebecca Clausen, and Brett Clark, *The Tragedy of the Commodity: Oceans, Fisheries, and Aquaculture* (New Brunswick, NJ: Rutgers University Press, 2015).

25. Foster, "Marx and the Rift," 5; Marx, *Capital*, 637–638, 860; Marx, *Capital*, vol. 3, 754, 959.

26. Foster, "Marx and the Rift," 4.

27. C. E. Colton, "Waste and Pollution: Changing Views and Environmental Consequences," in *The Illusory Boundary: Environment and Technology in History*, ed. Martin Reuss and Stephen H. Cutcliffe (Charlottesville: University of Virginia Press, 2010), 171–207.

28. Nathan McClintock, "Why Farm the City? Theorizing Urban Agriculture through a Lens of Metabolic Rift," *Cambridge Journal of Regions, Economy and Society* 3, no. 2 (July 1, 2010): 191–207.

29. Karl Polanyi, *The Great Transformation: The Political and Economic Origins of Our Time*, 2nd ed. (Boston: Beacon Press, 2001).

30. Longo, Clausen, and Clark, *Tragedy of the Commodity*.

31. Bruce Braun and Noel Castree, *Remaking Reality: Nature at the Millennium* (Routledge, 2005), 3.

32. C.S.A. (Kris) van Koppen, "Incorporating Nature in Environmental Sociology: A Critique of Bhaskar and Latour, and a Proposal," *Environmental Sociology* 3, no. 3 (July 3, 2017): 173–185.

33. Polanyi, *Great Transformation*.

34. David Harvey, *The Urbanization of Capital: Studies in the History and Theory of Capitalist Urbanization* (Baltimore: Johns Hopkins University Press, 1985); Marx, *Capital*; Melanie K. Yazzie, "Decolonizing Development in Diné Bikeyah: Resource Extraction, Anti-Capitalism, and Relational Futures," *Environment and Society* 9, no. 1 (September 1, 2018): 25–39.

35. David Harvey, *A Brief History of Neoliberalism* (Oxford: Oxford University Press, 2007).

36. Harvey, *Brief History of Neoliberalism*; David Harvey, "Realization Crises and the Transformation of Daily Life," *Space and Culture* 22, no. 2 (May 2019): 126–141.

37. Winona LaDuke, "Traditional Ecological Knowledge and Environmental Futures," *Colorado Journal of International Environmental Law and Policy* 5, no. 127 (1994): 127–148; Andrea Smith, "Indigeneity, Settler Colonialism, White Supremacy," in *Racial Formation in the Twenty-First Century*, ed. Daniel Martinez HoSang, Oneka LaBennett, and Laura Pulido (Berkeley: University of California Press, 2012), 66–90; Whyte, "Dakota Access Pipeline."

38. Kenneth A. Gould, David N. Pellow, and Allan Schnaiberg, *Treadmill of Production* (Boulder, CO: Routledge, 2008); Allan Schnaiberg, *The Environment: From Surplus to Scarcity* (New York: Oxford University Press, 1980).

39. Arthur P. J. Mol, David A. Sonnenfeld, and Gert Spaargaren, *The Ecological Modernisation Reader: Environmental Reform in Theory and Practice* (Routledge, 2009); Gert Spaargaren and Arthur P. J. Mol, "Sociology, Environment, and Modernity: Ecological Modernization as a Theory of Social Change," *Society & Natural Resources* 5, no. 4 (1992): 323–344.

40. For example, see Richard York and Eugene A. Rosa, "Key Challenges to Ecological Modernization Theory: Institutional Efficacy, Case Study Evidence, Units of Analysis, and the Pace of Eco-Efficiency," *Organization & Environment* 16, no. 3 (September 2003): 273–288.

41. Polanyi, *Great Transformation*.

42. LaDuke, "Traditional Ecological Knowledge"; Smith, "Indigeneity, Settler Colonialism, White Supremacy"; Whyte, "Dakota Access Pipeline."

43. M. Bianet Castellanos, "Introduction: Settler Colonialism in Latin America," *American Quarterly* 69, no. 4 (December 21, 2017): 777–781.

44. Aníbal Quijano, "Coloniality of Power and Eurocentrism in Latin America," *International Sociology* 15, no. 2 (June 1, 2000): 552.

45. Evelyn Nakano Glenn, "Settler Colonialism as Structure: A Framework for Comparative Studies of U.S. Race and Gender Formation," *Sociology of Race and Ethnicity* 1, no. 1 (January 1, 2015): 777.

46. Dina Gilio-Whitaker, *As Long As Grass Grows: The Indigenous Fight for Environmental Justice, Colonization to From Standing Rock* (Boston: Beacon Press, 2019).

47. George Steinmetz, "The Colonial State as a Social Field: Ethnographic Capital and Native Policy in the German Overseas Empire before 1914," *American Sociological Review* 73, no. 4 (August 1, 2008): 589.

48. Erich W. Steinman, "Decolonization Not Inclusion: Indigenous Resistance to American Settler Colonialism," *Sociology of Race and Ethnicity* 2, no. 2 (April 2016): 219–236.

49. Gilio-Whitaker, *As Long As Grass Grows*; Roxanne Dunbar-Ortiz, *An Indigenous Peoples' History of the United States* (Boston: Beacon Press, 2015); Kari Marie Norgaard, *Salmon and Acorns Feed Our People: Colonialism, Nature, and Social Action* (New Brunswick, NJ: Rutgers University Press, 2019).

50. For example, see Native Women's Wilderness, "Murdered and Missing Indigenous Women," https://www.nativewomenswilderness.org/mmiw.

51. Dorceta E. Taylor, "Black Farmers in the USA and Michigan: Longevity, Empowerment, and Food Sovereignty," *Journal of African American Studies* 22, no. 1 (2018): 49–76; Michelle Alexander, *The New Jim Crow: Mass Incarceration in the Age of Colorblindness* (New Press, 2011); Douglas A. Blackmon, *Slavery by Another Name: The Re-enslavement of Black Americans from the Civil War to World War II* (Anchor, 2009); Robert D. Bullard et al., "Toxic Wastes and Race at Twenty: Why Race Still Matters after All of These Years," *Environmental Law* 38, no. 2 (2008): 371; Thomas W. Mitchell, "From Reconstruction to Deconstruction: Undermining Black Landownership, Political Independence, and Community through Partition Sales of Tenancies in Common," *Northwestern University Law Review* 95 (2000): 505.

52. Meghan Elizabeth Kallman, "The 'Male' Privilege of White Women, the 'White' Privilege of Black Women, and Vulnerability to Violence: An Intersectional Analysis of Peace Corps Workers in Host Countries," *International Feminist Journal of Politics* 21, no. 4 (August 8, 2019): 566–594; George Jerry Sefa Dei and Arlo Kempf, *Anti-Colonialism and Education: The Politics of Resistance* (Sense, 2006).

53. LeQuesne, "Petro-hegemony."

54. Meghji, *Decolonizing Sociology*.

55. Achille Joseph Mbembe, "Decolonizing the University: New Directions," *Arts and Humanities in Higher Education* 15, no. 1 (February 1, 2016): 29–45.

56. Smith, *Decolonizing Methodologies*; Connell, "Decolonizing Sociology."

57. Robert Lee and Tristan George, "Land-Grab Universities," *High Country News*, March 30, 2020.

58. Summer Wilkie, "So You Want to Acknowledge the Land?," *High Country News*, April 22, 2021.

59. Michael Goldman, *Imperial Nature: The World Bank and Struggles for Social Justice in the Age of Globalization* (New Haven, CT: Yale University Press, 2006); Vandana Shiva, *Water Wars: Privatization, Pollution and Profit* (Berkeley, CA: North Atlantic Books, 2016).

60. Nadine Naguib Suliman, "The Intertwined Relationship between Power and Patriarchy: Examples from Resource Extractive Industries," *Societies* 9, no. 1 (February 1, 2019): 1–11.

61. Linda M. Lobao, Gregory Hooks, and Ann R. Tickamyer, *The Sociology of Spatial Inequality* (SUNY Press, 2007), 1.

62. Michael Omi and Howard Winant, *Racial Formation in the United States* (Routledge, 2014); R. S. Smith, "Giving Credit Where Credit Is Due: Dorothy Swaine Thomas and the 'Thomas Theorem,'" *American Sociologist* 26, no. 4 (Winter 1995): 9–28.

63. Kimberlé Crenshaw, "Mapping the Margins: Intersectionality, Identity Politics, and Violence against Women of Color," *Stanford Law Review* 43, no. 6 (July 1991): 1241–1299; Kimberlé Crenshaw, *On Intersectionality: Essential Writings* (New Press, 2017).

64. Mignon Duffy, "Doing the Dirty Work: Gender, Race, and Reproductive Labor in Historical Perspective," *Gender & Society* 21, no. 3 (June 1, 2007): 313–336; Rhacel Salazar Parreñas, "Migrant Filipina Domestic Workers and the International Division of Reproductive Labor," *Gender & Society* 14, no. 4 (August 2000): 560–580.

65. Langdon Winner, "Do Artifacts Have Politics?," *Daedalus* 109, no. 1 (1980): 121–136; James Ferguson, *The Anti-Politics Machine: Development, Depoliticization, and Bureaucratic Power in Lesotho* (University of Minnesota Press, 1994).

66. Thomas Piketty, *Capital in the Twenty-First Century*, trans. Arthur Goldhammer, reprint ed. (Cambridge, MA: Belknap Press, 2017).

67. Hari Bapuji, "Individuals, Interactions and Institutions: How Economic Inequality Affects Organizations," *Human Relations* 68, no. 7 (July 1, 2015): 1059–1083; Hari Bapuji and Lukas Neville, "Income Inequality Ignored? An Agenda for Business and Strategic Organization," *Strategic Organization* 13, no. 3 (August 1, 2015): 233–246.

68. Marie L. Besançon, "Relative Resources: Inequality in Ethnic Wars, Revolutions, and Genocides," *Journal of Peace Research* 42, no. 4 (July 1, 2005): 393–415; Christopher Cramer, "Does Inequality Cause Conflict?" *Journal of International Development* 15, no. 4 (2003): 397–412; Piketty, *Capital in the Twenty-First Century*; Kim A. Weeden and David B. Grusky, "Inequality and Market Failure," *American Behavioral Scientist* 58, no. 3 (March 1, 2014): 473–491; P. Gordon-Larsen, "Inequality in the Built Environment Underlies Key Health Disparities in Physical Activity and Obesity," *Pediatrics* 117, no. 2 (February 1, 2006): 417–424; Parreñas, "Migrant Filipina Domestic Workers."

69. Diane Sicotte, *From Workshop to Waste Magnet: Environmental Inequality in the Philadelphia Region* (New Brunswick, NJ: Rutgers University Press, 2016).

70. Anthony E. Ladd, ed., *Fractured Communities: Risk, Impacts, and Protest against Hydraulic Fracking in U.S. Shale Regions* (New Brunswick, NJ: Rutgers University Press, 2018); Stephanie A. Malin, *The Price of Nuclear Power: Uranium Communities and Environmental Justice* (New Brunswick, NJ: Rutgers University Press, 2015).

71. Tracy Perkins, "On Becoming a Public Sociologist: Amplifying Women's Voices in the Quest for Environmental Justice," in *Sociologists in Action on Inequalities: Race, Class and Gender*, ed. Shelley K. White, Jonathan M. White, and Kathleen Odell Korgen (Sage, 2014): 88–92.

72. Tracy E. Perkins, "Women's Pathways into Activism: Rethinking the Women's Environmental Justice Narrative in California's San Joaquin Valley," *Organization & Environment* 25, no. 1 (2012): 76–94.

73. Karen Bell, "Bread and Roses: A Gender Perspective on Environmental Justice and Public Health," *International Journal of Environmental Research and Public Health* 13, no. 10 (2016): 1005.

74. Shannon Elizabeth Bell and Yvonne A. Braun, "Coal, Identity, and the Gendering of Environmental Justice Activism in Central Appalachia," *Gender & Society* 24, no. 6 (2010): 794–813.

75. Taylor, "Women of Color"; Celene Krauss, "Women and Toxic Waste Protests: Race, Class and Gender as Resources of Resistance," *Qualitative Sociology* 16, no. 3 (1993): 247–262; Ducre, "Black Feminist Spatial Imagination."

76. Robert J. Brulle, "U.S. Environmental Movements," in *Twenty Lessons in Environmental Sociology*, ed. Kenneth A. Gould and Tammy L. Lewis, 2nd ed. (New York: Oxford University Press, 2015), 263–282; Kenneth A. Gould and Tammy L. Lewis, *Twenty Lessons in Environmental Sociology*, 2nd ed. (New York: Oxford University Press, 2015); Tammy L. Lewis, "Environmental Movements in the Global South," in *Twenty Lessons in Environmental Sociology*, ed. Kenneth A. Gould and Tammy L. Lewis, 2nd ed. (New York: Oxford University Press, 2015), 300–314; Sabrina McCormick, "The Sociology of Environmental Health," in *Twenty Lessons in Environmental Sociology*, ed. Kenneth A. Gould and Tammy L. Lewis, 2nd ed. (New York: Oxford University Press, 2015), 171–190.

77. Cody Ferguson, *This Is Our Land: Grassroots Environmentalism in the Late Twentieth Century* (New Brunswick, NJ: Rutgers University Press, 2015); David Naguib Pellow, *Total Liberation: The Power and Promise of Animal Rights and the Radical Earth Movement* (University of Minnesota Press, 2014); Dorceta E. Taylor, "The Rise of the Environmental Justice Paradigm: Injustice Framing and the Social Construction of Environmental Discourses," *American Behavioral Scientist* 43, no. 4 (January 1, 2000): 508–580.

78. Lina Álvarez and Brendan Coolsaet, "Decolonizing Environmental Justice Studies: A Latin American Perspective," *Capitalism Nature Socialism* 31, no. 2 (2020): 50–69; Gilio-Whitaker, *As Long As Grass Grows*; Laura Pulido and Juan De Lara, "Reimagining 'Justice' in Environmental Justice: Radical Ecologies, Decolonial Thought, and the Black Radical Tradition," *Environment and Planning E: Nature and Space* 1, no. 1–2 (2018): 76–98; Malin and Ryder, "Developing Deeply Intersectional Environmental Justice Scholarship"; David Naguib Pellow, *What Is Critical Environmental Justice?* (John Wiley & Sons, 2017); Hilda E. Kurtz, "Acknowledging the Racial State: An Agenda for Environmental Justice Research," *Antipode* 41, no. 4 (2009): 684–704; David Naguib Pellow and Robert J. Brulle, "Power, Justice, and the Environment: Toward Critical Environmental Justice Studies," in *Power, Justice, and the Environment: A Critical Appraisal of the Environmental Justice Movement*, ed. David N. Pellow and Robert J. Brulle (Cambridge, MA: MIT Press, 2005): 1–19.

79. See definitions for environmental justice at the Environmental Justice Network's website: https://www.ejnet.org/ej/.

80. Robert J. Brulle, *Agency, Democracy, and Nature: The U.S. Environmental Movement from a Critical Theory Perspective* (Cambridge, MA: MIT Press, 2000); Brulle, "U.S. Environmental Movements."

81. Beth Schaefer Caniglia, Robert J. Brulle, and Andrew Szasz, "Civil Society, Social Movements, and Climate Change," in *Climate Change and Society: Sociological Perspectives*, ed. Riley E. Dunlap and Robert J. Brulle (Oxford University Press, 2015).

82. Philip McMichael, *Development and Social Change: A Global Perspective*, 6th ed. (Los Angeles: Sage, 2016); Alexa J. Trumpy, "Subject to Negotiation: The Mechanisms behind Co-optation and Corporate Reform," *Social Problems* 55, no. 4 (November 2008): 480–500; Gay Seidman, "Transnational Labour Campaigns: Can the Logic of the Market Be Turned against Itself?," *Development and Change* 39, no. 6 (2008): 991–1003.

83. Madison Dapcevich, "Trader Joe's Phasing Out Single-Use Plastics Nationwide following Customer Petition," *EcoWatch*, March 6, 2019, https://www.ecowatch.com/trader-joes-plastic-waste-2630818452.html.

84. Alissa Cordner and Phil Brown, "A Multisector Alliance Approach to Environmental Social Movements: Flame Retardants and Chemical Reform in the United States," *Environmental Sociology* 1, no. 1 (January 2, 2015): 69–79.

85. David N. Pellow, "Environmental Justice and the Political Process: Movements, Corporations, and the State," *Sociological Quarterly* 42, no. 1 (2001): 47–67.

86. Andrew Szasz, *Shopping Our Way to Safety: How We Changed from Protecting the Environment to Protecting Ourselves*, 3rd ed. (University of Minnesota Press, 2007); Margaret M. Willis and Juliet B. Schor, "Does Changing a Light Bulb Lead to Changing the World? Political Action and the Conscious Consumer," *Annals of the American Academy of Political and Social Science* 644, no. 1 (November 2012): 160–190.

87. Laurence Cox and Alf Gunvald Nilsen, "Social Movements Research and the 'Movement of Movements': Studying Resistance to Neoliberal Globalisation," *Sociology Compass* 1, no. 2 (2007): 426.

88. Michael McQuarrie, "Community Organizations in the Foreclosure Crisis: The Failure of Neoliberal Civil Society," *Politics & Society* 41, no. 1 (March 2013): 76.

89. Taylor, *American Conservation Movement*.

90. Ferguson, *This Is Our Land*.

91. Phil Brown, *Toxic Exposures: Contested Illnesses and the Environmental Health Movement* (Columbia University Press, 2007); Phil Brown et al., "Embodied Health Movements: New Approaches to Social Movements in Health," *Sociology of Health & Illness* 26, no. 1 (2004): 50–80; Brown, Morello-Frosch, and Zavestoski, *Contested Illnesses*; Stephen Zavestoski et al., "Patient Activism and the Struggle for Diagnosis: Gulf War Illnesses and Other Medically Unexplained Physical Symptoms in the US," *Social Science & Medicine* 58, no. 1 (January 1, 2004): 161–175.

92. Alissa Cordner, *Toxic Safety: Flame Retardants, Chemical Controversies, and Environmental Health* (Columbia University Press, 2016).

93. Meghan Elizabeth Kallman and Scott Frickel, "Power to the People: Industrial Transition Movements and Energy Populism," *Environmental Sociology* 5, no. 3 (July 3, 2019): 255–268; Arthur P. J. Mol and Gert Spaargaren, "Environment, Modernity and the Risk-Society: The Apocalyptic Horizon of Environmental Reform," *International Sociology* 8, no. 4 (December 1, 1993): 431–459.

94. Fred L. Block, "Innovation and the Invisible Hand of Government," in *State of Innovation: The U.S. Government's Role in Technology Development*, ed. Fred L. Block and Matthew R. Keller (Routledge, 2015); Fred Block and Margaret Somers, "Beyond the Economistic Fallacy: The Holistic Social Science of Karl Polanyi," in *Vision and Method in Historical Sociology*, ed. Theda Skocpol (Cambridge University Press, 1984), 47–84; Meghan Elizabeth Kallman and Scott Frickel, "Nested Logics and Smart Meter Adoption: Institutional Processes and Organizational Change in the Diffusion of Smart Meters in the United States," *Energy Research & Social Science* 57 (November 1, 2019): 101249.

95. Harvey, *Brief History of Neoliberalism*.

96. Linda Lobao, Lazarus Adua, and Gregory Hooks, "Privatization, Business Attraction, and Social Services across the United States: Local Governments' Use of Market-Oriented, Neoliberal Policies in the Post-2000 Period," *Social Problems* 61, no. 4 (November 1, 2014): 644–672.

97. Pellow, *Total Liberation*.

98. Giorgio Agamben, *State of Exception*, trans. Kevin Attell, 1st ed. (Chicago: University of Chicago Press, 2005).

99. Dunbar-Ortiz, *Indigenous Peoples' History of the United States*; Kyle Powys Whyte, "Indigenous Experience, Environmental Justice and Settler Colonialism," SSRN Scholarly Paper (Rochester, NY: Social Science Research Network, April 25, 2016).

100. Katya Adler, "Iceland Puts Well-Being Ahead of GDP in Budget," BBC News, December 3, 2019, Europe, https://www.bbc.com/news/world-europe-50650155.

101. Kate Raworth, *Doughnut Economics: Seven Ways to Think Like a 21st-Century Economist* (White River Junction, VT: Chelsea Green, 2017).

102. Riley E. Dunlap and Robert J. Brulle, eds., *Climate Change and Society: Sociological Perspectives* (Oxford University Press, 2015); Intergovernmental Panel on Climate Change, "Global Warming of 1.5°C."

103. Rebecca Elliott, "The Sociology of Climate Change as a Sociology of Loss," *European Journal of Sociology* 59, no. 3 (December 2018): 301–337.

104. Dunlap and Brulle, *Climate Change and Society*; J. Timmons Roberts and Bradley Parks, *A Climate of Injustice: Global Inequality, North-South Politics, and Climate Policy* (Cambridge, MA: MIT Press, 2006).

105. Neil McCulloch and Radek Stefanski, "Fossil Fuel Subsidies Amount to Hundreds of Billions of Dollars a Year—Here's How to Get Rid of Them," *The Conversation US* (February 11, 2021).

106. Robert J. Brulle, "Institutionalizing Delay: Foundation Funding and the Creation of U.S. Climate Change Counter-Movement Organizations," *Climatic Change* 122, no. 4 (February 1, 2014): 681–694; Justin Farrell, "Corporate Funding and Ideological Polarization about Climate Change," *Proceedings of the National Academy of Sciences* 113, no. 1 (January 5, 2016): 92–97.

107. Diego Andreucci and Isabella M. Radhuber, "Limits to 'Counter-Neoliberal' Reform: Mining Expansion and the Marginalisation of Post-Extractivist Forces in Evo Morales's Bolivia," *Geoforum* 84 (August 1, 2017): 280–291; Naomi Klein, *This Changes Everything: Capitalism vs. the Climate* (Simon and Schuster, 2014).

108. Ladd, *Fractured Communities*; Malin, *Price of Nuclear Power*.

109. Lant Pritchett, Michael Woolcock, and Matt Andrews, "Looking Like a State: Techniques of Persistent Failure in State Capability for Implementation," *Journal of Development Studies* 49, no. 1 (January 2013): 3.

110. Meghan Elizabeth Kallman, *The Death of Idealism: Development and Anti-Politics in the Peace Corps* (Columbia University Press, 2020), 62.

111. Wainwright, *Decolonizing Development*, 13.

112. Martha Nussbaum and Amartya Sen, *The Quality of Life* (Clarendon Press, 1993); Amartya Sen, *Development as Freedom*, reprint ed. (New York: Anchor, 2000).

113. Rajesh Chandra, *Industrialization and Development in the Third World* (Routledge, 2003); Allen J. Scott and Michael Storper, *Pathways to Industrialization and Regional Development* (Routledge, 2005); World Bank, *70 Years Connecting Capital Markets to Development* (Washington, DC: International Bank for Reconstruction and Development/The World Bank, 2018), https://www.worldbank.org/en/about/unit/treasury/impact/70-years-connecting-capital-markets-to-development.

114. Christiane Struckmann, "A Postcolonial Feminist Critique of the 2030 Agenda for Sustainable Development: A South African Application," *Agenda* 32, no. 1 (January 2, 2018): 12–24.

115. Frances Fox Piven, "Can Power from Below Change the World?" *American Sociological Review* 73, no. 1 (February 2008): 1–14.

116. Raworth, *Doughnut Economics*.

117. Raworth, *Doughnut Economics*, 9.

3. FAILING PEOPLE AND THE PLANET

1. Wendy Brown, *In the Ruins of Neoliberalism: The Rise of Antidemocratic Politics in the West* (Columbia University Press, 2019).

2. Sean Illing, "Jared Kushner Says Government Should Be Run like a Company. Here's Why That's Wrong," Vox, March 29, 2017, https://www.vox.com/conversations/2017/3/29/15080846/donald-trump-jared-kushner-mitt-romney-business-politics.

3. David Harvey, *A Brief History of Neoliberalism* (Oxford University Press, 2007).

4. George Monbiot, "Neoliberalism—the Ideology at the Root of All Our Problems," *The Guardian*, Books, April 15, 2016, https://www.theguardian.com/books/2016/apr/15/neolibera lism-ideology-problem-george-monbiot.

5. F. A. Hayek, *The Road to Serfdom: Text and Documents; The Definitive Edition*, ed. Bruce Caldwell, 1st ed. (Chicago: University of Chicago Press, 2007).

6. Monbiot, "Neoliberalism—the Ideology."

7. Charles W. Mills, *The Racial Contract* (Ithaca, NY: Cornell University Press, 2014), 18–19.

8. Douglas Rushkoff, *Team Human* (New York: W. W. Norton, 2019), 9.

9. Rushkoff, *Team Human*.

10. Peter Wohlleben, *The Hidden Life of Trees: What They Feel, How They Communicate—Discoveries from a Secret World*, trans. Jane Billinghurst, 1st English ed. (Vancouver, Canada: Greystone Books, 2016).

11. David J. Buller, "Four Fallacies of Pop Evolutionary Psychology," *Scientific American* 300, no. 1 (January 2009): 74–81; Stevi Jackson and Amanda Rees, "The Appalling Appeal of Nature: The Popular Influence of Evolutionary Psychology as a Problem for Sociology," *Sociology* 41, no. 5 (October 1, 2007): 917–930.

12. Harvey, *Brief History of Neoliberalism*.

13. Harvey, *Brief History of Neoliberalism*; David Harvey, "Neoliberalism Is a Political Project," *Jacobin*, 2016.

14. Harvey, *Brief History of Neoliberalism*; Harvey, "Neoliberalism Is a Political Project."

15. Jamie Peck and Nik Theodore, "Variegated Capitalism," *Progress in Human Geography* 31, no. 6 (December 1, 2007): 731–772.

16. Neil Brenner, Jamie Peck, and Nik Theodore, "Variegated Neoliberalization: Geographies, Modalities, Pathways," *Global Networks* 10, no. 2 (2010): 182–222; Harvey, *Brief History of Neoliberalism*; Peck and Theodore, "Variegated Capitalism."

17. Stephen Gill, "New Constitutionalism, Democratisation and Global Political Economy," *Pacifica Review: Peace, Security & Global Change* 10, no. 1 (February 1, 1998): 23–38.

18. Peter Frumkin, *On Being Nonprofit: A Conceptual and Policy Primer* (Harvard University Press, 2005).

19. Harvey, *Brief History of Neoliberalism*.

20. Kimberly Amadeo, "What Was the Bank Bailout Bill? Cost, Impact, and How It Passed," The Balance, October 26, 2020, https://www.thebalance.com/what-was-the-bank-bailout -bill-3305675 (accessed May 6, 2021).

21. Manuel B. Aalbers, "Neoliberalism Is Dead . . . Long Live Neoliberalism!," *International Journal of Urban and Regional Research* 37, no. 3 (2013): 1083–1090.

22. Roxanne Dunbar-Ortiz, *An Indigenous Peoples' History of the United States* (Boston: Beacon Press, 2015); Dorceta E. Taylor, "American Environmentalism: The Role of Race, Class and Gender in Shaping Activism, 1820–1995," *Race, Gender & Class* 5, no. 1 (1997): 16–62.

23. "Uninsured Rates for the Nonelderly by Race/Ethnicity," 2019, Kaiser Family Foundation, https://www.kff.org/uninsured/state-indicator/nonelderly-uninsured-rate-by-raceethnicity/ ?currentTimeframe=0&sortModel=%7B%22colId%22:%22Location%22,%22sort%22:%22asc %22%7D (accessed May 6, 2021).

24. Carol Anderson, *One Person, No Vote: How Voter Suppression Is Destroying Our Democracy* (Bloomsbury, 2018); Barbara Harris Combs, "Black (and Brown) Bodies Out of Place: Towards a Theoretical Understanding of Systematic Voter Suppression in the United States," *Critical Sociology* 42, no. 4–5 (July 1, 2016): 535–549.

25. David Hursh, Joseph Henderson, and David Greenwood, "Environmental Education in a Neoliberal Climate," *Environmental Education Research* 21, no. 3 (April 3, 2015): 299–318; Jonathan D. Ostry, Prakash Loungani, and Davide Furceri, "Neoliberalism: Oversold?," *Finance*

and Development 53, no. 2 (June 2016): 38–41; Jamie Peck and Adam Tickell, "Jungle Law Breaks Out: Neoliberalism and Global-Local Disorder," *Area* 26, no. 4 (1994): 317–326.

26. Garrick Small and John Sheehan, "The Metaphysics of Indigenous Ownership: Why Indigenous Ownership Is Incomparable to Western Conceptions of Property Value," in *Indigenous Peoples and Real Estate Valuation,* ed. Robert A. Simons, Rachel Malmgren, and Garrick Small, Research Issues in Real Estate (Boston: Springer US, 2008), 103–119.

27. Wendy Nelson Espeland, *The Struggle for Water: Politics, Rationality, and Identity in the American Southwest* (University of Chicago Press, 1998); Robin Wall Kimmerer, *Braiding Sweetgrass: Indigenous Wisdom, Scientific Knowledge and the Teachings of Plants,* 1st paperback ed. (Minneapolis: Milkweed Editions, 2015); Dunbar-Ortiz, *Indigenous Peoples' History of the United States.*

28. Donald W. Zeigler, "The Alcohol Industry and Trade Agreements: A Preliminary Assessment," *Addiction* 104, no. S1 (2009): 13–26.

29. Dani Rodrik, *The Globalization Paradox: Why Global Markets, States, and Democracy Can't Coexist* (Oxford University Press, 2011).

30. Eliza Barclay and Sarah Frostenson, "The Ecological Disaster That Is Trump's Border Wall: A Visual Guide," Vox, April 10, 2017, https://www.vox.com/energy-and-environment/2017/4/10/14471304/trump-border-wall-animals.

31. Garrett Hardin, "The Tragedy of the Commons," *Science* 162, no. 3859 (1968): 1243–1248.

32. See also Meghan Elizabeth Kallman and Scott Frickel, "Power to the People: Industrial Transition Movements and Energy Populism," *Environmental Sociology* 5, no. 3 (2019): 255–268.

33. Steven Davis, *In Defense of Public Lands: The Case against Privatization and Transfer,* 1st ed. (Philadelphia: Temple University Press, 2018).

34. Anne Bonds and Joshua Inwood, "Beyond White Privilege: Geographies of White Supremacy and Settler Colonialism," *Progress in Human Geography* 40, no. 6 (December 1, 2016): 715–733; Jen Preston, "Neoliberal Settler Colonialism, Canada and the Tar Sands," *Race & Class* 55, no. 2 (October 1, 2013): 42–59; Kyle Whyte, "The Dakota Access Pipeline, Environmental Injustice, and U.S. Colonialism," *Red Ink: An International Journal of Indigenous Literature, Arts, & Humanities,* no. 19.1 (2017).

35. Jason Byrne and Jennifer Wolch, "Nature, Race, and Parks: Past Research and Future Directions for Geographic Research," *Progress in Human Geography* 33, no. 6 (December 1, 2009): 743–765; Taylor, "American Environmentalism."

36. Patricia Nelson Limerick, "A History of the Public Lands Debate," proceedings of conference, *Challenging Federal Ownership and Management: Public Lands and Public Benefits,* October 11–13, 1995, https://scholar.law.colorado.edu/challenging-federal-ownership-management/2.

37. Davis, *In Defense of Public Lands.*

38. Davis, *In Defense of Public Lands.*

39. Hardin, "Tragedy of the Commons."

40. Elinor Ostrom, *Governing the Commons: The Evolution of Institutions for Collective Action* (Cambridge University Press, 1990); Elinor Ostrom, "Coping with Tragedies of the Commons," *Annual Review of Political Science* 2, no. 1 (June 1, 1999): 493–535.

41. Terry L. Anderson and Donald R. Leal, "Free Market Environmentalism: Hindsight and Foresight," *Cornell Journal of Law and Public Policy* 8, no. 1 (1998): 111–134; Davis, *In Defense of Public Lands;* Richard L. Stroup, "Privatizing Public Lands: Market Solutions to Economic and Environmental Problems," *Public Land & Resources Law Review* 19 (1998): 79; Richard L. Stroup and John A. Baden, *Natural Resources: Bureaucratic Myths and Environmental Management* (San Francisco: Pacific Institute for Public Policy Research, 1983); Scott Lehmann, *Privatizing Public Lands* (Oxford University Press, 1995).

42. Davis, *In Defense of Public Lands.*

43. Chris D'Angelo and Alexander C. Kaufman, "The Trump Administration's Plans for Less Public Input, More Pipelines," *High Country News*, January 15, 2020, https://www.hcn.org/articles/climate-desk-the-trump-administrations-plans-for-less-public-input-more-pipelines; Chris D'Angelo, "Land Transfer Advocate and Longtime Agency Combatant Now Leads BLM," *High Country News*, August 8, 2019, https://www.hcn.org/articles/climate-desk-bureau-of-land-management-land-transfer-advocate-and-longtime-agency-combatant-now-leads-blm; Jonathan Thompson, "The Big Public Land Sell-Out," *High Country News*, January 31, 2018, https://www.hcn.org/issues/50.3/energy-industry-the-big-public-land-sell-out.

44. Michael Goldman, *Imperial Nature: The World Bank and Struggles for Social Justice in the Age of Globalization* (New Haven, CT: Yale University Press, 2006); Michael Goldman, "How 'Water for All!' Policy Became Hegemonic: The Power of the World Bank and Its Transnational Policy Networks," in "Pro-Poor Water? The Privatisation and Global Poverty Debate," ed. Nina Laurie, special issue, *Geoforum* 38, no. 5 (September 1, 2007): 786–800; Dieter Plehwe, "The Origins of the Neoliberal Economic Development Discourse," in *The Road from Mont Pelerin: The Making of the Neoliberal Thought Collective*, ed. Philip Mirowski and Dieter Plehwe (Cambridge, MA: Harvard University Press, 2009), 238–279.

45. Noel Castree, "Neoliberalising Nature: The Logics of Deregulation and Reregulation," *Environment and Planning A* 40, no. 1 (2008): 131–152.

46. Daniel M. Cook and Andrew J. Polsky, "Political Time Reconsidered: Unbuilding and Rebuilding the State under the Reagan Administration," *American Politics Research* 33, no. 4 (July 2005): 577–605.

47. Edward P. Fuchs, *Presidents, Management, and Regulation* (Englewood Cliffs, NJ: Prentice Hall, 1988).

48. Cook and Polsky, "Political Time Reconsidered."

49. Richard S. Newman, *Love Canal: A Toxic History from Colonial Times to the Present* (Oxford University Press, 2016).

50. Cook and Polsky, "Political Time Reconsidered," 532.

51. Cook and Polsky, "Political Time Reconsidered."

52. Leif Fredrickson et al., "History of US Presidential Assaults on Modern Environmental Health Protection," *American Journal of Public Health* 108, no. S2 (April 1, 2018): S95–S103.

53. Jerome McDonnell, "Trump Wants to Take a Red Pen to the National Environmental Policy Act," WBEZ, February 2020, https://www.wbez.org/shows/wbez-news/trump-wants-to-take-a-red-pen-to-the-national-environmental-policy-act/bb9dbec9-f91a-473c-a53a-71e88a09d40f.

54. Fredrickson et al., "History of US Presidential Assaults on Modern Environmental Health Protection"; Cook and Polsky, "Political Time Reconsidered."

55. Devin Henry, "EPA Gets Funding Boost in Obama's Budget," *The Hill*, February 9, 2016, https://thehill.com/policy/energy-environment/268759-epa-gets-funding-boost-in-obamas-budget.

56. Greta R. Krippner, "The Financialization of the American Economy," *Socio-Economic Review* 3, no. 2 (2005): 14.

57. Gerald A. Epstein, *Financialization and the World Economy* (Cheltenham, UK: Edward Elgar, 2005), 3.

58. See also Andrew Sayer, "Interrogating the Legitimacy of Extreme Wealth: A Moral Economic Perspective," in *Handbook on Wealth and the Super-Rich*, ed. Iain Hay and Jonathan V. Beaverstock (Edward Elgar, January 29, 2016), https://www.elgaronline.com/view/edcoll/9781783474035/9781783474035.00012.xml.

59. Sayer, "Interrogating the Legitimacy," 20.

60. See also Dan McArthur, "Book Review: *Why We Can't Afford the Rich* by Andrew Sayer," *British Politics and Policy at LSE* (blog), April 10, 2016, https://blogs.lse.ac.uk/politicsandpolicy /book-review-why-we-cant-afford-the-rich-by-andrew-sayer/.

61. Sayer, "Interrogating the Legitimacy."

62. Greta R. Krippner, *Capitalizing on Crisis: The Political Origins of the Rise of Finance* (Harvard University Press, 2011).

63. Elizabeth Elkin, "CME's First Water Futures Are Coming as U.S. West Burns," *Bloomberg Business*, September 17, 2020, https://financialpost.com/pmn/business-pmn/cmes-first -water-futures-contract-is-coming-with-west-on-fire.

64. Goldman, "How 'Water for All!' Policy Became Hegemonic"; Rhodante Ahlers and Vincent Merme, "Financialization, Water Governance, and Uneven Development," *Wiley Interdisciplinary Reviews: Water* 3, no. 6 (2016): 766–774; Karen Bakker, *Privatizing Water: Governance Failure and the World's Urban Water Crisis* (Ithaca, NY: Cornell University Press, 2010).

65. Elkin, "CME's First Water Futures Are Coming as U.S. West Burns"; Laura Paskus, *At the Precipice: New Mexico's Changing Climate* (Albuquerque: University of New Mexico Press, 2020).

66. Jennifer Clapp, "Financialization, Distance and Global Food Politics," *Journal of Peasant Studies* 41, no. 5 (September 3, 2014): 797–814.

67. Alex Loftus and Hug March, "Financialising Nature?," *Geoforum* 60 (March 1, 2015): 172–175; Philip McMichael, "The Land Grab and Corporate Food Regime Restructuring," *Journal of Peasant Studies* 39, no. 3–4 (July 1, 2012): 681–701; Stefan Ouma, Leigh Johnson, and Patrick Bigger, "Rethinking the Financialization of 'Nature,'" *Environment and Planning A: Economy and Space* 50, no. 3 (May 1, 2018): 500–511.

68. Harvey, *Brief History of Neoliberalism*.

69. Terressa A. Benz, "Toxic Cities: Neoliberalism and Environmental Racism in Flint and Detroit, Michigan," *Critical Sociology* 45, no. 1 (2019): 49–62; Gustavo A. García-López, "The Multiple Layers of Environmental Injustice in Contexts of (Un)natural Disasters: The Case of Puerto Rico Post-Hurricane Maria," *Environmental Justice* 11, no. 3 (2018): 101–108; Michael J. Mascarenhas, "Where the Waters Divide: Neoliberal Racism, White Privilege and Environmental Injustice," *Race, Gender & Class* 23, no. 3–4 (2016): 6–25; Isabel Altamirano-Jiménez, *Indigenous Encounters with Neoliberalism: Place, Women, and the Environment in Canada and Mexico* (UBC Press, 2013).

70. Thomas Piketty, *Capital in the Twenty-First Century*, trans. Arthur Goldhammer, reprint ed. (Cambridge, MA: Belknap Press, 2017); Thomas Piketty, *Capital and Ideology*, trans. Arthur Goldhammer (Cambridge, MA: Belknap Press, 2020).

71. Michael S. Kimmel, "Globalization and Its Mal(e)Contents: The Gendered Moral and Political Economy of Terrorism," *International Sociology* 18, no. 3 (September 1, 2003): 603–620.

72. Michael J. Sandel, *The Tyranny of Merit: What's Become of the Common Good?* (Farrar, Straus and Giroux, 2020).

73. Cedric J. Robinson. *Black Marxism*, rev. and updated 3rd ed.: *The Making of the Black Radical Tradition* (UNC Press Books, 2020); Oliver C. Cox. "Race and Caste: A Distinction," *American Journal of Sociology* 50, no. 5 (1945): 360–368. Also see Laura Pulido and Juan De Lara, "Reimagining 'Justice' in Environmental Justice: Radical Ecologies, Decolonial Thought, and the Black Radical Tradition," *Environment and Planning E: Nature and Space* 1, no. 1–2 (2018): 76–98.

74. Stephanie Leydon, "How a Long-Ago Map Created Racial Boundaries That Still Define Boston," GBH News, Boston, November 12, 2019, https://www.wgbh.org/news/local-news /2019/11/12/how-a-long-ago-map-created-racial-boundaries-that-still-define-boston (accessed May 6, 2021).

75. Charles W. Mills, "White Supremacy as Sociopolitical System: A Philosophical Perspective," in *White Out: The Continuing Significance of Racism*, ed. Ashley W. Doane and Eduardo Bonilla-Silva (Psychology Press, 2003).

76. Francine D. Blau and Lawrence M. Kahn, "The Gender Wage Gap: Extent, Trends, and Explanations," *Journal of Economic Literature* 55, no. 3 (September 2017): 789–865; Theodore J. Davis, "The Politics of Race and Educational Disparities in Delaware's Public Schools," *Education and Urban Society* 49, no. 2 (February 1, 2017): 135–162.

77. Henry A. Giroux, "Spectacles of Race and Pedagogies of Denial: Anti-Black Racist Pedagogy under the Reign of Neoliberalism," *Communication Education* 52, no. 3–4 (January 2003): 191–211.

78. SURJ, "White Supremacy Culture," Showing Up for Racial Justice, 2020, https://www.showingupforracialjustice.org/white-supremacy-culture.html.

79. Sandel, *Tyranny of Merit*.

80. Scott Jashik, "Productivity or Sexism?," Inside Higher Ed, August 18, 2014, https://www.insidehighered.com/news/2014/08/18/study-raises-questions-about-why-women-are-less-likely-men-earn-tenure-research (accessed May 6, 2021).

81. Chandra Talpade Mohanty, "Transnational Feminist Crossings: On Neoliberalism and Radical Critique," *Signs: Journal of Women in Culture and Society* 38, no. 4 (2013): 971.

82. Mohanty, "Transnational Feminist Crossings," 971.

83. For example, see Jill Harrison, "Abandoned Bodies and Spaces of Sacrifice: Pesticide Drift Activism and the Contestation of Neoliberal Environmental Politics in California," *Geoforum* 39, no. 3 (2008): 1197–1214.

84. Robert D. Bullard, *Dumping in Dixie: Race, Class, and Environmental Quality*, 3rd ed. (Routledge, 2018).

85. Marion Fourcade and Kieran Healy, "Moral Views of Market Society," *Annual Review of Sociology* 33, no. 1 (July 18, 2007): 285–311.

86. Pierre Bourdieu, "The Essence of Neoliberalism," *Le Monde diplomatique*, December 1, 1998, https://mondediplo.com/1998/12/08bourdieu.

87. Bourdieu, "Essence of Neoliberalism."

88. Alastair Ager and Joey Ager, "Faith and the Discourse of Secular Humanitarianism," *Journal of Refugee Studies* 24, no. 3 (September 1, 2011): 456–472; Manuel Castells, *The Rise of the Network Society* (John Wiley & Sons, 2011).

89. Monbiot, "Neoliberalism—the Ideology.".

90. Antonio Gramsci, *Selections from the Prison Notebooks of Antonio Gramsci* (New York: International, 1971).

91. adrienne maree brown, *Pleasure Activism: The Politics of Feeling Good* (Chico, CA: AK Press, 2019).

92. United Nations, "Millennium Development Goals Report" (New York: United Nations, 2015).

93. United Nations, "Millennium Development Goals Report," 15; World Bank, "Decline of Global Extreme Poverty Continues but Has Slowed," 2018, https://www.worldbank.org/en/news/press-release/2018/09/19/decline-of-global-extreme-poverty-continues-but-has-slowed-world-bank.

94. Yansui Liu, Jilai Liu, and Yang Zhou, "Spatio-Temporal Patterns of Rural Poverty in China and Targeted Poverty Alleviation Strategies," *Journal of Rural Studies* 52 (May 1, 2017): 66–75; Hualou Long and Yansui Liu, "Rural Restructuring in China," in "Rural Restructuring in China," ed. Hualou Long and Yansui Liu, special issue, *Journal of Rural Studies*, 47, part B (October 1, 2016): 387–391.

95. Sonali Jain-Chandra et al., "Inequality in China—Trends, Drivers and Policy Remedies," International Monetary Fund Working Paper No. 18/127, June 5, 2018, https://www.imf.org

/en/Publications/WP/Issues/2018/06/05/Inequality-in-China-Trends-Drivers-and-Policy
-Remedies-45878; "The Trouble with China's Anti-Poverty Efforts," *Bloomberg Business*,
August 18, 2018, https://www.bloomberg.com/news/articles/2018-08-08/the-trouble-with
-china-s-anti-poverty-efforts.

96. Yongji Xue et al., "Rural Reform in Contemporary China: Development, Efficiency, and
Fairness," *Journal of Contemporary China* (July 6, 2020): 1–17.

97. Michael Devitt, "CDC Data Show U.S. Life Expectancy Continues to Decline," AAFP News,
December 10, 2018, https://www.aafp.org/news/health-of-the-public/20181210lifeexpectdrop
.html.

98. Drew DeSilver, "For Most Americans, Real Wages Have Barely Budged for Decades,"
Pew Research Center, 2018, https://www.pewresearch.org/fact-tank/2018/08/07/for-most
-us-workers-real-wages-have-barely-budged-for-decades/.

99. Elise Gould, "State of Working America Wages, 2019," Economic Policy Institute, February 20, 2020, https://www.epi.org/publication/swa-wages-2019/ (accessed May 6, 2021).

100. Jason Hickel, "The True Extent of Global Poverty and Hunger: Questioning the Good
News Narrative of the Millennium Development Goals," *Third World Quarterly* 37, no. 5
(May 3, 2016): 749.

101. Nanda Kishore Kannuri and Sushrut Jadhav, "Generating Toxic Landscapes: Impact on
Well-Being of Cotton Farmers in Telangana, India," *Anthropology & Medicine* 25, no. 2 (May 4,
2018): 121–140; Jagjit Plahe, Sarah Wright, and Miriam Marembo, "Livelihoods Crises in
Vidarbha, India: Food Sovereignty through Traditional Farming Systems as a Possible Solu-
tion," *South Asia: Journal of South Asian Studies* 40, no. 3 (2017): 600–618.

102. Ostry, Loungani, and Furceri, "Neoliberalism: Oversold?"

103. Dylan Matthews, "You're Not Imagining It: The Rich Really Are Hoarding Economic
Growth," Vox, August 8, 2017, https://www.vox.com/policy-and-politics/2017/8/8/16112368
/piketty-saez-zucman-income-growth-inequality-stagnation-chart; Thomas Piketty, *Capital
in the Twenty-First Century*; Thomas Piketty, *Capital and Ideology*.

104. Clare Coffey et al., "Time to Care: Unpaid and Underpaid Care Work and the Global
Inequality Crisis," Oxfam Briefing Paper, January 2020, https://oi-files-cng-prod.s3.amazonaws
.com/nigeria.oxfam.org/s3fs-public/bp-time-to-care-inequality-200120-en.pdf.

105. Paul Almeida, "Climate Justice and Sustained Transnational Mobilization," *Globalizations*
16, no. 7 (November 10, 2019): 973–979; Richard Jones Jr. and Bernadette Marie Calafell, "Con-
testing Neoliberalism through Critical Pedagogy, Intersectional Reflexivity, and Personal Narrative: Queer Tales of Academia," *Journal of Homosexuality* 59, no. 7 (August 1, 2012): 957–981;
Norie Ross Singer, "Toward Intersectional Ecofeminist Communication Studies," *Communication Theory* 30, no. 3 (August 1, 2020): 268–289.

106. Anna Kaijser and Annica Kronsell, "Climate Change through the Lens of Intersectionality," *Environmental Politics* 23, no. 3 (May 4, 2014): 417–433; Natalie Osborne, "Intersectionality and Kyriarchy: A Framework for Approaching Power and Social Justice in Planning and
Climate Change Adaptation," *Planning Theory* 14, no. 2 (May 1, 2015): 130–151; Patricia E. Perkins, "Climate Justice, Gender and Intersectionality," in *Routledge Handbook of Climate Justice*,
ed. Tahseen Jafry (Routledge, 2018).

107. Karl Marx, *Economic and Philosophic Manuscripts of 1844*, trans. Martin Milligan, Great
Books in Philosophy (Amherst, NY: Prometheus Books, 1988), 203.

108. Marx, *Economic and Philosophic Manuscripts*, 80.

109. David Harvey, *A Companion to Marx's Capital*, 2nd impression ed. (London: Verso,
2010); Marx, *Economic and Philosophic Manuscripts*, 75.

110. Carole Boyce Davies, ed., *Claudia Jones: Beyond Containment*. (Banbury, UK: Ayebia
Clarke Publishing, 2011).

111. Cedric Robinson, *Black Marxism*; Robin D. G. Kelley, "What Did Cedric Robinson Mean by Racial Capitalism?," *Boston Review*, January 12, 2017, http://bostonreview.net /race/robin-d-g-kelley-what-did-cedric-robinson-mean-racial-capitalism (accessed May 7, 2021).

112. Karl Polanyi, *The Great Transformation: The Political and Economic Origins of Our Time*, 2nd ed. (Boston: Beacon Press, 2001).

113. Polanyi, *Great Transformation*, 60.

114. Harvey, "Neoliberalism Is a Political Project"; Nik Heynen and Paul Robbins, "The Neoliberalization of Nature: Governance, Privatization, Enclosure and Valuation," *Capitalism Nature Socialism* 16, no. 1 (March 1, 2005): 5–8; Monbiot, "Neoliberalism—the Ideology"; Ostry, Loungani, and Furceri, "Neoliberalism: Oversold?"; Ouma, Johnson, and Bigger, "Rethinking the Financialization of 'Nature.'"

115. Aalbers, "Neoliberalism Is Dead"; Philip Mirowski, *Never Let a Serious Crisis Go to Waste: How Neoliberalism Survived the Financial Meltdown* (Verso Books, 2013); Simon Springer, "Postneoliberalism?," *Review of Radical Political Economics* 47, no. 1 (March 1, 2015): 5–17.

4. HUMAN BEINGS, NOT HUMANS BUYING

1. Interestingly, after the French Revolution, *individualisme* was used pejoratively in France to gesture at social dissolution and anarchy and the elevation of individual interests above those of the collective. The word had a negative connotation among French nationalists, conservatives, reactionaries, liberals, and socialists alike. Charly Coleman, *The Virtues of Abandon: An Anti-Individualist History of the French Enlightenment* (Stanford University Press, 2014).

2. John D. McCarthy and Mayer N. Zald, "Resource Mobilization and Social Movements: A Partial Theory," *American Journal of Sociology* 82, no. 6 (1977): 1212–1241, 1218.

3. Beth Caniglia and JoAnn Carmin, "Scholarship on Social Movement Organizations: Classic Views and Emerging Trends," *Mobilization: An International Quarterly* 10, no. 2 (June 1, 2005): 201–212.

4. Robert J. Brulle, "U.S. Environmental Movements," in *Twenty Lessons in Environmental Sociology*, ed. Kenneth A. Gould and Tammy L. Lewis, 2nd ed. (New York: Oxford University Press, 2015), 263–282.

5. Brulle, "U.S. Environmental Movements."

6. Brulle, "U.S. Environmental Movements"; Dorceta E. Taylor, *The Rise of the American Conservation Movement: Power, Privilege, and Environmental Protection*, reprint ed. (Durham, NC: Duke University Press, 2016).

7. Roxanne Dunbar-Ortiz, *An Indigenous Peoples' History of the United States* (Boston: Beacon Press, 2015); Dina Gilio-Whitaker, *As Long As Grass Grows: The Indigenous Fight for Environmental Justice, From Colonization to Standing Rock* (Boston: Beacon Press, 2019).

8. Paul Mohai, David Pellow, and J. Timmons Roberts, "Environmental Justice," *Annual Review of Environment and Resources* 34, no. 1 (October 15, 2009): 405–430; David Naguib Pellow, *What Is Critical Environmental Justice?* (John Wiley & Sons, 2017).

9. Dorceta Taylor, "American Environmentalism: The Role of Race, Class and Gender in Shaping Activism, 1820–1995," *Race, Gender & Class* 5, no. 1 (1997): 16–62; Dorceta Taylor, *Toxic Communities: Environmental Racism, Industrial Pollution, and Residential Mobility* (NYU Press, 2014); Cody Ferguson, *This Is Our Land: Grassroots Environmentalism in the Late Twentieth Century* (New Brunswick, NJ: Rutgers University Press, 2015); Kyle Powys Whyte, "Indigenous Experience, Environmental Justice and Settler Colonialism," SSRN Scholarly Paper (Rochester, NY: Social Science Research Network, April 25, 2016); Kyle Powys Whyte, "Indigenous Environmental Movements and the Function of Governance

Institutions," SSRN Scholarly Paper (Rochester, NY: Social Science Research Network, April 25, 2016).

10. Jill Lindsey Harrison, "Co-opted Environmental Justice? Activists' Roles in Shaping EJ Policy Implementation," *Environmental Sociology* 1, no. 4 (2015): 241–255; Ryan Holifield, "Neoliberalism and Environmental Justice in the United States Environmental Protection Agency: Translating Policy into Managerial Practice in Hazardous Waste Remediation," *Geoforum* 35, no. 3 (May 1, 2004): 285–297; Stephanie A. Malin, *The Price of Nuclear Power: Uranium Communities and Environmental Justice* (New Brunswick, NJ: Rutgers University Press, 2015); Jill Lindsey Harrison, "Neoliberal Environmental Justice: Mainstream Ideas of Justice in Political Conflict over Agricultural Pesticides in the United States," *Environmental Politics* 23, no. 4 (2014): 650–669; Daniel Faber, *Capitalizing on Environmental Injustice: The Polluter-Industrial Complex in the Age of Globalization* (Rowman & Littlefield, 2008).

11. Jill Lindsey Harrison, "Co-opted Environmental Justice? Activists' Roles in Shaping EJ Policy Implementation," *Environmental Sociology* 1, no. 4 (2015): 241–255; Ryan Holifield, "Neoliberalism and Environmental Justice in the United States Environmental Protection Agency: Translating Policy into Managerial Practice in Hazardous Waste Remediation," *Geoforum* 35, no. 3 (May 1, 2004): 285–297; Stephanie A. Malin, *The Price of Nuclear Power: Uranium Communities and Environmental Justice* (New Brunswick, NJ: Rutgers University Press, 2015); Jill Lindsey Harrison, "Neoliberal Environmental Justice: Mainstream Ideas of Justice in Political Conflict over Agricultural Pesticides in the United States," *Environmental Politics* 23, no. 4 (2014): 650–669; Daniel Faber, *Capitalizing on Environmental Injustice: The Polluter-Industrial Complex in the Age of Globalization* (Rowman & Littlefield, 2008).

12. Richard J. Lazarus, "The Greening of America and the Graying of Environmental Law: Reflections on Environmental Law's First Three Decades in the United States," *Virginia Environmental Law Journal* 20, no. 1 (2001): 75–106; Daniel A. Mazmanian and Michael E. Kraft, *Toward Sustainable Communities: Transition and Transformations in Environmental Policy* (MIT Press, 2009).

13. Mazmanian and Kraft, *Toward Sustainable Communities*.

14. Lazarus, "Greening of America."

15. Robert D. Bullard, *Confronting Environmental Racism: Voices from the Grassroots* (South End Press, 1993); Mohai, Pellow, and Roberts, "Environmental Justice"; Phil Brown, *Toxic Exposures: Contested Illnesses and the Environmental Health Movement* (Columbia University Press, 2007); Julie Sze and Jonathan K. London, "Environmental Justice at the Crossroads," *Sociology Compass* 2, no. 4 (July 2008): 1331–1354.

16. Caniglia and Carmin, "Scholarship on Social Movement Organizations."

17. James M. Jasper, *The Art of Moral Protest: Culture, Biography, and Creativity in Social Movements* (Chicago: University of Chicago Press, 1997); Nella Van Dyke, Sarah A. Soule, and Verta A. Taylor, "The Targets of Social Movements: Beyond a Focus on the State," in *Authority in Contention*, ed. Daniel J. Myers and Daniel M. Cress, vol. 25 of *Research in Social Movements, Conflicts and Change* (Emerald Group, 2004), 27–51.

18. David N. Pellow, "Environmental Justice and the Political Process: Movements, Corporations, and the State," *Sociological Quarterly* 42, no. 1 (January 2001): 47–67; Philip McMichael, *Development and Social Change: A Global Perspective*, 6th ed. (Los Angeles: Sage, 2016).

19. Daniel Jaffee, "Weak Coffee: Certification and Co-optation in the Fair Trade Movement," *Social Problems* 59, no. 1 (February 2012): 94–116.

20. Thomas A. Lyson and Annalisa Lewis Raymer, "Stalking the Wily Multinational: Power and Control in the US Food System," *Agriculture and Human Values* 17, no. 2 (2000): 199–220; Carolina Toschi Maciel and Bettina Bock, "Modern Politics in Animal Welfare: The Changing

Character of Governance of Animal Welfare and the Role of Private Standards," *International Journal of Sociology of Agriculture and Food* 20, no. 2 (2013): 219–235.

21. Elizabeth A. Armstrong and Mary Bernstein, "Culture, Power, and Institutions: A Multi-Institutional Politics Approach to Social Movements," *Sociological Theory* 26, no. 1 (March 2008): 74–99.

22. Andrew Szasz, *Shopping Our Way to Safety: How We Changed from Protecting the Environment to Protecting Ourselves*, 3rd ed. (Minneapolis: University of Minnesota Press, 2007).

23. Robin Jane Roff, "Shopping for Change? Neoliberalizing Activism and the Limits to Eating Non-GMO," *Agriculture and Human Values* 24, no. 4 (November 1, 2007): 511–522; Rachel Slocum, "Consumer Citizens and the Cities for Climate Protection Campaign," *Environment and Planning A: Economy and Space* 36, no. 5 (May 2004): 763–782; Margaret M. Willis and Juliet B. Schor, "Does Changing a Light Bulb Lead to Changing the World? Political Action and the Conscious Consumer," *Annals of the American Academy of Political and Social Science* 644, no. 1 (November 2012): 160–190.

24. Maria Csutora, "The Ecological Footprint of Green and Brown Consumers: Introducing the Behaviour-Impact-Gap (BIG) Problem," *15th European Roundtable on Sustainable Consumption and Production*, 2012.

25. Szasz, *Shopping Our Way to Safety*.

26. Szasz, *Shopping Our Way to Safety*, 195.

27. Clive Barnett et al., "The Political Ethics of Consumerism." *Consumer Policy Review* 15, no. 2 (2005): 45–51; Gill Seyfang, "Sustainable Consumption, the New Economics and Community Currencies: Developing New Institutions for Environmental Governance," *Regional Studies* 40, no. 7 (October 1, 2006): 781–791; Janette Webb, "Seduced or Sceptical Consumers? Organised Action and the Case of Fair Trade Coffee," *Sociological Research Online* 12, no. 3 (May 2007): 73–85; Melissa R. Gotlieb and Chris Wells, "From Concerned Shopper to Dutiful Citizen: Implications of Individual and Collective Orientations toward Political Consumerism," *Annals of the American Academy of Political and Social Science* 644, no. 1 (November 2012): 207–219; Willis and Schor, "Does Changing a Light Bulb Lead to Changing the World?"

28. Gavin Parker, "The Role of the Consumer-Citizen in Environmental Protest in the 1990s," *Space and Polity* 3, no. 1 (May 1999): 67–83; Alberto Melucci, *Nomads of the Present: Social Movements and Individual Needs in Contemporary Society*, ed. John Keane and Paul Mier (Philadelphia: Temple University Press, 1989); Lisa A. Neilson and Pamela Paxton, "Social Capital and Political Consumerism: A Multilevel Analysis," *Social Problems* 57, no. 1 (February 2010): 5–24; Dietlind Stolle and Marc Hooghe, "Consumers as Political Participants? Shifts in Political Action Repertoires in Western Societies," in *Politics, Products and Markets: Exploring Political Consumerism, Past and Present* (London: Transaction Press, 2004), 265–288.

29. Jess Benhabib and Alberto Bisin, "Advertising, Mass Consumption and Capitalism," *Department of Economics NYU*, manuscript, 2000, 34; Julie Guthman, "The Polanyian Way? Voluntary Food Labels as Neoliberal Governance," *Antipode* 39, no. 3 (2007): 456–478.

30. Edward T. Walker, Andrew W. Martin, and John D. McCarthy, "Confronting the State, the Corporation, and the Academy: The Influence of Institutional Targets on Social Movement Repertoires," *American Journal of Sociology* 114, no. 1 (July 2008): 44; Alexa J. Trumpy, "Subject to Negotiation: The Mechanisms Behind Co-optation and Corporate Reform," *Social Problems* 55, no. 4 (November 2008): 480–500.

31. *Brewing Justice: Fair Trade Coffee, Sustainability, and Survival*, 1st ed. (University of California Press, 2007); Jaffee, "Weak Coffee."

32. Tim Bartley, "Certifying Forests and Factories: States, Social Movements, and the Rise of Private Regulation in the Apparel and Forest Products Fields," *Politics & Society* 31, no. 3 (September 1, 2003): 433–464; "Institutional Emergence in an Era of Globalization: The Rise of

Transnational Private Regulation of Labor and Environmental Conditions," *American Journal of Sociology* 113, no. 2 (September 1, 2007): 297–351; Jaffee, "Weak Coffee," 110.

33. Bo Yun Park, "Racialized Political Consumerism in the United States," in *The Oxford Handbook of Political Consumerism*, ed. Magnus Boström, Michele Micheletti, and Peter Oosterveer. Oxford: Oxford University Press, 2019), 681–697; Jennifer L. Fluri et al., "Accessing Racial Privilege through Property: Geographies of Racial Capitalism," *Geoforum* 127 (2020). https://doi.org/10.1016/j.geoforum.2020.06.013.

34. Richard H. Hall, "Professionalization and Bureaucratization," *American Sociological Review* 33, no. 1 (February 1, 1968): 92–104; Meghan Elizabeth Kallman, "Encapsulation, Professionalization and Managerialism in the Peace Corps," *International Public Management Journal* (June 17, 2019): 1–30; Meghan Elizabeth Kallman, *The Death of Idealism: Development and Anti-Politics in the Peace Corps* (Columbia University Press, 2020); Kevin T. Leicht and Mary L. Fennell, "The Changing Organizational Context of Professional Work," *Annual Review of Sociology* 23 (1997): 215–231; Harold L. Wilensky, "The Professionalization of Everyone?," *American Journal of Sociology* 70, no. 2 (1964): 137–158.

35. Angela M. Eikenberry and Jodie Drapal Kluver, "The Marketization of the Nonprofit Sector: Civil Society at Risk?," *Public Administration Review* 64, no. 2 (2004): 132–140; Patricia Mooney Nickel and Angela M. Eikenberry, "A Critique of the Discourse of Marketized Philanthropy," *American Behavioral Scientist* 52, no. 7 (March 1, 2009): 974–989; INCITE!, ed., *The Revolution Will Not Be Funded: Beyond the Non-Profit Industrial Complex*, reprint ed. (Durham, NC: Duke University Press, 2017); Nina Eliasoph, "'Close to Home': The Work of Avoiding Politics," *Theory and Society* 26, no. 5 (1997): 605–647; Kallman, *Death of Idealism*.

36. There are other examples of this internationally, such as with Zapotec communities. See, for example, Lynn Stephen, "Women's Weaving Cooperatives in Oaxaca: An Indigenous Response to Neoliberalism," *Critique of Anthropology* 25, no. 3 (2005): 253–278.

37. For example, see Ted Jojola, "Indigenous Planning and Community Development," *Traditional Dwellings and Settlement Review* 12, no. 1 (2000): 1–15.

38. Karianne Gomez, Tiffany Mawhinney, and Kimberly Betts, "Welcome to Gen Z" (Network of Executive Women and Deloitte, 2020).

39. Amy Kamenetz, "A New Look at the Lasting Consequences of Student Debt," National Public Radio, nprEd, April 4, 2017, https://www.npr.org/sections/ed/2017/04/04/522456671/a-new-look-at-the-lasting-consequences-of-student-debt.

40. Laura Parker, "Kids Suing Governments about Climate: It's a Global Trend," *National Geographic Environment*, June 26, 2019, https://www.nationalgeographic.com/environment/2019/06/kids-suing-governments-about-climate-growing-trend/.

41. Corrie Grosse and Brigid Mark, "A Colonized COP: Indigenous Exclusion and Youth Climate Justice Activism at the United Nations Climate Change Negotiations," in *From Student Strikes to the Extinction Rebellion*, ed. Benjamin J. Richardson (Edward Elgar, 2020), 146–170; Jenny Ritchie, "Movement from the Margins to Global Recognition: Climate Change Activism by Young People and in Particular Indigenous Youth," *International Studies in Sociology of Education* 30, no. 1–2 (2020): 1–20.

42. Alicia Donnellan Barraclough et al., "Stewards of the Future: Accompanying the Rising Tide of Young Voices by Setting Youth-Inclusive Research Agendas in Sustainability Research," *Sustainable Earth* 4, no. 1 (2021): 1–6; Heejin Han and Sang Wuk Ahn, "Youth Mobilization to Stop Global Climate Change: Narratives and Impact," *Sustainability* 12, no. 10 (2020): 4127; Bright Nkrumah, "Eco-Activism: Youth and Climate Justice in South Africa," *Environmental Claims Journal* (December 12, 2020): 1–23; Ritchie, "Movement from the Margins to Global Recognition."

43. For more from Nakate in her own words, read: Vanessa Nakate, *A Bigger Picture: My Fight to Bring a New African Voice to the Climate Crisis* (Boston: Mariner Books, 2021).

44. Kenya Evelyn, "Outrage at Whites-Only Image as Ugandan Climate Activist Cropped from Photo," *The Guardian*, World News, January 25, 2020, https://www.theguardian.com /world/2020/jan/24/whites-only-photo-uganda-climate-activist-vanessa-nakate.

45. For more information, see: https://www.unescogreencitizens.org/projects/vash-green -schools-project/.

46. Tidings Ndhlovu, "Corporate Social Responsibility and Corporate Social Investment: The South African Case," *Journal of African Business* 12 (March 2011): 72–92; Nelson Mandela, "Document 186, Statement by Mr. Nelson Mandela, President of the National Congress, to the Special Committee against Apartheid," in *The United Nations and Apartheid, 1948–1994*, vol. 1, Blue Books Series (New York: United Nations, Department of Public Information, 1994), 477–479; Francis Njubi Nesbitt, *Race for Sanctions: African Americans against Apartheid, 1946–1994* (Indiana University Press, 2004); Paul Lansing, "The Divestment of United States Companies in South Africa and Apartheid," *Nebraska Law Review* 60, no. 2 (1981): 304–326.

47. Bill McKibben, "The Case for Fossil-Fuel Divestment: On the Road with the New Generation of College Activists Fighting for the Environment," *Rolling Stone*, February 22, 2013, https://www.rollingstone.com/politics/politics-news/the-case-for-fossil-fuel-divestment -100243/.

48. Noam Bergman, "Impacts of the Fossil Fuel Divestment Movement: Effects on Finance, Policy and Public Discourse," *Sustainability* 10, no. 7 (July 2018): 1–18.

49. Kathy Hipple, "IEEFA Update: Fiduciary Duty and Fossil Fuel Divestment," Institute for Energy Economics and Financial Analysis, October 22, 2019, https://ieefa.org/ieefa-update -fiduciary-duty-and-fossil-fuel-divestment/.

50. Jennie C. Stephens, Peter C. Frumhoff, and Leehi Yona, "The Role of College and University Faculty in the Fossil Fuel Divestment Movement," *Elementa: Science of the Anthropocene* 6, no. 41 (May 18, 2018): 1–12.

51. Elizabeth Shogren, "College Divestment Campaigns Creating Passionate Environmentalists," National Public Radio, May 10, 2013, https://www.npr.org/2013/05/10/182599588/college -divestment-campaigns-creating-passionate-environmentalists.

52. Kim Parker and Ruth Igielnik, "On the Cusp of Adulthood and Facing an Uncertain Future: What We Know about Gen Z So Far," Pew Research Center, May 14, 2020, https:// www.pewresearch.org/social-trends/2020/05/14/on-the-cusp-of-adulthood-and-facing-an -uncertain-future-what-we-know-about-gen-z-so-far-2/.

53. Jeff Corntassel, "Toward Sustainable Self-Determination: Rethinking the Contemporary Indigenous-Rights Discourse," *Alternatives* 33, no. 1 (2008): 105–132; Jeff Corntassel, "Re-envisioning Resurgence: Indigenous Pathways to Decolonization and Sustainable Self-Determination," *Decolonization: Indigeneity, Education & Society* 1, no. 1 (2012): 86–101; Taiaiake Alfred and Jeff Corntassel, "Being Indigenous: Resurgences against Contemporary Colonialism," *Government and Opposition* 40, no. 4 (2005): 597–614; Michelle Daigle, "Awawanenitakik: The Spatial Politics of Recognition and Relational Geographies of Indigenous Self-Determination," *Canadian Geographer/Le Géographe Canadien* 60, no. 2 (2016): 259–269; Stephanie Gutierrez, "An Indigenous Approach to Community Wealth Building: A Lakota Translation" (Washington, DC: Democracy Collaborative, November 2018).

54. Pierre Bourdieu, "The Essence of Neoliberalism," *Le Monde diplomatique*, December 1, 1998, https://mondediplo.com/1998/12/08bourdieu.

5. DEMOCRATIZING THE COMMONS BY BUILDING COMMUNITIES

1. Crystal Arnold, Jennifer Atchison, and Anthony McKnight, "Reciprocal Relationships with Trees: Rekindling Indigenous Wellbeing and Identity through the Yuin Ontology of Oneness,"

Australian Geographer (2021): 1–17; Isabel Carvalho et al., "Learning from a More-than-Human Perspective: Plants as Teachers," *Journal of Environmental Education* 51, no. 2 (2020): 144–155; David Naguib Pellow, *Total Liberation: The Power and Promise of Animal Rights and the Radical Earth Movement* (University of Minnesota Press, 2014).

2. Don Grant, Andrew Jorgenson, and Wesley Longhofer, *Super Polluters: Tackling the World's Largest Sites of Climate-Disrupting Emissions* (New York: Columbia University Press, 2020); Damian Carrington, "Humanity Has Wiped Out 60% of Animal Populations since 1970, Report Finds," *The Guardian*, Environment, October 30, 2018, https://www.theguardian.com /environment/2018/oct/30/humanity-wiped-out-animals-since-1970-major-report-finds; Rob Nixon, "The Great Acceleration and the Great Divergence: Vulnerability in the Anthropocene," *Profession*, Modern Language Association, March 2014, https://profession.mla.org /the-great-acceleration-and-the-great-divergence-vulnerability-in-the-anthropocene/; Steven Davis, *In Defense of Public Lands: The Case against Privatization and Transfer* (Philadelphia: Temple University Press, 2018); John Bellamy Foster and Brett Clark, "The Robbery of Nature: Capitalism and the Metabolic Rift," *Monthly Review: An Independent Socialist Magazine* 70, no. 3 (August 7, 2018): 1–20.

3. David Naguib Pellow, *Total Liberation*; Robin Wall Kimmerer, *Braiding Sweetgrass: Indigenous Wisdom, Scientific Knowledge and the Teachings of Plants* (Minneapolis: Milkweed Editions, 2015).

4. Kyle Powys Whyte, "Our Ancestors' Dystopia Now: Indigenous Conservation and the Anthropocene," in *Routledge Companion to the Environmental Humanities*, ed. Ursula K. Heise, John Christensen, and Michelle Niemann (New York: Routledge, 2017), 206–215; Tess Riley, "Just 100 Companies Responsible for 71% of Global Emissions, Study Says," *The Guardian*, Guardian Sustainable Business, July 10, 2017, https://www.theguardian.com/sustainable -business/2017/jul/10/100-fossil-fuel-companies-investors-responsible-71-global-emissions -cdp-study-climate-change; Paul Griffin, "CDP Carbon Majors Report, 2017" (Carbon Majors Database and Climate Accountability Institute, 2017).

5. Philip J. Landrigan et al., "The Lancet Commission on Pollution and Health," *Lancet* 391, no. 10119 (February 2018): 462–512.

6. Kyle Powys Whyte, "Indigenous Experience, Environmental Justice and Settler Colonialism," SSRN Scholarly Paper (Rochester, NY: Social Science Research Network, April 25, 2016).

7. Roxanne Dunbar-Ortiz, *An Indigenous Peoples' History of the United States* (Boston: Beacon Press, 2015); Eve Tuck and K. Wayne Yang, "Decolonization Is Not a Metaphor," *Decolonization: Indigeneity, Education & Society* 1, no. 1 (2012): 1–40; Denise Ferreira da Silva, "On Heat: Rising Temperatures May Provide a Guide for Thinking through How the Colonial, the Racial and the Capitalist Are Deeply—and Materially—Implicated and Intertwined," *Canadian Art*, October 29, 2018, https://canadianart.ca/features/on-heat/; Howard Zinn, *A People's History of the United States* (New York: Harper Perennial Modern Classics, 2005).

8. Dunbar-Ortiz, *An Indigenous Peoples' History of the United States*; Kimmerer, *Braiding Sweetgrass*; Nicole Bell, "Anishinaabe Bimaadiziwin: Living Spiritually with Respect, Relationship, Reciprocity, and Responsibility," in *Contemporary Studies in Environmental and Indigenous Pedagogies* ed. Andrejs Kulnieks, Dan Roronhiakewen Longboat, and Young Young (Brill | Sense, 2013), 89–108; Laurie Anne Whitt et al., "Belonging to Land: Indigenous Knowledge Systems and the Natural World," *Oklahoma City University Law Review* 26 (2001): 701.

9. David Feeny et al., "The Tragedy of the Commons: Twenty-Two Years Later," *Human Ecology* 18, no. 1 (March 1990): 4; quoted in Susana Narotzky, "What Kind of Commons Are the Urban Commons?," *Focaal* 2013, no. 66 (June 1, 2013): 123.

10. Karl Polanyi, *The Great Transformation: The Political and Economic Origins of Our Time*, 2nd ed. (Boston: Beacon Press, 2001).

11. Henri Lefebvre, "Le droit à la ville," *L Homme et la société* 6, no. 1 (1967): 30; Philippe Eynaud, Maïté Juan, and Damien Mourey, "Participatory Art as a Social Practice of Commoning to Reinvent the Right to the City," *VOLUNTAS: International Journal of Voluntary and Nonprofit Organizations* 29, no. 4 (August 1, 2018): 621–636.

12. Cf. Neil Brenner, *New State Spaces: Urban Governance and the Rescaling of Statehood* (Oxford: Oxford University Press, 2004); David Harvey, *Rebel Cities: From the Right to the City to the Urban Revolution* (New York: Verso, 2012).

13. Cf. Kurt Iveson, "Cities within the City: Do-It-Yourself Urbanism and the Right to the City," *International Journal of Urban and Regional Research* 37, no. 3 (2013): 941–956; Pauline Lipman, *The New Political Economy of Urban Education: Neoliberalism, Race, and the Right to the City* (Taylor & Francis, 2013); Don Mitchell, *The Right to the City: Social Justice and the Fight for Public Space* (Guilford Press, 2003).

14. Jürgen Habermas, *The Structural Transformation of the Public Sphere: An Inquiry into a Category of Bourgeois Society*, 6th ed. (Cambridge, MA: MIT Press, 1991).

15. David Treuer, "Return the National Parks to the Tribes: The Jewels of America's Landscape Should Belong to America's Original Peoples," *Atlantic*, May 2021, https://www.theatlantic.com/magazine/archive/2021/05/return-the-national-parks-to-the-tribes/618395/.

16. Garrett Hardin, "The Tragedy of the Commons," *Science* 162, no. 3859 (1968): 1243–1248.

17. Hardin, "Tragedy of the Commons," 1244.

18. See also Feeny et al., "Tragedy of the Commons"; Arthur F. McEvoy, "Toward an Interactive Theory of Nature and Culture: Ecology, Production, and Cognition in the California Fishing Industry," *Environmental Review: ER* 11, no. 4 (Winter 1987): 289–305.

19. Elinor Ostrom, *Governing the Commons: The Evolution of Institutions for Collective Action* (Cambridge University Press, 1990); Elinor Ostrom, "Coping with Tragedies of the Commons," *Annual Review of Political Science* 2, no. 1 (June 1, 1999): 493–535; Vandana Shiva, *Water Wars: Privatization, Pollution and Profit* (Berkeley, CA: North Atlantic Books, 2016).

20. Deborah Curran, "Indigenous Processes of Consent: Repoliticizing Water Governance through Legal Pluralism," *Water* 11, no. 3 (2019): 571; Evans Shoko and Maheshvari Naidu, "Peace-Based Informal Practices around Shared Communal Water Resources in Tyrone Village of Mhondoro-Ngezi, Zimbabwe," *International Journal of African Renaissance Studies—Multi-, Inter- and Transdisciplinarity* 13, no. 2 (2018): 77–91; L. Jane McMillan and Kerry Prosper, "Remobilizing Netukulimk: Indigenous Cultural and Spiritual Connections with Resource Stewardship and Fisheries Management in Atlantic Canada," *Reviews in Fish Biology and Fisheries* 26, no. 4 (2016): 629–647; Stefano B. Longo, Rebecca Clausen, and Brett Clark, *The Tragedy of the Commodity: Oceans, Fisheries, and Aquaculture* (New Brunswick, NJ: Rutgers University Press, 2015); Deborah McGregor, "Traditional Knowledge and Water Governance: The Ethic of Responsibility," *AlterNative: An International Journal of Indigenous Peoples* 10, no. 5 (2014): 493–507; Stefano B. Longo and Rebecca Clausen, "The Tragedy of the Commodity: The Overexploitation of the Mediterranean Bluefin Tuna Fishery," *Organization & Environment* 24, no. 3 (2011): 312–328; Fiona McCormack, "Fish Is My Daily Bread: Owning and Transacting in Maori Fisheries," in *Anthropological Forum* 20, no. 1 (2010): 19–39.

21. Polanyi, *Great Transformation*.

22. Adrienne Roberts, "Privatizing Social Reproduction: The Primitive Accumulation of Water in an Era of Neoliberalism," *Antipode* 40, no. 4 (2008): 535–560.

23. Fred Pearce, *When the Rivers Run Dry: Water—the Defining Crisis of the Twenty-First Century*, rev., updated ed. (Boston: Beacon Press, 2018).

24. Maude Barlow, *Whose Water Is It, Anyway? Taking Water Protection into Public Hands* (ECW Press, 2019); Maude Barlow and Tony Clarke, *Blue Gold: The Fight to Stop the Corporate Theft of the World's Water* (New Press, 2014); Peter Gleick, *Bottled and Sold: The Story behind Our Obsession with Bottled Water*, 1st ed. (Washington, DC: Island Press, 2010); Abrahm Lustgarten, "Liquid Assets," *ProPublica*, February 9, 2016, https://www.propublica .org/article/can-wall-street-solve-the-water-crisis-in-the-west; Shiva, *Water Wars*.

25. Shiva, *Water Wars*.

26. Makere W. Stewart-Harawira, "Troubled Waters: Maori Values and Ethics for Freshwater Management and New Zealand's Fresh Water Crisis," *Wiley Interdisciplinary Reviews: Water* 7, no. 5 (2020): e1464; Veronica Strang, "The Rights of the River: Water, Culture and Ecological Justice," in *Conservation: Integrating Social and Ecological Justice*, ed. Helen Kopnina and Haydn Washington (New York: Springer, 2020), 105–119; Piergiorgio Di Giminiani and Marcelo González Gálvez, "Who Owns the Water? The Relation as Unfinished Objectivation in the Mapuche Lived World," *Anthropological Forum* 28, no. 3 (2018): 199–216; Elizabeth Macpherson and Felipe Clavijo Ospina, "The Pluralism of River Rights in Aotearoa, New Zealand, and Colombia," *Journal of Water Law* 25, no. 6 (2020): 283–293; Erin L. O'Donnell and Julia Talbot-Jones, "Creating Legal Rights for Rivers," *Ecology and Society* 23, no. 1 (2018); Julian S. Yates, Leila M. Harris, and Nicole J. Wilson, "Multiple Ontologies of Water: Politics, Conflict and Implications for Governance," *Environment and Planning D: Society and Space* 35, no. 5 (2017): 797–815; Anne Salmond, "Tears of Rangi: Water, Power, and People in New Zealand," *HAU: Journal of Ethnographic Theory* 4, no. 3 (2014): 285–309; James D. K. Morris and Jacinta Ruru, "Giving Voice to Rivers: Legal Personality as a Vehicle for Recognizing Indigenous People's Relationship to Water?," *Australian Indigenous Law Review* 14, no. 2 (2010): 49–62.

27. Karen Bakker, *Privatizing Water: Governance Failure and the World's Urban Water Crisis* (Ithaca, NY: Cornell University Press, 2010); Michael Goldman, *Imperial Nature: The World Bank and Struggles for Social Justice in the Age of Globalization* (New Haven, CT: Yale University Press, 2006).

28. Bakker, *Privatizing Water*.

29. Goldman, *Imperial Nature*; Michael Goldman, "How 'Water for All!' Policy Became Hegemonic: The Power of the World Bank and Its Transnational Policy Networks," *Geoforum* 38, no. 5 (September 2007): 786–800.

30. Barlow and Clarke, *Blue Gold*.

31. Barlow, *Whose Water Is It, Anyway?*; Lustgarten, "Liquid Assets"; Shiva, *Water Wars*.

32. Stephanie A. Malin et al., "The Right to Resist or a Case of Injustice? Meta-Power in the Oil and Gas Fields," *Social Forces* 97, no. 4 (June 1, 2019): 1811–1838.

33. Marie Cusick, "Millions Own Gas and Oil under Their Land. Here's Why Only Some Strike it Rich," National Public Radio, March 15, 2018, https://www.npr.org/2018/03/15 /592890524/millions-own-gas-and-oil-under-their-land-heres-why-only-some-strike-it-rich; Malin et al., "The Right to Resist or a Case of Injustice?"; Stephanie A. Malin and Kathryn Teigen DeMaster, "A Devil's Bargain: Rural Environmental Injustices and Hydraulic Fracturing on Pennsylvania's Farms," *Journal of Rural Studies* 47 (October 1, 2016): 278–290; Bethany McLean, *Saudi America: The Truth about Fracking and How It's Changing the World* (New York: Columbia Global Reports, 2018).

34. Jonathan Thompson, "The Big Public Land Sell-Out," *High Country News*, January 31, 2018, https://www.hcn.org/issues/50.3/energy-industry-the-big-public-land-sell-out.

35. P. Andrew Jones and Tom Cech, *Colorado Water Law for Non-Lawyers* (Boulder: University Press of Colorado, 2009).

36. Pearce, *When the Rivers Run Dry*; Meghan Elizabeth Kallman, "Leadership, Inclusion, and Group Decision-Making in HONK! Bands," in *HONK! A Street Band Renaissance of*

Music and Activism, ed. Reebee Garofalo, Erin T. Allen, and Andrew Snyder (New York: Routledge, 2020), 292.

37. Miatta Fahnbulleh, "The Neoliberal Collapse," *Foreign Affairs*, January 2, 2020, https://www.foreignaffairs.com/articles/united-kingdom/2019-12-10/neoliberal-collapse.

38. Valérie Fournier, "Commoning: On the Social Organisation of the Commons," *M@n@gement* 16, no. 4 (2013): 433–453.

39. William Julius Wilson, *When Work Disappears: The World of the New Urban Poor*, 1st ed. (New York: Vintage Books, 1997).

40. Robert J. Gordon and Michael Butler Murray, *The Rise and Fall of American Growth: the U.S. Standard of Living Since the Civil War*, The Princeton Economic History of the Western World (Princeton University Press, Brilliance Audio, 2016), unabridged audiobook, 30 hr., 14 min.; Saskia Sassen, *The Global City: New York, London, Tokyo*, 2nd ed. (Princeton University Press, 2013).

41. Fournier, "Commoning."

42. Philippe Eynaud, Maïté Juan, and Damien Mourey, "Participatory Art as a Social Practice of Commoning to Reinvent the Right to the City," *VOLUNTAS: International Journal of Voluntary and Nonprofit Organizations* 29, no. 4 (June 8, 2018): 621–636.

43. Cf. Richard Florida, *The Rise of the Creative Class: And How It's Transforming Work, Leisure, Community, and Everyday Life* (New York: Basic Books, 2002).

44. Jamie Peck, "Struggling with the Creative Class," *International Journal of Urban and Regional Research* 29, no. 4 (2005): 740–770; see also Johannes Novy and Claire Colomb, "Struggling for the Right to the (Creative) City in Berlin and Hamburg: New Urban Social Movements, New 'Spaces of Hope'?," *International Journal of Urban and Regional Research* 37, no. 5 (2013): 1816–1838.

45. Reebee Garofalo, Erin T. Allen, and Andrew Snyder, eds., *HONK! A Street Band Renaissance of Music and Activism* (New York: Routledge, 2020); Amelia Mason, "In an Era of Protest, HONK! Fest's Activist Roots Come into Focus," WBUR, October 5, 2017, http://www.wbur.org/artery/2017/10/05/honk-fests-activist-roots.

46. Kallman, "Leadership, Inclusion, and Group Decision-Making in HONK! Bands."

47. Mick Burns, *Keeping the Beat on the Street: The New Orleans Brass Band Renaissance* (Baton Rouge, LA: LSU Press, 2008).

48. BMOL, "Benevolent Societies," Black Men of Labor, 2018, http://thebmol.org/bmol-history/benevolent-societies/.

49. Second line parades are descendants of New Orleans jazz funerals. The term "second line" refers to people who join into a parade. Those who are hosting an event are the "first line" of the parade. At a jazz funeral, this would be family of the deceased, the hearse, and the band. Those who follow the procession, often dancing and singing, are the "second line." Joel Dinerstein, "Second Lining Post-Katrina: Learning Community from the Prince of Wales Social Aid and Pleasure Club," *American Quarterly* 61, no. 3 (2009): 615–637.

50. HONK! Fest, "About—What Is HONK!?," 2018, http://honkfest.org/about/.

51. Kallman, "Leadership, Inclusion, and Group Decision-Making in HONK! Bands."

52. Nick Estes, *Our History Is the Future: Standing Rock versus the Dakota Access Pipeline, and the Long Tradition of Indigenous Resistance* (Verso, 2019); Chas Jewett and Mark Garavan, "Water Is Life—an Indigenous Perspective from a Standing Rock Water Protector," *Community Development Journal* 54, no. 1 (2019): 42–58; Temryss MacLean Lane, "The Frontline of Refusal: Indigenous Women Warriors of Standing Rock," *International Journal of Qualitative Studies in Education* 31, no. 3 (2018): 197–214; Deborah McGregor, "Indigenous Women, Water Justice and Zaagidowin (Love)," *Canadian Woman Studies* 30, no. 2–3 (2015); Kim Anderson, Barbara Clow, and Margaret Haworth-Brockman, "Carriers of Water: Aboriginal

Women's Experiences, Relationships, and Reflections," *Journal of Cleaner Production* 60 (2013): 11–17; Deborah McGregor, "Anishnaabe-kwe, Traditional Knowledge, and Water Protection," *Canadian Woman Studies* 26, no. 3 (2008).

53. Kyle Ferrar and Kirk Jalbert, "Air Pollution in the Bay Area's Refinery Corridor," *Frac-Tracker Alliance*, Articles, April 29, 2016, https://www.fractracker.org/2016/04/air-pollution-refinery-corridor/.

54. Susie Cagle, "Richmond v Chevron: The California City Taking On Its Most Powerful Polluter," *The Guardian*, Environment, October 9, 2019, https://www.theguardian.com/environment/2019/oct/09/richmond-chevron-california-city-polluter-fossil-fuel.

55. Ferrar and Jalbert, "Air Pollution in the Bay Area's Refinery Corridor."

56. Cagle, "Richmond v Chevron."

57. Cagle, "Richmond v Chevon"; Ferrar and Jalbert, "Air Pollution in the Bay Area's Refinery Corridor."

58. Cagle, "Richmond v Chevron."

59. Erica Chenoweth, *The Success of Nonviolent Civil Resistance*, TEDxBoulder (Boulder, CO, 2013), YouTube, https://www.youtube.com/watch?v=YJSehRlU34w.

60. Normally, we would use the phrasing "Havasupai Tribal nation" to recognize and honor Tribal sovereignty, but we are using the term "Havasupai Tribe" in deference to the term they use to describe themselves on materials like their website. For instance, see https://www.theofficialhavasupaitribe.com.

61. Ophelia Watahomigie-Corliss, "Uranium Mining Threatens Our Home, the Grand Canyon," *High Country News*, April 14, 2020, https://www.hcn.org/articles/indigenous-affairs-mining-uranium-mining-threatens-our-home-the-grand-canyon.

62. There is a great deal of research on this. See the references immediately following, especially from the Southwest Research and Information Center.

63. See the Southwest Research and Information Center's clearinghouse, http://www.sric.org/; Stephanie A. Malin, *The Price of Nuclear Power: Uranium Communities and Environmental Justice* (New Brunswick, NJ: Rutgers University Press, 2015); Traci Brynne Voyles, *Wastelanding: Legacies of Uranium Mining in Navajo Country* (University of Minnesota Press, 2015); Anita Moore-Nall, "The Legacy of Uranium Development on or near Indian Reservations and Health Implications Rekindling Public Awareness," *Geosciences* 5, no. 1 (2015): 15–29; Stefanie Raymond-Whish et al., "Drinking Water with Uranium below the US EPA Water Standard Causes Estrogen Receptor–Dependent Responses in Female Mice," *Environmental Health Perspectives* 115, no. 12 (2007): 1711–1716.

64. Amber Reimondo, "Canyon Mine: Why No Uranium Mine Is 'Safe' for the Grand Canyon Region," *Grand Canyon Trust*, Reports, April 27, 2020, https://www.grandcanyontrust.org/Canyon-Mine-Report.

65. Uranium Watch, "White Mesa Mill License Renewal," last updated September 19, 2017, https://www.uraniumwatch.org/whitemesamill.licenserenewal.htm; Malin, *Price of Nuclear Power*.

66. Stephanie Malin, "Before the US Approves New Uranium Mining, Consider Its Toxic Legacy," *The Conversation*, February 22, 2018, http://theconversation.com/before-the-us-approves-new-uranium-mining-consider-its-toxic-legacy-91204.

6. MORE THAN THE MARKET

1. Noel Castree, "Neoliberalising Nature: The Logics of Deregulation and Reregulation," *Environment and Planning A* 40, no. 1 (January 2008): 131–152.

2. Karl Polanyi, *The Great Transformation: The Political and Economic Origins of Our Time*, 2nd ed. (Boston: Beacon Press, 2001).

3. Gareth Dale, "Double Movements and Pendular Forces: Polanyian Perspectives on the Neoliberal Age," *Current Sociology* 60, no. 1 (January 1, 2012): 3–27; Stephanie A. Malin, *The Price of Nuclear Power: Uranium Communities and Environmental Justice* (New Brunswick, NJ: Rutgers University Press, 2015).

4. Émile Durkheim, *Suicide: A Study in Sociology*, trans. George Simpson and John A. Spaulding (New York: Free Press, 1979).

5. Alan Collins et al., "Suicide, Sentiment and Crisis," *Social Science Journal*, April 25, 2019.

6. Kate Raworth, *Doughnut Economics: Seven Ways to Think like a 21st-Century Economist* (White River Junction, VT: Chelsea Green, 2017). See additional explanation in the last section of chapter 2.

7. Raworth, *Doughnut Economics*, 9.

8. Donella Meadows, *Thinking in Systems: A Primer* (White River Junction, VT: Chelsea Green, 2008); Harold B. Weiss, "Overshoot: The Ecological Basis of Revolutionary Change," *Public Health Reports* 124, no. 1 (2009): 167–168.

9. Ana Moragues-Faus et al., "Building Diverse, Distributive, and Territorialized Agrifood Economies to Deliver Sustainability and Food Security," *Economic Geography* 96, no. 3 (2020): 219–243; Patrick Léon Gross, "Better Together? How the Doughnut Economics Action Lab Organizes Communities for Transformative Action" (2020); James Fenelon and Jennifer Alford, "Envisioning Indigenous Models for Social and Ecological Change in the Anthropocene," *Journal of World-Systems Research* 26, no. 2 (2020): 372; Kyle Powys Whyte, "Settler Colonialism, Ecology, and Environmental Injustice," *Environment and Society* 9, no. 1 (2018): 125–144; Mark Ericson, "International Indigenous Youth Cooperative (IIYC): Youth, Cultural Sustainability, Resilience, and Survivance," *Journal of American Indian Education* 55, no. 3 (2016): 111–133; Kekuhi Kealiikanakaoleohaililani and Christian P. Giardina, "Embracing the Sacred: An Indigenous Framework for Tomorrow's Sustainability Science," *Sustainability Science* 11, no. 1 (2016): 57–67; Ushnish Sengupta, "Indigenous Cooperatives in Canada: The Complex Relationship between Cooperatives, Community Economic Development, Colonization, and Culture," *Journal of Entrepreneurial and Organizational Diversity* 4, no. 1 (2015): 121–152; Ushnish Sengupta, Marcelo Vieta, and John Justin McMurtry, "Indigenous Communities and Social Enterprise in Canada," *Canadian Journal of Nonprofit and Social Economy Research* 6, no. 1 (2015): 104–123; Mehana Blaich Vaughan and Peter M. Vitousek, "Mahele: Sustaining Communities through Small-Scale Inshore Fishery Catch and Sharing Networks," *Pacific Science* 67, no. 3 (2013): 329–344; John Curl, *For All the People: Uncovering the Hidden History of Cooperation, Cooperative Movements, and Communalism in America* (PM Press, 2012); Rauna Kuokkanen, "Indigenous Economies, Theories of Subsistence, and Women: Exploring the Social Economy Model for Indigenous Governance," *American Indian Quarterly* 35, no. 2 (2011): 215–240; Fikrit Berkes, Johan Colding, and Carl Folke, "Rediscovery of Traditional Ecological Knowledge as Adaptive Management," *Ecological Applications* 10, no. 5 (2000): 1251–1262.

10. Naomi Klein, *Fences and Windows: Dispatches from the Front Lines of the Globalization Debate* (New York: Picador, 2002).

11. David Bollier, "The Rediscovery of the Commons," *Upgrade* 4, no. 3 (2003): 10–12.

12. Brenna Bhandar, *Colonial Lives of Property: Law, Land, and Racial Regimes of Ownership* (Duke University Press, 2018); Patrick Wolfe and Lindsey Schneider, "There's Something in the Water: Salmon Runs and Settler Colonialism on the Columbia River," *American Indian Culture and Research Journal* 37, no. 2 (January 1, 2013): 149–164.

13. James K. Boyce et al., "Power Distribution, the Environment, and Public Health: A State-Level Analysis," *Ecological Economics* 29, no. 1 (April 1, 1999): 127–140; Tim G. Holland, Garry D. Peterson, and Andrew Gonzalez, "A Cross-National Analysis of How Economic Inequality Predicts Biodiversity Loss," *Conservation Biology* 23, no. 5 (2009): 1304–1313; Gregory M. Mikkelson, Andrew Gonzalez, and Garry D. Peterson, "Economic Inequality Predicts Biodiversity Loss," *PLoS ONE* 2, no. 5 (May 16, 2007): e444; Raworth, *Doughnut Economics*; see citations from notes 9 and 12; Myles Lennon, "Postcarbon Amnesia: Toward a Recognition of Racial Grief in Renewable Energy Futures," *Science, Technology, & Human Values* 45, no. 5 (2020): 934–962.

14. Raworth, *Doughnut Economics*.

15. Daniel Boffey, "Amsterdam to Embrace 'Doughnut' Model to Mend Post-Coronavirus Economy," *The Guardian*, World News, April 8, 2020, https://www.theguardian.com/world/2020/apr/08/amsterdam-doughnut-model-mend-post-coronavirus-economy; Kate Raworth, "Introducing the Amsterdam City Doughnut," *Exploring Doughnut Economics* (blog), April 8, 2020, https://www.kateraworth.com/2020/04/08/amsterdam-city-doughnut/.

16. Jordan B. Kinder, "Solar Infrastructure as Media of Resistance, or, Indigenous Solarities against Settler Colonialism," *South Atlantic Quarterly* 120, no. 1 (2021): 63–76; Nikki Luke and Nik Heynen, "Community Solar as Energy Reparations: Abolishing Petro-Racial Capitalism in New Orleans," *American Quarterly* 72, no. 3 (2020): 603–625; Michael Maruca, "From Exploitation to Equality: Building Native-Owned Renewable Energy Generation in Indian Country," *William & Mary Environmental Law and Policy Review* 43 (2018): 391; Myles Lennon, "Decolonizing Energy: Black Lives Matter and Technoscientific Expertise amid Solar Transitions," *Energy Research & Social Science* 30 (2017): 18–27; Shalanda H. Baker, "Mexican Energy Reform, Climate Change, and Energy Justice in Indigenous Communities," *Natural Resources Journal* 56, no. 2 (2016): 369–390.

17. Chelsea Schelly, *Dwelling in Resistance: Living with Alternative Technologies in America* (New Brunswick, NJ: Rutgers University Press, 2017).

18. Malin, *Price of Nuclear Power*; Stephanie A. Malin et al., "Free Market Ideology and Deregulation in Colorado's Oil Fields: Evidence for Triple Movement Activism?," *Environmental Politics* 26, no. 3 (May 4, 2017): 521–545.

19. Malin, *Price of Nuclear Power*; Stephanie A. Malin and Becky Alexis-Martin, "Embedding the Atom: Pro-Neoliberal Activism, Polanyi, and Sites of Acceptance in American Uranium Communities," *Extractive Industries and Society*, January 10, 2019.

20. Arlie Russell Hochschild, *Strangers in Their Own Land: Anger and Mourning on the American Right* (New York: New Press, 2016).

21. Malin et al., "Free Market Ideology."

22. Malin et al., "Free Market Ideology."

23. Andrew Curley, "Unsettling Indian Water Settlements: The Little Colorado River, the San Juan River, and Colonial Enclosures," *Antipode* 53, no. 3 (2021): 705–723; Leanne Betasamosake Simpson, *As We Have Always Done: Indigenous Freedom through Radical Resistance* (University of Minnesota Press, 2017); Kyle Powys Whyte, "Indigenous Climate Change Studies: Indigenizing Futures, Decolonizing the Anthropocene," *English Language Notes* 55, no. 1 (2017): 153–162; Kyle Powys Whyte, "Justice Forward: Tribes, Climate Adaptation and Responsibility," in *Climate Change and Indigenous Peoples in the United States: Impacts, Experiences, and Actions*, ed. Julie Koppel Maldonado, Benedict Colombi, and Rajul Pandya (Springer, 2013): 9–22; Vaughan and Vitousek, "Mahele: Sustaining Communities"; Anna J. Willow, *Strong Hearts, Native Lands: The Cultural and Political Landscape of Anishinaabe Anticlearcutting Activism* (SUNY Press, 2012).

24. Nick Estes, "Fighting for Our Lives: #NoDAPL in Historical Context," *The Red Nation*, September 18, 2016, https://therednation.org/fighting-for-our-lives-nodapl-in-context/; Erich

Steinman, "Why Was Standing Rock and the #NoDAPL Campaign So Historic? Factors Affecting American Indian Participation in Social Movement Collaborations and Coalitions," *Ethnic and Racial Studies* 42, no. 7 (May 19, 2019): 1070–1090; Dina Gilio-Whitaker, *As Long As Grass Grows: The Indigenous Fight for Environmental Justice, From Colonization to Standing Rock* (Boston: Beacon Press, 2019).

25. Nick Estes, "Fighting for Our Lives: #NoDAPL in Historical Context," *The Red Nation*, September 18, 2016, https://therednation.org/fighting-for-our-lives-nodapl-in-context/; Erich Steinman, "Why Was Standing Rock and the #NoDAPL Campaign So Historic? Factors Affecting American Indian Participation in Social Movement Collaborations and Coalitions," *Ethnic and Racial Studies* 42, no. 7 (May 19, 2019): 1070–1090; Gilio-Whitaker, *As Long As Grass Grows*.

26. Estes, "Fighting for Our Lives."

27. Roxanne Dunbar-Ortiz, *An Indigenous Peoples' History of the United States* (Boston: Beacon Press, 2015); Estes, "Fighting for Our Lives."

28. Dunbar-Ortiz, *Indigenous Peoples' History*; Estes, "Fighting for Our Lives."

29. Curley, "Unsettling Indian Water Settlements"; Kyle Powys Whyte, "Indigenous Environmental Justice: Anti-colonial Action through Kinship," in *Environmental Justice: Key Issues*, ed. Brendan Coolsaet (London: Routledge, 2020): 266–278; Gilio-Whitaker, *As Long as Grass Grows*; Nick Estes, *Our History Is the Future: Standing Rock versus the Dakota Access Pipeline, and the Long Tradition of Indigenous Resistance* (Verso, 2019); Chas Jewett and Mark Garavan, "Water Is Life—an Indigenous Perspective from a Standing Rock Water Protector," *Community Development Journal* 54, no. 1 (2019): 42–58; Temryss MacLean Lane, "The Frontline of Refusal: Indigenous Women Warriors of Standing Rock," *International Journal of Qualitative Studies in Education* 31, no. 3 (2018): 197–214; Michelle Daigle, "Resurging through Kishiichiwan," *Decolonization: Indigeneity, Education & Society* 7, no. 1 (2018): 159–172; Kyle Powys Whyte, "The Dakota Access Pipeline, Environmental Injustice, and US Colonialism," *Red Ink: An International Journal of Indigenous Literature, Arts, & Humanities*, no. 19.1 (2017); Dina Gilio-Whitaker, "Idle No More and Fourth World Social Movements in the New Millennium," *South Atlantic Quarterly* 114, no. 4 (2015): 866–877; Kathleen Pickering Sherman, James Van Lanen, and Richard T. Sherman, "Practical Environmentalism on the Pine Ridge Reservation: Confronting Structural Constraints to Indigenous Stewardship," *Human Ecology* 38, no. 4 (2010): 507–520.

30. Sitting Bull College, "Standing Rock Statistical Profile," https://sittingbull.edu/sitting-bull-college/students/library/standing-rock-statistical-profile/.

31. Dana E. Powell, *Landscapes of Power: Politics of Energy in the Navajo Nation* (Duke University Press, 2018); Melanie K. Yazzie, "Decolonizing Development in Diné Bikéyah: Resource Extraction, Anti-capitalism, and Relational Futures," *Environment and Society* 9, no. 1 (September 1, 2018): 25–39; Dana E. Powell and Dáilan J. Long, "Landscapes of Power: Renewable Energy Activism in Diné Bikéyah," *Indians & Energy: Exploitation and Opportunity in the American Southwest* (2010): 231–262; Dana E. Powell, "Technologies of Existence: The Indigenous Environmental Justice Movement," *Development* 49, no. 3 (2006): 125–132.

32. See also Sakihitowin Awasis, "'Anishinaabe Time': Temporalities and Impact Assessment in Pipeline Reviews," *Journal of Political Ecology* 27, no. 1 (2020): 830–852; Steven McLeod, "To Sell 'Reconciliation': 8th Fire, Idle No More and the Possibilities of Reconciliation," *TOPIA: Canadian Journal of Cultural Studies* 33 (2015): 7–28; Karl Gardner and Richard Peters, "Toward the 8th Fire: The View from Oshkimaadziig Unity Camp," *Decolonization: Indigeneity, Education & Society* 3, no. 3 (2014); Chris Paci, "Lighting the Eighth Fire: The Liberation, Resurgence, and Protection of Indigenous Nations," *Canadian Journal of Native Studies* 29, no. 1–2 (2009): 307.

33. Winona LaDuke, "Indigenous Power: A New Energy Economy," *Race, Poverty & the Environment* 13, no. 1 (2006): 6–10.

34. For example, see their website at http://www.honorearth.org/.

35. For more on this, see: Winona LaDuke, *To Be a Water Protector: The Rise of the Wiindigoo Slayers* (Ponsford, MN: Spotted Horse Press, 2020).

36. Winona's Hemp and Heritage Farm, "Our Heritage," June 7, 2020, https://www.winonashemp.com/our-heritage.

37. Anishinaabe Agriculture Institute, "Harvest Update Report" (Osage, MN: Anishinaabe Agriculture Institute, December 2019), http://anishinaabeagriculture.org/reports.

38. Robin Wall Kimmerer, *Braiding Sweetgrass: Indigenous Wisdom, Scientific Knowledge and the Teachings of Plants* (Minneapolis: Milkweed Editions, 2015). See especially the chapter titled "The Three Sisters" to learn more.

39. Eunhee Choi et al., "Task Force Report: A Review of Hemp as a Sustainable Agricultural Commodity: Tools and Recommendations for Winona LaDuke's Hemp Farm and Sovereign Native American Tribes" (Seattle: University of Washington, The Henry M. Jackson School of International Studies, 2018), https://digital.lib.washington.edu/researchworks/handle/1773/43756.

40. Patricia Hill Collins, "The Difference That Power Makes: Intersectionality and Participatory Democracy," in *The Palgrave Handbook of Intersectionality in Public Policy*, ed. Olena Hankivsky and Julia S. Jordan-Zachery (Cham, Switzerland: Palgrave Macmillan, 2019), 167–192; Kishi Animashaun Ducre, "The Black Feminist Spatial Imagination and an Intersectional Environmental Justice," *Environmental Sociology* 4, no. 1 (January 2, 2018): 22–35; Stephanie A. Malin and Stacia S. Ryder, "Developing Deeply Intersectional Environmental Justice Scholarship," *Environmental Sociology* 4, no. 1 (January 2, 2018): 1–7; David Naguib Pellow, *What Is Critical Environmental Justice?* (John Wiley & Sons, 2017); David Naguib Pellow, "Toward a Critical Environmental Justice Studies: Black Lives Matter as an Environmental Justice Challenge," *Du Bois Review* 13, no. 2 (2016): 221–236; Sumi Cho, Kimberlé Williams Crenshaw, and Leslie McCall, "Toward a Field of Intersectionality Studies: Theory, Applications, and Praxis," *Signs: Journal of Women in Culture and Society* 38, no. 4 (2013): 785–810; Kishi Animashaun Ducre, "Greening Sociology," in *Greening the Academy: Ecopedagogy through the Liberal Arts*, ed. Samuel Day Fassbinder, Anthony J. Nocella II, and Richard Kahn (Brill | Sense, 2012): 33–45; Kimberlé Crenshaw, "Mapping the Margins: Intersectionality, Identity Politics, and Violence against Women of Color," *Stanford Law Review* 43, no. 6 (July 1991): 1241–1299. Also see our extensive review and list of further citations in chapter 2 of this book.

41. Michelle Daigle, "Tracing the Terrain of Indigenous Food Sovereignties," *Journal of Peasant Studies* 46, no. 2 (2019): 297–315; Jennifer M. Sumner, Derya Tarhan, and J. J. McMurtry, "Eating in Place: Mapping Alternative Food Procurement in Canadian Indigenous Communities," *Journal of Agriculture, Food Systems, and Community Development* 9, no. B (2019): 239–250; Leah Penniman, *Farming While Black: Soul Fire Farm's Practical Guide to Liberation on the Land* (Chelsea Green Publishing, 2018); Monica M. White, *Freedom Farmers: Agricultural Resistance and the Black Freedom Movement* (UNC Press, 2018); Simpson, *As We Have Always Done*; Charlotte Coté, "'Indigenizing' Food Sovereignty: Revitalizing Indigenous Food Practices and Ecological Knowledges in Canada and the United States," *Humanities* 5, no. 3 (2016): 57; Kristin Reynolds and Nevin Cohen, *Beyond the Kale: Urban Agriculture and Social Justice Activism in New York City*, vol. 28 (University of Georgia Press, 2016); Sam Grey and Raj Patel, "Food Sovereignty as Decolonization: Some Contributions from Indigenous Movements to Food System and Development Politics," *Agriculture and Human Values* 32, no. 3 (2015): 431–444; Gail P. Meyers, "Decolonizing a Food System: Freedom Farmers' Market as a Place for Resistance and Analysis," *Journal of Agriculture, Food Systems, and Community Development* 5, no. 4 (2015): 149–152; Joni Adamson, "Medicine Food: Critical Environmental Justice Studies, Native North American Literature, and the Movement for Food Sovereignty," *Environmental*

Justice 4, no. 4 (2011): 213–219; Monica M. White, "Sisters of the Soil: Urban Gardening as Resistance in Detroit," *Race/Ethnicity: Multidisciplinary Global Contexts* 5, no. 1 (2011): 13–28.

42. Soul Fire Farm, Mission statement, www.soulfirefarm.org.

43. Soul Fire Farm Co-Directors, *Soul Fire Farm Annual Report* (2019), 4.

44. Roxana Hegeman, "USDA to Begin Paying Off Loans of Minority Farmers in June," Associated Press, May 21, 2021, https://apnews.com/article/ks-state-wire-business-race-and -ethnicity-91c9f6147cb0afab1650f4ddf49e86d1?fbclid=IwAR2YnTNSYO84fLiNiqKgaYSRM GoxBkJs4wIPah7EW2qaRuCwz4qPGjeufIo.

45. To learn more about this process, read Penniman, *Farming While Black.*

46. Soul Fire Farm, "Strategic Goals: Uproot Racism in the Food System," About, https:// www.soulfirefarm.org/about/goals/.

47. Soul Fire Farm, "Farming Practices," The Land, https://www.soulfirefarm.org/theland /farmingpractices/.

48. Pellow, *What Is Critical Environmental Justice?*

7. CONCLUSION

1. Saeed Ahmed, "There Have Been, on Average, 10 Mass Shootings in the U.S. Each Week This Year," National Public Radio, National, May 10, 2021, https://www.npr.org/2021/05/10 /995380788/there-have-been-on-average-10-mass-shootings-in-the-u-s-each-week-this-year.

2. Michelle M. Jacob et al., "Indigenous Cultural Values Counter the Damages of White Set-tler Colonialism," *Environmental Sociology* (2020): 1–13; Sarah Marie Wiebe, "Sensing Policy: Engaging Affected Communities at the Intersections of Environmental Justice and Decolo-nial Futures," *Politics, Groups, and Identities* 8, no. 1 (2019): 181–193; Jules M. Bacon, "Settler Colonialism as Eco-social Structure and the Production of Colonial Ecological Violence," *Environmental Sociology* 5, no. 1 (2019): 59–69; J. Kēhaulani Kauanui, "'A Structure, Not an Event': Settler Colonialism and Enduring Indigeneity," *Lateral* 5, no. 1 (2016); Sarah Marie Wiebe, *Everyday Exposure: Indigenous Mobilization and Environmental Justice in Canada's Chemical Valley* (UBC Press, 2016); Anne Bonds and Joshua Inwood, "Beyond White Privi-lege: Geographies of White Supremacy and Settler Colonialism," *Progress in Human Geogra-phy* 40, no. 6 (December 1, 2016): 715–733.

3. David Lloyd and Patrick Wolfe, "Settler Colonial Logics and the Neoliberal Regime," *Set-tler Colonial Studies* 6, no. 3 (2016): 109–118.

4. David Schlosberg and David Carruthers, "Indigenous Struggles, Environmental Justice, and Community Capabilities," *Global Environmental Politics* 10, no. 4 (2010): 12–35.

5. Deborah McGregor, "Mino-Mnaamodzawin: Achieving Indigenous Environmental Jus-tice in Canada," *Environment and Society* 9, no. 1 (2018): 7–24; Kyle Powys Whyte, "On the Role of Traditional Ecological Knowledge as a Collaborative Concept: A Philosophical Study," *Eco-logical Processes* 2, no. 1 (December 2013); Linda Robyn, "Indigenous Knowledge and Technol-ogy: Creating Environmental Justice in the Twenty-First Century," *American Indian Quarterly* (2002): 198–220; Ta-Nehisi Coates, "The Case for Reparations," *Atlantic*, June 2014, https:// www.theatlantic.com/magazine/archive/2014/06/the-case-for-reparations/361631/; Neema Kudva and Kajri Misra, "Gender Quotas, the Politics of Presence, and the Feminist Project: What Does the Indian Experience Tell Us?," *Signs: Journal of Women in Culture and Society* 34, no. 1 (September 1, 2008): 49–73; Shirley Leung, "Chelsea Is About to Become the Country's Big-gest Experiment in Giving Out No-Strings-Attached Checks," *Boston Globe*, October 17, 2020, https://www.bostonglobe.com/2020/10/17/business/chelsea-is-about-become-countrys -biggest-experiment-giving-out-no-strings-attached-checks/; Donna Lu, "Universal Basic Income Seems to Improve Employment and Well-Being," *New Scientist*, May 6, 2020,

https://www.newscientist.com/article/2242937-universal-basic-income-seems-to-improve
-employment-and-well-being/.

6. Restorative Practices Trust, "The Whanganui Restorative Practices Trust," n.d., Restorative Practices Whanganui, https://restorativepracticeswhanganui.co.nz/trust/; see also
Jenny Saywood, "Whanganui: Respectful Relationships at the Heart of Our City—a Story
from New Zealand," *International Journal of Restorative Justice* 2, no. 2 (2019): 320–324.

7. Saywood, "Whanganui."

8. Restorative Practices Trust, "Whanganui Restorative Practices Trust."

9. Eleanor Ainge Roy, "New Zealand River Granted Same Legal Rights as Human Being," *The
Guardian*, March 16, 2017, https://www.theguardian.com/world/2017/mar/16/new-zealand
-river-granted-same-legal-rights-as-human-being.

10. Aldon D. Morris, *The Origins of the Civil Rights Movement: Black Communities Organizing for
Change* (New York: Free Press, 1986); Doug McAdam, "Recruitment to High-Risk Activism:
The Case of Freedom Summer," *American Journal of Sociology* 92, no. 1 (July 1, 1986): 64–90.

11. Morris, *Origins of the Civil Rights Movement*. On love, see: McGregor, "Indigenous Women."

12. Bianca DiJulio et al., "Loneliness and Social Isolation in the United States, the United
Kingdom, and Japan: An International Survey," *KFF* (blog), August 30, 2018, https://www.kff
.org/other/report/loneliness-and-social-isolation-in-the-united-states-the-united-kingdom
-and-japan-an-international-survey/; Zoya Gervis, "Why the Average American Hasn't Made
a New Friend in Five Years," *Digitalhub* (blog), May 9, 2019, https://www.swnsdigital.com
/2019/05/why-the-average-american-hasnt-made-a-new-friend-in-five-years/.

13. Francesca Polletta, *Freedom Is an Endless Meeting: Democracy in American Social Movements* (Chicago: University of Chicago Press, 2004).

14. Robin Wall Kimmerer, *Braiding Sweetgrass: Indigenous Wisdom, Scientific Knowledge, and
the Teachings of Plants* (Minneapolis: Milkweed Editions, 2013), 328.

15. Neil E. Klepeis et al., "The National Human Activity Pattern Survey (NHAPS): A
Resource for Assessing Exposure to Environmental Pollutants," *Journal of Exposure Science &
Environmental Epidemiology* 11, no. 3 (July 2001): 231–252; Theodore Roszak, Mary E. Gomes,
and Allen D. Kanner, eds., *Ecopsychology: Restoring the Earth, Healing the Mind* (San Francisco: Sierra Club Books, 1995); Kimmerer, *Braiding Sweetgrass*, 358.

16. Michael Carolan, *The Real Cost of Cheap Food*, 2nd ed. (London: Routledge, 2018).

17. Jeremy Woods et al., "Energy and the Food System," *Philosophical Transactions of the
Royal Society B: Biological Sciences* 365, no. 1554 (September 27, 2010): 2991–3006.

18. Dale Allen Pfeiffer, *Eating Fossil Fuels: Oil, Food, and the Coming Crisis in Agriculture* (New
Society Publishers, 2006), 67.

19. Leung, "Chelsea Is About to Become the Country's Biggest Experiment"; Rachel Treis-
man, "California Program Giving $500 No-Strings-Attached Stipends Pays Off, Study Finds,"
National Public Radio, March 4, 2021, https://www.npr.org/2021/03/04/973653719/california
-program-giving-500-no-strings-attached-stipends-pays-off-study-finds.

20. Malini Ranganathan and Eve Bratman, "From Urban Resilience to Abolitionist Climate
Justice in Washington, DC," *Antipode* 53, no. 1 (2021): 115–137.

21. Joanna Macy and Chris Johnstone, *Active Hope: How to Face the Mess We're in without
Going Crazy* (Novato, CA: New World Library, 2012); Rebecca Solnit, *Hope in the Dark: Untold
Histories, Wild Possibilities* (Chicago: Haymarket Books, 2016).

22. Macy and Johnstone, *Active Hope*.

23. Meghan Kallman and Terry Clark, *The Third Sector: Community Organizations, NGOs, and
Nonprofits* (University of Illinois Press, 2016); Alexis de Tocqueville, *Democracy in America*,
Dover Thrift Edition (Mineola, NY: Dover, 2017).

24. Solnit, *Hope in the Dark*, 7.

INDEX

AIM. *See* American Indian Movement

Allende, Salvador, 52

American Indian Foods, 135

American Indian Movement (AIM), 142

American Rescue Plan, 159

animal rights movement, 78

Anishinaabe Agriculture Institute, 147, 149

barbell economies, 112

Bears Ears National Monument, 58

Beauvoir, Simone de, 5

benevolent societies, 113

Bezos, Jeff, 61

Biden, Joe: commitment articulated by administration of, 159; election of, 3; leasing of land to oil and gas companies under leadership of, 108–109; loan payoff program for minority farmers announced by administration of, 152; problems addressed by, 58; social and environmental protections addressed by, 72

biomimicry, 135

Black Dirt Farm Collective, 152

Black Hills Act of 1877, 141

Black Lives Matter movement, 39, 92, 158

Black Marxism: The Making of the Black Radical Tradition, 70

Bollier, David, 135

Bourdieu, Pierre, 102

Brown, Jessica, 90

Brown, Phil, 41

Brown, Wendy, 48

Bush, George (Vice President), 59

Cabot Creamery Co-operative, 135

California Farmer Justice Collaborative, 152

Cannon Ball Community Solar Farm, 142–143

capitalism: barriers erected by, 136; by-products of, 33; colonialism and, 37; contradictions of, 90; definition of, 32; difference between other systems and, 71; dis-embeddedness and, 132, 137; as driver of climate crises, 122; elite-centered, 16; exploitation and, 10, 28; first contradiction of, 34; fundamentalist form of, 9; global, 31, 33; guiding logic of, 43; industrial, 23, 35, 44; Keynesian, 53; labor and, 30; neoliberalism as variety of, 52–55; racial, 13, 28, 38, 43, 64, 70, 80, 95, 135; resistance to, 10, 39, 120; stubbornness of, 138; system that rejects, 149; Treadmill of Production theory of, 34

case studies, 21–22; climate justice (Uganda), 83–88; collection action (renewing of), 81–101; Community Solar, 140–147; Grand Canyon (threat of uranium mining near), 124–129; Indigenized Energy, 140–147; Lakota nation (approaches to collective community-building by), 96–101; oil refineries, intergenerational equity amid (Indigenous), 116–124; Soul Fire Farm, 152–157; Standing Rock, 140–147; Thunder Valley Community Development Corporation, 96–101; water protection (Indigenous-led action for), 116–124; Water Protectors (Havasupai Tribal nation's), 124–129; Winona's Hemp and Heritage Farm, 147–152; youth divestment movement (U.S.), 88–96; youth-led activism, 81–83

Catton, William, 134

Central European Free Trade Agreement, 56

chattel slavery, 36

Chauvin, Derek, 3, 159

Chavez, Cesar, 12

Chenoweth, Erica, 118

Chevron, 117

Chicago Boys, 52

Citizens United v. FEC, 54, 76

city models (restorative). *See* Whanganui Restorative Justice Trust

Clark, Brett, 30

Clausen, Rebecca, 30

Clean Air Act of 1970, 78

Clean Water Act, 39, 78, 137

ABOUT THE AUTHORS

STEPHANIE A. MALIN is an environmental sociologist specializing in the community impacts of resource extraction and energy production and in environmental justice, environmental health, and the social effects of market-based economies. Stephanie serves as an associate professor of sociology at Colorado State University in Fort Collins. She is the author of *The Price of Nuclear Power: Uranium Communities and Environmental Justice* and a cofounder and co-director of the Center for Environmental Justice at CSU.

MEGHAN ELIZABETH KALLMAN is a sociologist and assistant professor at the School for Global Inclusion and Social Development and affiliated faculty in the Department of Sociology at the University of Massachusetts Boston. She studies organizations and institutional change, clean technology, and community and international development. She is the author of *The Death of Idealism: Development and Anti-Politics in the Peace Corps* and is a state senator of Rhode Island.

Printed in the United States
by Baker & Taylor Publisher Services